Papers of the Fifty-Fourth Algonquian Conference

Actes du cinquante-quatrième Congrès des Algonquinistes

PAPERS OF THE ALGONQUIAN CONFERENCES

ACTES DU CONGRÈS DES ALGONQUINISTES

54

Papers of the Fifty-Fourth Algonquian Conference

Actes du cinquante-quatrième Congrès des Algonquinistes

EDITED BY Inge Genee, Monica Macaulay, and Natalie Weber

MICHIGAN STATE UNIVERSITY PRESS | EAST LANSING

♾ The paper used in this publication meets the minimum requirements
of ANSI/NISO Z39.48-1992 (R 1997) (Permanence of Paper).

Michigan State University Press
East Lansing, Michigan 48823-5245

Library of Congress Cataloging-in-Publication Data
Names: Algonquian Conference (54th : 2022 : University of Colorado Boulder) | Genee, Inge, editor.
| Macaulay, Monica Ann, editor. | Weber, Natalie (Linguist), editor.
Title: Papers of the fifty-fourth Algonquian Conference = Actes du cinquante-quatrième Congrès
des Algonquinistes / Inge Genee, Monica Macaulay, and Natalie Weber, editors.
Other titles: Actes du cinquante-quatrième Congrès des Algonquinistes
Description: East Lansing : Michigan State University Press, 2025. |
Series: Papers of the Algonquian Conference | Includes bibliographical references.
Identifiers: LCCN 2024038541 | ISBN 9781611865295 (paperback) | ISBN 9781609177805
Subjects: LCSH: Algonquian languages—Congresses. | Algonquian Indians—Congresses. |
LCGFT: Conference papers and proceedings.
Classification: LCC PM601 .A44 2022 | DDC 497/.3—dc23/eng/20241010
LC record available at https://lccn.loc.gov/2024038541

Cover design by Erin Kirk
Cover detail of a quill box is used courtesy of Julie L. Loehr

---

Visit Michigan State University Press at *www.msupress.org*

Contents

Preface

The University of Colorado Boulder was honored to host the 54th Algonquian Conference from October 20–23, 2022, our first time hosting this particular conference. The lead conference organizers were Andrew Cowell (Linguistics), Kristen Carpenter (CU Law School), and Alexis Palmer (Linguistics). Key funding for the conference was provided by an Innovative Seed Grant from the CU Research and Innovation Office (RIO), with additional major support coming from the Department of Linguistics, the Law School, and the Center for Native American and Indigenous Studies (CNAIS). This support allowed us to include a number of invited Indigenous keynote speakers and panelists, many from outside the normal attendees at the Algonquian Conference. The support also allowed us to present a special theme for the conference—the International Decade of Indigenous Languages (IDIL). The contributions of Kristen Carpenter and others at the Law School (notably Ariel Barbieri-aghib and Ellen Thurston) allowed us to bring a unique legal and human rights perspective to the conference, which we hope can be continued in future years, and allowed us to benefit from many in-kind contributions from the Law School. Special thanks are also extended to Laura Michaelis-Cummings, Chair of Linguistics.

In addition to the more traditional papers published in this volume of the conference proceedings, some of the keynotes and special panel discussions around the IDIL have been published in the *Colorado Environmental Law Journal*, as part of an effort to provide rapid recommendations on goals and best practices for the IDIL. These contributions came from a number of individuals outside of the normal academic circles of the Algonquian Conference (lawyers, tribal leaders and representatives, computer scientists, non-Algonquian specialists) as well as from Algonquianists. They are presented in the form of edited transcripts of the actual oral presentations and discussions that went on at the special IDIL-oriented sessions of the conference. This 2023 volume of the *Environmental Law Journal* complements the academic papers included in this volume, and readers may be interested in consulting that publication.

Finally, we would like to thank the previous hosts of the Algonquian Conference, who shared valuable information on budget, organization and processes with us at CU Boulder, making the conference a much easier event to manage than would have otherwise been the case.

Additional Conference Papers

In addition to the papers published in this volume, the following papers were presented at the conference:

Antti Arppe, Jolene Poulin, Atticus Harrigan, Katherine Schmirler, Daniel Dacanay, Rose Makinaw. *êkosi ê-nêhiyawi-pîkiskwêcik maskwacîsihk*—Towards a Spoken Dictionary of Maskwacîs Cree.

George Blanchard, Anastasia Miller-Youst, Joel Barnes, Carl Schaefer, Terry Hinsley. Shawnee Prosody for Pedagogy.

Ksenia Bogomolets. Phonological and Morpho-Phonological Properties of Vowel Harmony in Arapaho.

Joe Bryan, Seth Greer, Andy Cowell. The Colorado Indigenous Geographies Project: Challenges of Multi-lingual Geographical Documentation and Public Presentation.

Vincent Collette. Loanwords between Iroquoian and Algonquian Languages.

Rose-Marie Déchaine and Sonja Frazier. Discourse Syntax of an Ojibwe Narrative.

Sonja Frazier. A Rolling Stone Gathers No Moss, But Does A Skull? Applying Mühlbauer's (2008) Analysis to Ditibitigwaan: The Rolling Skull.

Christopher Hammerly, Sonja Frazier, Giancarlo Sierra, Scott Parkhill, Harrison Porteous, Chad Quinn. A Text-to-Speech System and Indigenous Avatar for Border Lakes Ojibwe.

Atticus G. Harrigan, Miikka Silfverberg, Antti Arppe. Resampling a Small Corpus to Build a Neural Model of Plains Cree.

Maude Harvey. Obviation in First Person Narrative in South East Cree.

Ryan Henke. A First Look at the Child Acquisition of Relational Verbs in Northern East Cree.

Dominik Kadlec. Developing a Computational Model of Blackfoot Morphology: Why It Is Important and How We Can Learn from It.

Corinne Kasper and Robert Eugene Lewis. The Potawatomi Complementizer System.

Polina Kasyonova. Cree Theme Sign is a Portmanteau.

Maria Mazzoli. Towards a Psycholinguistically Grounded Analysis of Stem Structure in Algonquian Languages: Incorporated Nouns, Medials, Concrete Finals and Their Cognitive Reality.

Cherry Meyer and Anna Whitney. Semantic Effects of VII Finals /-aa/ and /-ad/ on Medials.

Aandeg Muldrew. Understanding the *e-* Conjunct in Northwestern Ojibwe

Daniel G. Nolett, Philippe Charland, Christopher A. Roy. Louis Tahamont in Masardis, Maine, June 8, 1860.

Chad Quinn, Mike Parkhill, Christopher Hammerly. An Integrated Learning Platform for Border Lakes Ojibwe.

Jolene Poulin, Antti Arppe, Atticus Harrigan, Katherine Schmirler, Daniel Dacanay, Eddie Antonio Santos, Ansh Dubey, Andrew Neitsch, Daniel Hieber, Arok Wolvengrey. *itwêwina*: Towards a Morphologically Intelligent and User-Friendly On-line Dictionary of Plains Cree.

Christopher A. Roy. Tales of Abenaki Romance in New York State.

Leksi Scarr. A New Look at Prenouns in Menominee.

Lucy Thomason. 'As Soon As He Set Eyes on One, He Started Pretending That One Is His Mother': Inflectional Indefinites and Derived Indefinites in Meskwaki.

Irina Wagner. Grammatical Diversity as Means to Tellership Rights in Arapaho Conversational Storytelling.

Natalie Weber. How Synchronic Analysis Informs Subgrouping: Against Proto-Algonquian-Blackfoot.

D.H. Whalen, Christian DiCanio, Wei-Rong Chen. Variable Realization of the Arapaho Glottal Stop, Despite Its Being Distinctive and Frequent.

Yadong Xu. A Comparison of Formative Elements in Nishnaabemwin, Plains Cree, and Kickapoo.

The Discourse Status of Sole Proximates

Irene Appelbaum

In this paper, I describe a conflict in the literature on obviation concerning a proximate NP when it is the sole NP in a clause. The conflict is not limited to discussion of any one particular language. Thus, although my examples are drawn from previously published work on Meskwaki and from Ktunaxa narratives, the problem is found in analyses of languages exhibiting obviation, quite broadly. The conflict is this: Obviation is identified as a phenomenon requiring the presence of at least two NPs in a sentence. This implies that an NP that is the only NP in a sentence does not participate in obviation. Yet referents of such sole NPs are often characterized as exhibiting discourse prominence—the hallmark of proximate referents in the context of obviation. The problem with such sole NPs, then, is that they seem to be both capable and incapable of having discourse-prominent referents. The first aim of this paper is simply to make explicit this conflict implicit in our current accounts of how obviation functions. The second aim is to offer an avenue for resolving this conflict. I will suggest that we retain the assumption that obviation presupposes a second NP, but reject the requirement that it must appear in the same clause or sentence. Instead, I will suggest that a proximate NP that is the sole NP in a sentence can be said to participate in obviation as long as there is an obviative NP in a neighboring sentence. This obviative NP may be in a prior or subsequent clause and it may include the sole proximate's own status in surrounding clauses. This change allows us to say that such sole proximates may have a discourse-prominent referent, while retaining the view that obviation is a contrast between two NPs. Additionally, the amended view allows us to distinguish degrees of discourse prominence in different patterns of obviation. I conclude by highlighting a consequence of this approach—namely, that we often can't tell the discourse status of a sole NP in a clause independent of the surrounding text.

Description of the Problem

All Algonquian languages, and the language isolate Ktunaxa, exhibit obviation. Obviation functions somewhat differently in individual Algonquian languages, and there are also differences between how obviation functions in Algonquian languages and in Ktunaxa.[1] Nevertheless, there are core assumptions about obviation that are largely language-independent. Among these is the assumption that obviation is only applicable in contexts where there are at least two third persons in a clause or a sentence. For Blackfoot, Bliss describes the context for obviation as "a clause containing multiple third persons" (2005:61). Of Algonquian, generally, Oxford says obviation is applicable "when a clause contains multiple third person referents" (2019:16), and Dryer describes obviation as operating in Ktunaxa "in every sentence containing more than one third person participant" (1994:65).

What it means to say obviation is "applicable" in such contexts is that every third person in sentences containing at least two third persons is identified as proximate or obviative, with the constraint that only one NP may be proximate. Crucially, the referent of the NP identified as proximate is thought to outrank the referents of the obviatives in terms of discourse prominence. Other terms used to capture the idea of discourse prominence are "most central to the discourse" (Dahlstrom 2015:128), "most discourse-central" (Wolvengrey 2005:424), "more discourse-salient" (Bliss 2017:1), or simply "more prominent" (Goddard 1990:335).

"Discourse prominence," in turn, is said to encode a range of meanings that cross-cut the particular language being discussed. These meanings include the "topic" (Dahlstrom 1996:122; Oxford 2017:2; Wolvengrey 2005:424; Dryer 1996:14; Bliss 2005:65) or "focus" (Wolfart 1973:17; Bliss 2005:65) of the sentence, the character with whom the speaker has the most "sympathy" (Thomason 2003:98) or "empathy" (Dahlstrom 2017:52, n.d.:3–22), or whose "point of view" (Thomason 2003:98, Dahlstrom 2017:52) is being represented. In addition, the "main character" (Dahlstrom n.d.:3–20) or "hero" (Dahlstrom n.d.:8–7) of a narrative is often said to be the referent of a discourse-prominent proximate.

Thus, obviation is widely understood as a binary opposition within a clause or sentence containing at least two third-person NPs, wherein the referent of one is singled out as proximate and thought to be discourse prominent, and all others are identified as obviative.

In terms of morphological encoding, the obviative is always the marked member of the proximate/obviative opposition. In Ktunaxa, and in most Algonquian languages, the proximate is zero-marked. For example, the Ktunaxa form *kławła* 'grizzly bear' has no suffix either when it appears in contrast to an obviative NP, as in (1), or when it is the only NP in its clause, as in (2).[2]

(1) Ktunaxa

n-ułpał-ni	skinku¢-s	sił	¢xa-s-i	**kławła.**[3]
IND-hear-IND	Coyote-OBV	ASP	talk-OBV-IND	**Grizzly.Bear**

'Grizzly Bear (prox) heard Coyote (obv) talking.' (Boas 2005:140, line 4, emphasis added)

(2) Ktunaxa

qanax-i	**kławła.**
go.along-IND	**Grizzly.Bear**

'Grizzly Bear went along.' (Boas 2005:56, line 8, emphasis added)

In some Algonquian languages, the proximate has a distinct suffix. But even in these cases, the proximate is still unmarked in the sense that it is formally identical to the simple third-person form outside the context of obviation. For example, in Meskwaki, the proximate (singular) form has the suffix *-a* and the obviative (singular) has the suffix *-ani*. So, in (3), *ehkwe·w-a* 'woman' is proximate. Insofar as this proximate has a suffix, we can say it is more marked than the Ktunaxa proximate, which lacks a suffix altogether. But insofar as the same suffix also appears when an NP is the sole NP in its clause in Meskwaki, as in (4), we can say the proximate is nevertheless the unmarked member of the pair.

(3) Meskwaki

ehkwe·w-a kaka·čim-e·-w-a neniw-ani

woman-SG joke.with-DIR-3-SG man-OBV

'The woman (PROX) joked with the man (OBV).' (Dahlstrom n.d.:3–13, emphasis added)

(4) Meskwaki

še·ški=meko **ehkwe·w-a** e·h-wača·nota·-t-i

only=EMPH **woman-SG** AOR-do.cooking-3-MODE

'The women did nothing but cook.' (Dahlstrom n.d.:3–16, emphasis added)

Significantly, this single third-person form is also referred to as 'proximate'. As Goddard notes: "The proximate is the unmarked third-person category; if there is only one third person in a context, it can only be proximate" (Goddard 1990:317).

This fact—that single NPs are also identified as proximate—is not problematic in itself. However, it follows from this fact that identifying an NP as proximate does not by itself indicate that the referent of the NP participates in obviation. If the NP is the only NP in the sentence, it is, by definition, proximate; however, since obviation requires the presence of a second NP in the sentence, in the current understanding, such NPs cannot participate in obviation.

Admittedly, this leaves open the possibility that such sole proximates may be discourse-prominent, INDEPENDENT of the context of obviation. But in such a case, we would be forced to posit two parallel kinds of discourse-prominent proximates—ones that occur in the context of obviation and others that occur as sole proximates in a clause—and positing duplicate discourse systems seems otherwise unmotivated. So we seem to be forced to the conclusion that a proximate that is the sole NP in its clause cannot participate in obviation and therefore cannot be considered discourse prominent. Dahlstrom is explicit on this point. She says, "It is important to note that if the context contains only one third person, proximate morphology does not signal anything about discourse status" (n.d.:3–12).

The difficulty with this position is that it conflicts with analyses of texts where discourse prominence is often attributed to the referent of an NP that is the sole NP in its clause. Indeed, we find that in such cases, these single third persons are said to serve largely the same range of discourse functions as when proximates occur in the context of obviation: expressing topic or point of view, or identifying a main character. Let's look at some examples.

Sole Proximates and Textual Analyses

In example (5), from Meskwaki, 'Wisahkeha' is the sole third person in the sentence.

(5) Meskwaki
wi·sahke·ha=ke·hi wa·natohka=meko e·hkehči-nepa·či.
Wi·sahke·ha=and peacefully=emph greatly-sleep.3/AOR
'As for **Wi·sahke·ha**, he was peacefully sound asleep.' (Dahlstrom n.d.:8–7, emphasis added)

It is therefore proximate, by default. In other words, it fits the characterization of a morphological-only proximate. But in her description of this example, Dahlstrom (n.d.:8–7) explains the proximate status as due to the referent being the main character. She says, "At this point in the story, Wisahkeha is the main character and is THEREFORE referred to by proximate forms" (n.d.:8–7, emphasis added). The point here is not of course that main characters cannot appear in intransitive clauses, but rather that if the noun is proximate because of its discourse status as a main character, then proximate status is here serving a discourse function absent the requisite presence of a second third person in the clause.

In example (6), also from Meskwaki, once again, there is only one third-person referent: the Sioux, indexed with the proximate, animate form, *i·nikike·hi* 'those', and with the intransitive agreement, *owa·či* '3PL/AOR'.

(6) Meskwaki
i·niki=ke·hi, "aya·pami·-yakwe.
those.PROX.ANIM=moreover go.back-21/SUBJ
ke-i·h-nawači-memekwatahw-a·pena," e·h-iy-owa·či.
2-FUT-stop.to-beat.up-21>3/IND AOR-say.thus-3PL/AOR
'And **those** [**Sioux**]: "When we go back we'll stop to beat him up," **they** said.'[4]
(Dahlstrom 2015:122)

In this example, too, the proximate occurs outside the context of obviation and hence outside the context in which it can be said to signal discourse prominence. Nevertheless, the proximate status is interpreted as having the frequent discourse-prominence meaning of point of view. Dahlstrom explains, "Earlier in the story this group of Sioux is referred to with obviative NPs but here, where their speech and POINT OF VIEW are represented, they gain proximate status" (2015:122, emphasis added).

In the Meskwaki sequence in (7) and (8), Goddard (1984) clearly identifies the shift from the obviative *owi:ye:hani* 'someone' in (7) to the proximate *i:na* 'that man' in (8), as a proximate shift in which the proximate is the sole third person in the sentence.[5]

(7) Meskwaki
o:ni **owi:ye:hani** taši-a:hkwe:nite, kosemete, mani=ča:h=ki:wawita pya:te pepikwe:škwi, i:na:mihtahi=pi anwe:we:htaki.
'Now, if **someone** [**OBV, i.e., of the enemy**] is being fierce, if he [OBV] is feared, (and) if the one [PROX] who has this flute with him comes, he [PROX] would blow it.' (Goddard 1984:278, emphasis added)

(8) Meskwaki
o:ni **i:na** ke:ko:h=meko išawisa.
'Then something would happen to **that man** [PROX].' (Goddard 1984:278, emphasis added)

As the only third person, we expect the proximate to be interpreted as a morphological-only proximate. But Goddard (1984:279) is explicit in attributing a discourse function to the referent. He says, "It is clear that the proximate shift at this point has an IMPORTANT DISCOURSE FUNCTION, shifting the FOCUS of the narrative to the enemy warrior and describing the effect of the flute-playing from his POINT OF VIEW" (1984:279, emphasis added).

The examples just described illustrate that how we characterize obviation—as a discourse opposition between two NPs in a sentence—may clash with how we interpret obviation in the context of narratives—as a discourse phenomenon applicable in a clause with only one NP. Note that I am not calling into question the accuracy of these textual analyses. I am simply pointing out that insofar as they attribute a discourse function to sole NPs in a sentence, they are at odds with the widely accepted assumption that the discourse functions of obviation require the presence of two NPs in a clause. So, once again, the dilemma is that examples such as these presuppose that the sole NP of a clause can have a discourse-prominent referent, while the core characterization of obviation as an opposition between at least two NPs in a clause implies that it cannot.

This conflict has not, as far as I know, been previously identified. While attention is sometimes drawn to the discourse status of referents in sole-proximate clauses, it is not their status as sole proximates that is at issue. It is taken for granted that referents of sole NPs in a clause may be discourse prominent. Instead, the noteworthy point is only that such examples have minor characters as referents and minor characters would not seem to be good candidates for discourse prominence. The response here is usually to highlight the temporary nature of the discourse-prominent status in these cases (Goddard 1990:326, 330; Dahlstrom 1996:123, n.d.:3–20). Now, it is true both that minor characters are sometimes the referents of such single third persons and that when they are, their tenure as proximate is often brief. In the following, I discuss minor characters further, but in the present context, the problem is not that minor or peripheral characters sometimes exhibit discourse prominence, it's that ANY referents of single third persons do.

One could try to resolve the conflict by claiming that such clauses—whether with minor or major characters as referents—are infrequent and, hence, may be discounted as exceptions. The problem with this response is that it seems to be false. Clauses with a sole discourse-prominent NP are common. Indeed, proximate-shift sentences in which a new discourse-prominent referent is said to be introduced are usually of this kind. That is, it has often been noted (Goddard 1990; Dahlstrom 2014; Appelbaum 2021) that it is the norm for proximate shifts to occur with a single third-person NP in the clause. So, the problem with treating such clauses as exceptions is that it requires us to discount as exceptions clauses that are both common and central to tracking the discourse structure of a narrative—namely, proximate-shift sentences.

Toward a Solution

I think the key to getting beyond this standoff is to expand the domain of obviation. Instead of requiring that two NPs be present in a single clause or sentence, we should allow that the second NP—an obviative NP—may be in a prior or subsequent clause and, moreover, that this obviative NP and the sole proximate NP may have the same referent. That is, on the view I'm suggesting, the change from an NP being obviative in one clause to being a sole proximate in another clause is sufficient to allow that the sole proximate participates in obviation. However, in cases where the neighboring obviative refers to the same character as the sole proximate NP does, we can say that the proximate NP is relatively less discourse prominent than when the neighboring obviative refers to a second referent.

Broadening the context for obviation allows us to bring together our characterization of obviation as requiring two NPs, on the one hand, and our analyses of texts and understanding of proximate shifts, on the other, for what motivates the assumption that obviation only applies in the context of two NPs is that discourse status is an irreducibly relative notion. Attributions of discourse status presuppose some kind of comparison case. On the traditional understanding of obviation, this comparison must be a second NP syntactically realized in the same clause or sentence. Thus, when an NP appears as the sole NP in a clause, its referent cannot be identified as discourse prominent. However, if we allow that the second, that is, obviative, NP may be outside the syntactically realized clause, the requirements for discourse prominence are met even if there is only a single NP in a given clause. Let's look at an example.

In the sequence here, from a Ktunaxa narrative (Boas 2005), the main character, Yawukikam̓, meets Crane, a minor character. Examples (9) and (10) contain transitive sentences in which *yawuki·kam* is proximate and *qaspiłu'ks* 'Crane' is obviative.

(9) Ktunaxa
    łaxan̓xu'-ni [yawuki·kam][6] [qaspiłu'k-s].
    catch.up.to-IND [Yawukikam] [Crane-OBV]
    '[Yawukikam] reached [Crane (OBV)].' (Boas 2005:122, line 33)

(10) Ktunaxa
    qakił-ni [yawuki·kam] [qaspiłu'k-s].
    say.to-IND [Yawukikam] [Crane-OBV]
    '[Yawukikam] said to [Crane (OBV)].' (Boas 2005:122, line 34)

In (11), when Crane speaks, the NP referring to him becomes proximate, but the quotative verb is now detransitivized, so 'Crane' is the sole third person in the sentence. In the subsequent sentence, example (12), *qaspiłu'ks* 'Crane' is once again obviative.[7]

(11) Ktunaxa
qaki'-ni qaspiłu'k "...".
say-IND Crane "..."
'Crane said, "...".' (Boas 2005:122, line 35)

(12) Ktunaxa
q̓akpakitxu'-ni [yawuki·kam] qaspiłu'k-s
strike.down-IND [Yawukikam] Crane-OBV
'[Yawukikam] knocked Crane down.' (Boas 2005:122, lines 39, 40)

This pattern is typical of the temporary discourse status minor characters often have, mentioned earlier. In such scenarios, an obviative NP becomes a sole proximate for one clause and then returns to being obviative in the following clause. If our understanding of obviation allows us to compare the sole proximate to its own status in the previous clause, we can say that this sole proximate participates in obviation and that its status as proximate represents a discourse upgrade for the referent relative to its own status as obviative in the previous clause.

However, on the traditional understanding of obviation as requiring two NPs in the same clause, we are forced to deny that the referent of this sole proximate NP exhibits discourse status at all. Although analyses of this type of passage may make reference to the obviative status of the referent in the prior (or subsequent) clause, the requirement that the two NPs be found in the same clause prevents us from considering this obviative when determining the discourse status of the sole proximate NP.

A different pattern of obviation is typical in cases where the sole NP refers to a main character. In these cases, the sole proximate NP is followed by another sentence (or multiple sentences) in which it continues to be proximate but in which it is now accompanied by a second obviative NP. For example, in (13), from just earlier in the same Ktunaxa narrative, the main character, Yawukikam, is referred to by a proximate NP that is the only NP in the clause.

(13) Ktunaxa
qahanax-i [yawuki·kam].
go.along-IND [Yawukikam]
'[Yawukikam] went along.' (Boas 2005:122, line 33)

But in the next clause, example (14), the NP *yawuki·kam* continues to be proximate, but now a second NP, *qaspiłu'ks* 'Crane', is present as obviative. In this case, we can say that when *yawuki·kam* is the sole NP in its clause, as in (13), it is discourse prominent because of the presence of an obviative in the subsequent clause.

(14) Ktunaxa
n-ułpał-ni qaspiłu'k-s s-nawasxunak-s-i.
IND-hear-IND Crane-OBV CONT-sing-OBV-IND
'[He] heard Crane (OBV) singing.' (Boas 2005:123, lines 33, 34)

While the traditional approach does not allow us to say a sole NP in a sentence is discourse prominent in either of the patterns just shown, the present approach allows us to say that the sole NP is discourse prominent in both cases. On the other hand, there would seem to be a difference in the discourse status of the NP in each of these sequences. That is, in both scenarios, we are considering the discourse status of an NP in the same type of sentence—one in which it is the only NP—and in both cases, we can say the sole NP is discourse prominent because there is an obviative in a nearby sentence providing a contrast case. But it would also be desirable to be able to capture the intuitive difference in discourse status between these two types of cases, and the present approach allows us to do that as well. While in both cases there is an obviative in a nearby sentence, in the former case, the obviative has the same referent as the proximate that is the sole NP in its sentence. In the latter case, however, the obviative in the subsequent clause refers to a different referent. This difference allows us to say that the sole proximate in the latter type of scenario is more discourse prominent than a sole proximate in the former type of scenario.

Attributing different degrees of discourse prominence to the referent in each of these cases seems justified because in the former type of case the proximate is only more discourse prominent than its own prior and/or subsequent status, while in the latter case the proximate is more discourse prominent than another character. It is important to note that by identifying these patterns as typical for minor and major characters, respectively, I am not claiming that the characters are minor or major *in virtue of* whether the contrasting obviative refers to a second character. Instead, I am claiming that this contrast between same or different referent for the obviative determines whether the single proximate NP is more or less discourse prominent, and that it is an advantage of this approach that major characters end up having more discourse prominence relative to minor characters even when both types of character appear in the same type of sole NP clause.

The current approach also allows us to capture scenarios in which the NPs in successive sole-proximate clauses are alternately (fully) discourse prominent. That is, it allows us to describe scenarios where there is a genuine change in which character is most discourse prominent. For example, in the sequence that follows, *nasu'kin* 'chief' is the sole NP in its clause in (15) and, in (18), *ni·ȼuq̓-s* 'Duck' is the sole NP.[8]

(15) Ktunaxa
taxa-s k-ȼiłmiyit-s n-'anaxam̓-ni **nasu'kin** n-'uxtik.
then-OBV SUB-evening-OBV IND-go.out-IND **chief** IND-defecate
'Then, in the evening, the chief went out to defecate.' (Boas 2005:126, line 103, emphasis added)

(16) Ktunaxa
n-aqankił-ni **ni·ȼuq̓-s.**
IND-call.out.to-IND **Duck-OBV**
'[He] called out to Duck (obv).' (Boas 2005:126, line 104)

(17) Ktunaxa
qakił-ni "...".
say̓.to-IND "..."
'[He (Chief] said to [him (Duck, obv)] "...".' (Boas 2005:126, line 104)

(18) Ktunaxa
n-'anaxam̓-ni **ni·ȼuq̓.**
IND-go.out-IND **Duck**
'Duck went out.' (Boas 2005:126, line 105, emphasis added)

(19) Ktunaxa[9]
qawxał-qałuqka-łam̓-ni 'a·k̓ałaxikp-'is-is ni'-s **nasu'kin-s.**
in.that.place-cut.s.one.there-with.head-IND anus-3.POSS-OBV the-OBV **CHIEF-OBV**
'[He] cut the chief's (OBV) anus (OBV) with his head.'[9] (Boas 2005:123, lines 105, 106, emphasis added)

In each case, the sole, and therefore proximate NP, is followed by a clause in which it is again proximate but in which there is additionally a contrasting obviative NP. In (16), *ni·¢uq́-s* 'Duck' appears as the obviative, and in (19), *nasu'kin-s* 'chief' does. So, because the proximate NP in (15), *nasu'kin* 'chief', appears in the context of another referent as obviative in (16), we can say Chief is more discourse prominent than he would have been if (16) did not have an obviative referring to another character. Similarly, we can say that Duck is more discourse prominent in (18) than it would have been if *ni·¢uq́* 'Duck' did not occur in the context of a nearby obviative referring to a different character in example (19). In other words, the sole proximates in their respective clauses are both fully discourse prominent.

In addition to capturing the situation in which the discourse status of a sole NP may be more or less discourse prominent than that of another sole NP, the present approach also lets us capture the situation in which successive sole NPs are equally (fully) discourse prominent, though at different points in the story. It is important to emphasize that I am only suggesting relative differences in degrees of discourse prominence, other things being equal.

Now, to be sure, other analyses of texts make frequent, detailed reference to the discourse status of such sole proximates over successive clauses. These analyses illuminate the range of uses of obviation and its richness as a discourse resource. My claim is simply that these descriptions, unlike the alternative suggested here, are at odds with a view of obviation in which the contrast between proximate and obviative NPs must be found in the same sentence.

Objection and Reply

The conflict I discuss in this paper depends on a view of obviation in which two NPs must be present in a single clause or sentence. If the domain within which these two NPs must occur is not limited to a single clause or sentence, then there is no necessary conflict when discourse prominence is attributed to referents of NPs that are the sole NP in their clause. So, my criticism applies only to views that explicitly identify the context for obviation as a single clause or sentence. But—so the objection goes—not all characterizations of obviation do. For example, describing obviation in Meskwaki, Dahlstrom simply refers to "CONTEXTS containing more than one third person referent" (2015:128, emphasis added), and Wolvengrey describes obviation in Plains Cree as applying "in ANY SITUATION in which two or more third person participants are present" (2005:424, emphasis added). My reply to this objection is to acknowledge that in such descriptions there is no necessary conflict, but to point out that such accounts are atypical, and that even in these, the nature and consequences of such an expanded domain for obviation are not made explicit or developed.

Summary and Conclusion

According to the traditional view, the context for obviation is two NPs within a clause or sentence. This implies that obviation is not operative in clauses containing only a single NP. If obviation is not operative in such clauses, there is no reason to treat such single NPs as discourse prominent despite their default status as proximate. In the analyses of texts, however, discourse prominence is often attributed to proximates that are the sole NP in their clause, and, moreover, the most typical type of proximate-shift sentence is of this kind. In the face of this conflict, I have suggested that we might broaden the context for obviation to include a second, obviative NP in a prior and/or subsequent clause. I have argued that as long as there is a comparison NP somewhere nearby, we can say that the conditions for obviation are met and we can therefore attribute discourse prominence to such sole NPs in a clause. I have also suggested that we should distinguish cases where the contrasting obviative has the same referent as the sole proximate NP from those where the obviative has a different referent, and that in the latter case, the sole NP is more discourse prominent than in the former case, other things being equal.

One implication of the approach I am suggesting is that we may not be able to tell that an NP that is the sole NP in its clause is discourse prominent (or whether it is relatively more or relatively less discourse prominent) at the time that the clause occurs. It may be only after a subsequent sentence that we can determine the discourse status of the referent in the previous clause. While this may seem to be a drawback of this approach, I believe it is an appropriate consequence, for when we tell a story, we often do not know from sentence to sentence how it will develop. Depending on what transpires in successive sentences, we may be forced to reinterpret a previous one. Indeed, this is true not only for events of storytelling, but for any event of discursive interaction.

NOTES

1. See Dryer (1992).
2. The following abbreviations are used in interlinear glosses: 2 = second person, 21 = first person inclusive plural, 3 = third person, ANIM = animate, AOR = aorist, ASP = aspect, CONT = continuous, DIR = direct, EMPH = emphatic, FUT = future, IND = (independent) indicative, NP = noun phrase, OBV = obviative, PL = plural, POSS = possessive, PROX= proximate, SG=singular, SUB=subordinate, SUBJ = subjunctive.
3. For this and subsequent Ktunaxa examples, I have updated Boas's original orthography.
4. The quoted material is considered "a separate world of discourse" (Dahlstrom 2017:45), so for present purposes, the NPs contained therein are ignored.
5. This example and example (8) are presented as in Goddard's original, without interlinear glossing.
6. Ktunaxa does not have third-person pronouns, so if the full NP is not used—as is commonly the case—one or both NPs will not be overtly expressed at all; here and in the following I have put the full NPs in brackets for ease of presentation.
7. I omit the material in direct quotes as irrelevant to the examples.
8. In Ktunaxa, certain adverbs (as in (15)), especially *taxa* 'then', can take the obviative suffix.
9. We know from earlier in the story that Duck has put flint on his head.

REFERENCES

Appelbaum, Irene. 2021. The Importance of Being Not-Obviative. *Papers of the 50th Algonquian Conference*, ed. by Monica Macaulay and Margaret Noodin, pp. 5–22. East Lansing: Michigan State University Press.

Bliss, Heather. 2005. Topic, Focus, and Point of View in Blackfoot. *Proceedings of the 24th West Coast Conference on Formal Linguistics*, ed. by John Alderete, Chung-Hye Han, and Alexei Kochetov, pp. 61–69. Somerville, MA: Cascadilla Proceedings Project.

Bliss, Heather. 2017. Dependencies in Syntax and Discourse: Obviation in Blackfoot and Beyond. *Working Papers of the Linguistics Circle of the University of Victoria* 27(1):1–26.

Boas, Franz. 2005 [1918]. *Kutenai Tales*. Ann Arbor: University of Michigan Library, Digital General Collection. http://name.umdl.umich.edu/ACK2029.0001.001.

Dahlstrom, Amy. 1996. Narrative Structure of a Fox Text. *Nikotwâsik iskwâhtêm, pâskihtêpayih! Studies in Honour of H.C. Wolfart*, ed. by John D. Nichols and Arden C. Ogg, pp. 113–162. Winnipeg: Algonquian and Iroquoian Linguistics Memoirs, vol. 13.

Dahlstrom, Amy. 2014 [1991]. *Plains Cree Morphosyntax*. London: Routledge.

Dahlstrom, Amy. 2015. Highlighting Rhetorical Structure through Syntactic Analysis: An Illustrated Meskwaki Text by Alfred Kiyana. *New Voices for Old Words: Algonquian Oral Literatures*, ed. by David J. Costa, pp. 118–197. Lincoln: University of Nebraska Press.

Dahlstrom, Amy. 2017. Obviation and Information Structure in Meskwaki. *Papers of the 46th Algonquian Conference 2014*, ed. by Monica Macaulay and Margaret Noodin, pp. 39–54. East Lansing: Michigan State University Press.

Dahlstrom, Amy. [n.d.] *Meskwaki Syntax*. Manuscript, University of Chicago. https://lucian.uchicago.edu/blogs/adahlstrom/publications-2/selected-manuscripts.

Dryer, Matthew. 1992. A Comparison of the Obviation Systems of Kutenai and Algonquian. *Papers of the 23rd Algonquian Conference*, ed. by William Cowan, pp. 119–163. Ottawa: Carleton University Press.

Dryer, Matthew. 1994. The Discourse Function of the Kutenai Inverse. *Voice and Inversion*, ed. by T. Givon, pp. 65–99. Amsterdam: John Benjamins Publishing.

Dryer, Matthew. 1996. Grammatical Relations in Ktunaxa (Kutenai). *The Belcourt Lecture Delivered before the University of Manitoba on 24 February 1995*. Winnipeg: Voices of Rupert's Land.

Goddard, Ives. 1984. The Obviative in Fox Narrative Discourse. *Papers of the 15th Algonquian Conference*, ed. by William Cowan, pp. 273–286. Ottawa: Carleton University Press.

Goddard, Ives. 1990. Aspects of the Topic Structure of Fox Narratives: Proximate Shifts and the Use of Overt and Inflectional NPs. *International Journal of American Linguistics* 56(3):317–340.

Oxford, Will. 2017. Proximate DP, Obviative KP: Balancing the Morphosyntax and Pragmatics of Obviation. *Proceedings of the 2017 Annual Conference of the Canadian Linguistic Association*, ed. by Andrew Alexander Monti, pp. 1–15. https://cla-acl.ca/pdfs/actes-2017/Oxford_W.2017CLAProceedingsPaper.pdf.

Oxford, Will. 2019. Algonquian. *Routledge Handbook of North American Languages*, ed. by Daniel Siddiqi, Michael Barrie, Jason Haugen, and Eric Mathieu. New York: Routledge.

Thomason, Lucy. 2003. *The Proximate and Obviative Contrast in Meskwaki*. PhD thesis, University of Texas at Austin.

Wolfart, H.C. 1973. *Plains Cree: A Grammatical Study*. Transactions of the American Philosophical Society 63(5). Philadelphia.

Wolvengrey, Arok. 2005. Inversion and the Absence of Grammatical Relations in Plains Cree. *Morphosyntactic Expression in Functional Grammar*, ed. by Casper de Groot and Kees Hengeveld, pp. 419–445. Berlin: De Gruyter Mouton. https://www.degruyter.com/document/doi/10.1515/9783110920833.419/html.

Michipicoten Anishinaabemowin

An Autoethnographic Approach to Language Documentation

John-Paul Chalykoff

Michipicoten First Nation is located in northeastern Ontario, from the northeastern shore of Lake Superior to the interior of northeastern Algoma. *Noopiming dazhi-ininiwag* is one of the terms George Kah-Ge-Ga-Gah-Bowh Copway used to describe the Anishinaabeg who "reside in the interior of the shores of Lake Superior, in the North" (Ningewance and Valentine 2013). Gray and Morrison explain that the term also had a sometimes teasing, sometimes pejorative meaning of "hicks" or "backwoodsmen" for being "considered more rustic and less sophisticated than their more southerly counterparts" (2019:11). In some sources, Michipicoten shows up as *Mishibikwadinaang*, the Grand Hill (Lippert and Engel 2015) [*mishi-* 'giant'; *bikwadinaa* (VII) 'it is a knoll, is a hill' (Ojibwe People's Dictionary n.d.)]; it is a little different at the local level. From speaking with local elders from Michipicoten First Nation, Batchewana First Nation, Pic Mobert First Nation, and Chapleau Ojibway, the speakers all refer to it as *Michipigodong*. William "Bill" Swanson, an elder from Michipicoten First Nation, would go a step further and refer to it more specifically as *Michipigodong Ziibiing*, emphasizing the Michipicoten River.

As documentation of language in and around Michipicoten remains limited, there is a need to move forward in this work. This is a pilot project building off of vocabulary items that I have learned through family and community. They are shared in an autoethnographic format (Bishop 2020; Whitinui 2013) and interwoven with Indigenous storytelling (Kovach 2009, 2021; Simard 2020).

Michipicoten has a complex community dynamic due to being composed of two subgroups. Gray and Morrison state that Michipicoten was historically divided into two subgroupings, distinguished from one another by land-use practices, with the coastal group consuming more fish along the coast, while the interior group would primarily stay inland, moving further into the interior during the winter. Even though the two groups lived different lifestyles, they were not separate, but connected through intermarriage and clan/*doodem* kinship (2019:5–6).

Research Approach

This pilot study utilizes an autoethnographic approach (Bishop 2020; Whitinui 2013), while also weaving Indigenous storytelling throughout (Kovach 2009, 2021; Simard 2020). As a researcher who is also a member of Michipicoten First Nation, I draw from oral history, family stories, and historical reports and documents to build out initial findings on Ojibwe spoken in the northeastern region of Lake Superior. These findings are described by sharing stories, in which many of these little pieces of language emerged. Indigenous autoethnography offers a means to gather and share language in a community-oriented way (Whitinui 2013). Although this is a small first step, this research nonetheless sets a path for future work.

Margaret Kovach (Nêhiyaw and Saulteaux) shares that "stories remind us of who we are and of our belonging" (2009:94) while discussing stories as Indigenous methodology. She goes further in stating, "Story nurtures relationship. Story kindles reciprocity. Story compels responsibility. Story thrives where there is respect. Story is a gift. And in research, this changes everything" (Kovach 2021:156). Paul Whitinui (Maori) explains that "Indigenous autoethnography by its very definition asks to consider epistemological perspectives equally and to draw together self (auto), ethno (nation), and writing (graphy)" (2013:12). Bishop (Gamilaroi) argues that "the concept of 'self' needs broadening to recognise that this is a bigger entity than an individual" (2020:6). With this, the concept of auto/self expands beyond the limits of the individual. The language/vocabulary that I will be sharing throughout consists of words that I have learned from the family and community. There is a mix of community knowledge interwoven with academic research. Elements of storytelling will be incorporated throughout. Simard (Anishinaabe), referencing Koch (1998), shares that "storytelling is a lived process designed to facilitate change, whether internal or external, within an individual, family, community, nation or environment" (2020:141). Simard continues that "through reflection and praxis, storytelling methods allow for the discovery of social meanings related to the natural process of cultural development" (2020:141). Bishop reminds us that as Indigenous researchers "we are responsible and accountable first and foremost to our families, community members, Elders, Ancestors, and Country" (2020:4), something that I strive for in this work as well.

Ojibwe Dialects

Much of the data presented in this paper was not gathered using a systematic predetermined method. What I share has come from family and community, and is limited in quantity. However, family and community members will often speak of "our dialect." While it can be difficult to define a community's understanding of a dialect, most know that there are things that make our communities' variations different from what we often learn in available classes.

What separates a dialect from a language is quite complex. Linguists usually rely on some measure of mutual intelligibility, but that may vary between speakers. There is, however, a community level of understanding of dialects that I have come to pick up throughout the years of being in language learning circles that I want to emphasize. My understanding, and thus my interpretation, of when most speak of dialect is usually in the context of "our dialect" and "not our dialect." While I imagine it would be hard for many of them to define what separates dialects, many of them do understand there are differences. I recall sitting in a room of speakers from Batchewana First Nation in 2011 trying to come up with a mutual translation on a topic in a way that reflected how Batchewana speakers would say it. Some would pull words from published dictionaries for discussion, and one of the older elders would say "that's not our language," but meaning it in a dialectal way. The boundaries of "our dialect" and "their dialect" are complex, but it is usually implicitly understood that there are things that distinguish the way they speak from more "dominant" dialects.

Anishinaabemowin in and around Michipicoten First Nation has so far had little to no language documentation. Rand Valentine's dissertation *Ojibwe Dialect*

Relationships (1994) is the deepest study into Ojibwe dialects. Unfortunately, he was not able to make it to Michipicoten during his time of study. While much more analysis would be needed to be able to say more definitively, Michipicoten would most likely fit into the North of Lake Superior dialect as described by Valentine, where neighboring communities such as Pic Mobert First Nation (Netmizaaggamig Nishnaabeg), Pic Heron First Nation (Biigtigong Nishnaabeg), and Batchewana First Nation are discussed (1994:437–442). Valentine states that there are three broad dialectal groups: a northern group, a southern group, and a third transitional group that displays features of north and south. He identifies the North of Lake Superior as an area where some of the transitional features are displayed (1994:39–40). However, while North of Lake Superior does display some northern features, it is primarily a southern dialect, being more closely related to Chippewa, which includes communities around Minnesota and Wisconsin (1994:46). In personal communication, Valentine (in 2015) stated that evidence showed that Pic Mobert First Nation was situated there for a long time, because they had traits that combined elements from northern and southern dialects. In my own travels in the region, I did notice that Pic Mobert First Nation was where certain features began showing up, such as *nindoonjii* instead of *nindoonjibaa* for 'I am from someplace'. Michipicoten, which is east of Pic Mobert, still uses *nindoonjibaa*. With Michipicoten being the next neighbor over from Pic Mobert, there is a strong possibility that it also falls into that transitional area with northern and southern features being found.

Much of the language presented in this paper comes from discussions I have had with family, extended family, and community elders. Some of it comes from childhood memories, while other pieces come from listening to family members speak over the years.

My grandmother, Frances Beaupré (née Tangie), lost her fluency in childhood. Her grandmother, Mary Matchinini, raised her for the first five years of her life, and spoke to her in Anishinaabemowin. However, after her grandmother's passing, she was no longer spoken to in the language. She carried memories from this time for the rest of her life, remembering her grandmother. Even later in life, certain speakers would spark memories back to my grandmother of her own grandmother speaking to her. Some speakers from Garden River would bring that memory back. It also came up while driving through Manitoba and hearing Ojibwe spoken on the radio: "That sounds like my grandma!" These are some of the breadcrumb clues that my grandmother left behind.

Emerging Language Patterns

"Story is a gift" (Kovach 2021:156). Much of the vocabulary that will be shared here, I heard through story and discussion. Some of it was around the dinner table. Some of it in a hospital room. Some of it from visiting in a community center. Some of it around a community fire. I present the following words in an autoethnographic form. Each of these words or phrases has a little story associated with how I heard it, and I have labeled these as either "inland" or "coastal," depending on the subgroup affiliation of the community member from whom I heard them. I have more words and phrases labeled as "inland," since my family is from the inland group.

tootoosh 'nipple, breast' (inland)

This is the first Ojibwe word I recall from memory. Growing up, my siblings and I did not know or use the word *nipple* or *breast*, we just said *tootoosh* (with the softer -oo- sound like in the English word *boot*). I did not realize until years later that it was Ojibwe until taking Anishinaabemowin classes, and eventually put two and two together that *doodoosh* (with the harder pronunciation of -oo- like in the English word *boat*) and *tootoosh* were the same thing.

Quackegezick/Quackegesick (Gwekigiizhig) 'Turnover Day' (family name) (inland)

My grandmother's maternal line is Quackegezick. The name has been spelled a variety of ways over the years, but Quackegezick is how it was spelled on my great-grandmother Rosie Quackegezick's wedding certificate with my great-grandfather Rennison Tangie. My grandma would translate it as meaning 'Turnover Day.' It was not until recent years, when reading a historical report where I saw an alternate spelling, Gwekigijig (Gray and Morrison 2019:42), that I understood more of the pieces in the term. I could see the *gwek-* root, meaning 'to turn or change direction' (Ojibwe People's Dictionary n.d.), and *giizhig* meaning 'day.'

pezhik, niizhin, nisin, niiwin, naanan, ningodaachin, niizhwaachin, nishwaachin, zhaangchin, mitaachin 'one, two, three, four, five, six, seven, eight, nine, ten' (inland)

This is how my great-grandfather taught my mother, aunts, and uncles how to count in Ojibwe. As my family began taking Anishinaabemowin classes later in life, they began to notice that the way most classes counted was quite different from how their grandpa Rennison Tangie had taught them. Most classes would have some variation of the much more common *bezhig, niizh, niswi, niiwin, naaanan, ningodwaaswi, niizhiwaaswi, nishwaaswi, zhaangswi, midaaswi.* Some would try saying that it was Oji-Cree or Cree. Whenever they were asking Cree speakers, it was different from how they counted. My grandmother's brother, John Tangie, would insist: "It's Ojibwe! I know Oji-Cree, and that's not what we speak! It's Ojibwe!" We saw/heard some examples of *niizhin* and *nisin* from Patricia Ningewance's (Lac Seul First Nation) materials (2004:16), but we never heard anyone use the variations of the words for six to ten. It was not until 2016 while attending the immersion camp Eshki-Nishnaabemjig, when fellow participants John and Patsy Turner from Temagami First Nation shared how they count differently in their community, that I found an example of another community that counts the same way my great-grandfather had taught our family. John Turner had said it is how Algonquins count (personal communication 2016). Valentine only documents three communities using *midaachin/mitaachin*: Biscotasing, ON, Temagami, ON, and Winneway, QC, all of which are interior communities (1994:886).

gi-zaagi'in 'I love you' (inland)

I was on the search for language remembered by family, trying to gather anything I could. I was speaking with Patricia Tangie. My grandmother and her father, Allan Tangie, were siblings. She remembered having written down words and terms her father had shared with her when he was still living, but could not find the notebook. However, she remembered specifically how he said "I love you"—*gi-zaagi'in.* I could hear the glottal stop; it was not the shortened form *gzaagin.*

kayaashk 'seagull' (inland)

In her last few years, my grandma started to develop dementia. As she progressed into it, some Ojibwe she heard during her childhood would sometimes return to her. One time while she was visiting with my family household—I remember her sitting at the dinner table—she said *kayaashk* 'seagull.' It seemed to please her, remembering the word. I had noticed she pronounced it with the *k*- at the front instead of the *g*-.

gwiiwizens 'boy' (inland)

I remember going to visit a cousin, Abe Quackegesick, in the hospital. He was my grandmother's age. He was hesitant to share in the language. There were still painful memories associated with speaking, and he was also hesitant with his language skill. During our conversation, he did however end up saying *gwiiwizens* 'boy.' I distinctly remember hearing that short vowel intact, compared to the shortened form *gwiizens*.

n'mooshkine 'I'm full' (coastal)

I remember sitting beside elder Bill Swanson during dinner break between a long day of council meetings. After he was done eating, he patted his belly and said "*n'mooshkine*!" 'I'm full!' We had a good laugh together. I have heard him use *ndebsinii* as well, which is the word more commonly associated with being full from eating, but I always enjoyed when he would use *n'mooshkine* because it has more of a visual of being full to the brim: real stuffed kind of full. The personal pronoun marker *n-* (I/me) is usually barely audible, with just a hint of it.

engaach go 'taking it easy/take it easy' (coastal)

Elder Dave Swanson is one of the firekeepers in the community. When sitting around the fire with him, or catching up with him somewhere, whether it be in the community or downtown, it is rare to not hear him say "*engaach go*," when asked how he was doing; "taking it easy." It is also how he ends a lot of conversations, telling them to "*engaach go*," to "take it easy!"

"Zaagaate biidaasamose!" 'Sunshine's walking this way!' (coastal)

While I was visiting with elder Joe Swanson in the hospital back in 2016, he started sharing some stories of his childhood that he remembered. He spoke of an elder who would tease his brother Dave by calling him *Zaagaate*. Joe would say that Dave hated being called that as a child. Whenever Dave would be walking by as a child, the elder would proclaim "*Zaagaate biidaasamose*!" 'Sunshine's walking this way!' Joe would say that Dave would then usually turn and walk the other way. Joe shared that this elder from his childhood would also tease his cousin Emerson Riel when he was a child as well by calling him *Daawaa*, like Odaawaa/Ottawa. The initial short vowel *o-* was not pronounced in Joe's story, highlighting a possible pattern of syncopation/weak vowel deletion.

Michipigodong 'Michipicoten First Nation' (coastal/inland)

Many people are usually curious about the definition of Michipicoten. I heard and saw a number of translations over the years myself. I sometimes heard it was in reference to *Mishi-Bizhiw*, the great water lynx/panther we see at the Agawa Pictographs. If you do a quick Google search, you will find the 'Big Bluffs' translation from a number of sources. *Mishibikwadinaang*, the Grand Hill, has been showing up quite a bit more as a common one (Lippert and Engel 2015).

It was not until 2011 that I started asking local speakers from the region to get a local sense of the term. I first asked speaker Mary Allen (in 2011) from Batchewana First Nation how she would say Michipicoten in Ojibwe. I can still remember it clearly: *Michipigodong*. She had trouble trying to translate it; she pictured something like a hidden or secret valley in her mind. I had an opportunity to revisit this in 2015/2016 and got to ask some other speakers from the region. While visiting Pic Mobert First Nation/Netmizaaggamig Nishnaabeg, I had asked a speaker there how she would say Michipicoten in Ojibwe. She also said *Michipigodong*. She also had trouble translating it. While I was visiting Chapleau Ojibway elder Eva Memegos (in 2016), living in Chapleau Cree First Nation, she repeated the same thing. When asked how she would translate, she giggled, saying it sounded more French to her, and had trouble translating it. When I was elected to council for Michipicoten in 2017, I got to listen to elder councillor William "Bill" Swanson, and he shared the same thing, but went on to add that he remembered hearing it as *Michipigodong Ziibiing*, referencing the Michipicoten River. This is in reference to the old Michipicoten River community that was forcibly removed from the river site. However, he also had trouble translating it. Part of me wonders if it is similar to how *Baawating* (Sault Ste Marie/the place of the rapids) was shortened from *Baawitigong*, with *Michipigodong* possibly being a shortened localized version of *Mishibikwadinaang*.

boogijimin 'beans' (lit. 'the farting fruit') (inland)

This is perhaps one of my favorite words I had learned from my grandma. Sometimes around the dinner table, she would share stories. Often, they were stories about her life. Sometimes they were little nuggets of what she remembered "the older ones" would say. She recounted being a child listening to the older ones talking about beans. She would laugh recalling them calling it *boogijimin*, 'the farting fruit.' Just a very simple word from a quiet memory, yet I will never forget it.

Conclusion and Future Work

Remembering: This is the goal of documenting language. Recalling an earlier Kovach teaching, "Story compels responsibility" (2021:156), the stories of language shared above all remind me of my own responsibility in language documentation around Michipicoten. I estimate that there are perhaps five to ten language speakers in the area, and that is a more generous estimation. Time is truly of the essence. There are some clear next steps to take with the work. While the COVID-19 pandemic caused complications and delays, there is a window to begin working on language initiatives at the community level again.

There is a need to reconnect with the language speakers in Michipicoten and neighboring communities. Valentine's dissertation will be used as a model to gather vocabulary, as it is still an important piece and will help to connect where Michipicoten fits on the dialect spectrum. I am not trained in language documentation, but there is little time to lose, as there is a need to gather and document.

Connections with language speakers need to be rekindled. There is such a lack of vocabulary and other materials collected that it will be crucial to try gathering more. Utilizing Valentine's dissertation as a starting point to gather terms and vocabulary will be a valuable benchmark. From that benchmark, this pilot study can expand into a broader study involving gathering as much as possible to try to better situate Michipicoten's dialect grouping.

In the context of a pilot study, an autoethnographical approach is a jumping point from which to reinforce relationships and emphasize stories. However, further research employing methods including open-ended interviews and a conversation method (Kovach 2010) is needed. Valentine's survey will be utilized as the basis for gathering language data (1994:xv–xxiii). At this stage of research, I leverage autoethnography as a way to advocate for the importance of language documentation. Every single word truly does have a story behind it. We do not always need a story, but we do need the words, the sounds, the sayings, and however much else we can preserve while we still can. Language documentation is not an easy endeavor to begin, especially without training. I hope some of this work can offer processes of what can be done to begin working with speakers in our communities in language documentation/preservation, with the larger goal of deeper studies as a path toward the continuance of language.

REFERENCES

Bishop, Michelle. 2020. "Don't Tell Me What to Do." Encountering Colonialism in the Academy and Pushing Back with Indigenous Autoethnography. *International Journal of Qualitative Studies in Education*. https://www.tandfonline.com/doi/full/10.1080/09518398.2020.1761475

Gray, Susan E., and James Morrison. 2019. History of Michipicoten First Nation. Michipicoten First Nation.

Koch, Tina. 1998. Storytelling: Is it Really Research? *Journal of Advanced Nursing* 28:1182–1190. Doi: 10.1046/j.1365-2648.1998.00853.x

Kovach, Margaret. 2009. *Indigenous Methodologies: Characteristics, Conversations, and Contexts*. Toronto: University of Toronto Press.

Kovach, Margaret. 2010. Conversation Method in Indigenous Research. *First Peoples Child & Family Review* 5(1):40–48.

Kovach, Margaret. 2021. *Indigenous Methodologies: Characteristics, Conversations, and Contexts*, 2nd ed. Toronto: University of Toronto Press.

Lippert, Charles, and Jordan Engel. 2015. The Great Lakes: An Ojibwe Perspective. *The Decolonial Atlas*. https://decolonialatlas.wordpress.com/2015/04/14/the-great-lakes-in-ojibwe-v2.

Ningewance, Patricia. 2004. *Gookom's Language: Learning Ojibwe*. Mazinaate, Inc.

Ningewance Nadeau, Patricia, and J. Randolph Valentine. 2013. *Western Ojibwe Dictionary*. [Software.]

Ojibwe People's Dictionary. n.d. [Vocabulary, roots/morphemes]. https://ojibwe.lib.umn.edu.

Simard, Estelle. 2020. Critical Indigenous Ways of Knowing: Research, Narratives, and Self-Actualisation. *International Journal of Critical Indigenous Studies* 13(2):135–153. https://ijcis.qut.edu.au/article/view/1636/1002

Valentine, J. Randolph. 1994. Ojibwe Dialect Relationships. PhD thesis, University of Texas at Austin.

Whitinui, Paul. 2013. Indigenous Autoethnography: Exploring, Engaging, and Experiencing "Self" as a Native Method of Inquiry. *Journal of Contemporary Ethnography* 43(4): 1–32.

Initial Short Vowels and Language Change in Miami-Illinois

David J. Costa

The changes undergone by the vowels of Proto-Algonquian as they appear in Miami-Illinois are for the most part unproblematic. The long vowels of Proto-Algonquian appear almost unchanged in Miami-Illinois, with the main exception of long *ee* usually shifting to *ii* after *k* (Costa 2003:135–136). Miami-Illinois short vowels show a considerably more complex development, with word-initial short vowels showing the most elaborate development of all. The loss and merger of many word-initial short vowels in modern Miami-Illinois means that their full history can only be discerned by consulting the missionary materials on old Illinois, dating from around 1690 to 1720. In the past few years, the data in these dictionary manuscripts has been entered into an online database known as ILDA (Miami Tribe of Oklahoma 2017), making Illinois data more easily accessible than ever before (https://mc.miamioh.edu/ilda-myaamia). In this paper, I will lay out the Illinois reflexes of the word-initial short vowels of Proto-Algonquian, showing what grammatical conditioning, analogy, and sound shifts they were already undergoing by the old Illinois period, which will serve to highlight the dialect variation that is rife in these manuscripts. Additionally, I will discuss the considerably simplified reflexes these vowels have in modern Miami-Illinois (the

1790s to the present).[1] This will be done by citing relevant examples from the Illinois and modern Miami-Illinois corpus, which spans 200 years, comparing maximally archaic forms to more innovative forms.

Word-Initial Proto-Algonquian *o

In the earliest records of Illinois, from the late 17th/early 18th century, there are already only two contrastive word-initial short vowels, *a* and *i*. In Proto-Algonquian, *a, *i, and *o all contrasted word initially, but by the earliest Illinois records, short *o* has already disappeared from word-initial position, merging into *a* by sound law (see Costa 2003:141–143).[2] Miami-Illinois *a* is the only reflex of word-initial Proto-Algonquian *o ever seen in Miami-Illinois nouns and adverbs, to the point where *a* is by far the most common word-initial vowel in the language. However, in verbs, this has been disturbed by analogy; as explained in Costa (2003:404–411), verb stems that had initial *o in Proto-Algonquian are variously reflected in Miami-Illinois with either *a* (the phonologically regular treatment) as seen in (1), *wi* (2), or, rarely, long *oo* (3).[3] The latter two treatments arise from analogical leveling: The reanalysis with *wi* is backformed from the form **o*-initial verbs regularly take in initial change (namely, *wee*), and the forms with *oo* are generalized from forms taking person prefixes, after which *oo* is expected on a comparative basis (see Costa 2003:407, 411). In examples (1) through (3), (a) gives the word-initial form, (b) gives the form after a person prefix, (c) gives the form with initial change, and in (d) I give the reconstructed Proto-Algonquian stem.

(1) a. *ahpwaaro* 'smoke!' (LB ‹ap8aro›)
b. *nintahpwaa* 'I smoke' (Gr ‹nitap8a›, LB ‹nintap8o›)
c. *eehpwaayaani* 'I smoke' (LB ‹ehpoeian›)
d. < PA stem *ospwa·- (see Goddard 1982:28)

(2) a. *wihšiwa* 'she gets married' (LB ‹8ichi8o›)
b. *niwehši* 'I (woman) get married.' (Gr/LB ‹ni8echi›)
c. *weehšita* 'she gets married' (LB ‹8echita›)
d. < PA stem *oʔši- 'marry, take a husband (of a woman)' (Goddard 1973:48).[4]

(3) a. *oonsaaweewi* 'it is yellow, brown' (Gr/LB/P ‹8nsa8e8i›)
b. *nintoonsaahsaan* 'I tan it (a hide)' (Gr ‹nit8nsassan›)
c. *oonsaayosita* 'he is yellow, brown' (Gr ‹8nsaï8sita›, LB ‹8nsai8sita›)
d. < PA initial *osa·- 'yellow, brown'[5]

These are the normal patterns found with **o*-initial verbs in modern Miami-Illinois, as well as the most common forms seen in the old Illinois sources. However, in Illinois, one sees other strategies as well. One such development, very likely archaic, is the contracting of *ni-* 'first person' + *we-* sequences to *noo-*;[6] for example, for the TI stem *weraskinatoo-* 'fill it up, load it' (4a), the missionary sources attest both uncontracted *niweraskinatoo* 'I fill it up, load it' (4b) and the presumably older contracted form in (4c).[7]

(4) a. TI stem *weraskinatoo-* 'fill it up, load it'
b. *niweraskinatoo* 'I fill it up, load it' (Gr ‹ni8eraskinat8›)
c. *nooraskinatoon* 'I fill it up, load it' (P ‹n8raskinat8n›)

Some Illinois dialects take this further still, reanalyzing the *noo-* contractions of verbs with initial PA *ni* + **o-* (especially those with the initial *wer-*) as part of the stem, and thus superadding prefixal *ni-* and *ki-* to this in the first person. This is demonstrated in (5) with the TI stem *werahotoo-* 'put it on, bind it up', with the form (5b) with the full first person prefix, and the reanalyzed form in (5c).

(5) a. stem *werahotoo-* 'put it on, bind it up'
b. *niwerahatoo* 'I put it on, bind it up' (Gr ‹ni8irahat8›, D ‹niwälahato›)
c. *ninoorahotoo* 'I put it on, bind it up' (LB ‹nin8rah8t8›)

Similarly, for the usual AI stem *wereekiniko-* 'dress a hide', one sees both the first person prefixed form in (6b) and the contracted form in (6c).

(6) a. stem *wereekiniko-* 'dress a hide'
b. *niwereekiniko* 'I dress a hide' (Gr ‹ni8erekinig8›, LB ‹ni8erikineg8›)
c. *ninooreekiniko* 'I dress a hide' (Gr/LB ‹nin8rekinig8›)

Likewise, for the AI stem *weraapinti-* 'pull a bowstring into position', two different first person alternates are attested: (7b) with the full prefix and the contracted form in (7c).

(7) a. stem *weraapinti-* 'pull a bowstring into position'
b. *niweraapinti* 'I pull a bowstring into position' (Gr/LB ‹ni8erapinti›)
c. *ninooraapinti* 'I pull a bowstring into position' (LB ‹nin8rapinti›)

Proof that this *noo-* is generalized to second person forms as well is seen in the AI stem *weraskini-* 'be filled' in (8).

(8) a. stem *weraskini-* 'be filled' (AI)
b. *kinooraskinimwa* 'you (pl.) are filled, (it) is filled with you (pl.)'[8] (Gr ‹kin8raskinem8a›)

Word-Initial Proto-Algonquian *i

The Illinois development of word-initial Proto-Algonquian *i is more complex than that of *o, with nouns and adverbs undergoing a slightly different treatment from to that of verbs. For convenience, I will describe three different types of word-initial *i forms in Illinois: forms deriving from PA *ir- and *iθ-, those from *iHk- (where 'H' signifies any PA consonant that can precede *k other than *n), and those from PA *išp-.

Word-Initial Proto-Algonquian *ir and *iθ

In the oldest Illinois records, word-initial *i* is written interchangeably as either ‹i› or ‹e›. Nouns deriving from word-initial Proto-Algonquian *iren- are transcribed most often with word-initial ‹i›, but also sometimes with ‹e›. For example, for *ireniwa* 'man' in (9a), from PA *irenyiwa, one sees original Illinois transcriptions with the initial vowel rendered both ‹i› and ‹e›:

(9) a. *ireniwa* 'man' (Gr/LB/P ‹ireni8a›, LB ‹erêni8o›)
b. < PA *irenyiwa 'man' (see Bloomfield 1946:87)

Likewise, for Illinois *irenaswa* ‘buffalo’ and words derived from it, one usually finds forms written with initial ‹i› (10a), but also there is at least one form written with ‹e› (10b).

(10) a. *irenaswa* ‘buffalo’ (Gr ‹irenans8a›, LB ‹irenans8o›)
b. *irenaswayi* ‘buffalo hide’ (Gr ‹irenans8eï›, LB ‹erenans8ie›)
c. < pseudo-PA *irenoswa, *irenoswayi (Goddard 2002:61)

Since short **i* and **e* did not contrast word-initially in Proto-Algonquian, this scribal variation between ‹e› and ‹i› is almost certainly not phonologically significant in Illinois, and merely represents attempts to render a phoneme that either was intermediate between *e* and *i*, or was in free variation between these two sounds.

Proto-Algonquian verb stems beginning with the very common initial *iθ-/*iš- ‘thus’ follow the same patterns of development in both Illinois and the modern language: word initially, the vowel appears as *i* at all time periods, though again this is variably written as ‹i› and ‹e› in Illinois (11a); after person prefixes, this vowel always appears as *e* (11b,c); and when undergoing initial change, it appears as *ii* (11d).

(11) a. *išiteeheewa* ‘he thinks so’ (Gr ‹ichitehe8a›, LB/R ‹echitehe8a›)
b. *nintešiteehee* ‘I think so’ (Gr/R ‹nitechitehe›, LB ‹nintechitehe›)
c. *kitešiteehee* ‘you think so’ (LB ‹kitechitehe›)
d. *iišiteeheeci* ‘he thinks so’ (Gr ‹ichitehetchi›, Mc ‹ī‘cítä‘ätc^{i}‘›)
e. pseudo-PA stem *išite·he·- ‘think so’ (cf. Meskwaki *išite·he·wa* ‘he thinks’)

Displaying a different pattern from both Proto-Algonquian *iren- and *iθ-/*iš- are Illinois words deriving from PA *iθo·h- ‘point at, aim’ as seen in the TA stem *iθo·hw- ‘point at him’ (Goddard 2002:62) in (12), and the noun *iθo·hikani ‘forefinger’ (Ives Goddard personal communication 2020) in (13). In contrast with the Illinois development of *iθ- ‘thus’ (which strictly by normal sound change one would expect it to be homophonous with), verbs and nouns derived from the PA initial *iθo·h- have been reanalyzed in all Miami-Illinois records with stem-initial *a* ((12a,b) and (13a)), with a corresponding initial change vowel *ee* (12c).[9]

(12) a. *aroohwi* 'point at him, aim at him!' (P ‹ar8h8i›)
b. *nintaroohwaa* 'I point at him, aim at him' (Gr ‹nitar8h8a›, LB ‹nintar8^{h}a›)
c. *eeroohonta* 'he is pointed at, aimed at' (Gr ‹er8h8nta›)
d. < PA *iθo·hwe·wa 'he points at him' (Goddard 2002:62, 2003:182)

(13) a. *nintarohwirenciaakani* 'my index finger' (Gr ‹nitar8h8irintchiagane›, LB ‹nitar8irintchiagane›, P ‹nitar8h8rintchiagane›)[10]
b. cf. PA *iθo·hikani 'forefinger' (Ives Goddard personal communication 2020) and Ojibwe *inoohikaninj* 'index finger'

The replacement of noun-initial PA **i* with *a* is occasionally seen in the late Illinois records as well. It is most common in LeBoullenger's dictionary, the language of which is notably less archaic than that of Largillier's dictionary (which was written perhaps 30 years earlier). For example, for 'earthen pot made by the Indians', Largillier has an *i*-initial form (14a), compared to the more innovative *a*-initial inanimate equivalent LeBoullenger gives (14b).

(14) a. *irenahkihkwa* 'earthen pot made by the Indians' (Gr ‹irenakic8a›)
b. *arenahkihkwi* 'earthen pot made by the Indians' (LB ‹arena kic8e›)

Similarly, for 'plums', Largillier has an archaic *i*-initial form (15a), while LeBoullenger has an innovative *a*-initial form (15b).[11]

(15) a. *ireniminiiki* 'plums' (Gr ‹ireniminiki›)
b. *areniminiiki* 'plums' (LB ‹areniminiki›)

Occasionally this goes so far in the LeBoullenger manuscript as to lead to the complete deletion of word-initial *i in nouns; for example, the Illinois word for 'rat' is *i*-initial in most of its attestations (16a), though an innovative plural form with the initial vowel deleted is attested once by LeBoullenger (16b).[12]

(16) a. *irenakoohsia* 'rat' (Gr ‹irenac8ssia›, LB/P ‹irenag8ssia›)
b. *rénakoohsiwaki* 'rats' (LB ‹rênac8ssi8oki›)

By the 1790s onward, word-initial *i* is never found on Miami-Illinois nouns anymore: It is replaced with *a*, which in turn is often deleted entirely, especially by the late

19th century. Thus, for Miami-Illinois ‘man’ (see also (9)), the Illinois sources all attest initial *i* (17a), which is shifted in the early modern sources to *a* (17b), which is, in turn, deleted by the early 19th century and thereafter (17c).

(17) a. *ireniwa* ‘man’ (Gr/LB/P ‹ireni8a›, LB ‹erêni8o›)
b. *alenia* ‘man’ (Hk ‹alenja›, BB ‹ahlanuah›, Tr ‹ulāāneeau›)
c. *lénia* ‘man’ (Tr ‹lāāneeau›, Gt ‹lénia›, Mc ‹länyá^{n}›)
d. < PA *irenyiwa ‘man’ (see Bloomfield 1946:87)

Similarly, while the Illinois word for ‘buffalo’ is always *i*-initial (18a), and see also (10) above, a few sources from the early modern period give it with initial *a* (18b), but some early modern sources and all sources from the late 19th and early 20th centuries give it as consonant-initial (18c).

(18) a. *irenaswa* ‘buffalo’ (Gr ‹irenans8a›, P ‹irenans8›, LB ‹irenans8o›)
b. *alenaswa* ‘buffalo’ (V ‹alanantsoua›, Tr ‹ulaanāūzwau›)
c. *lénaswa* ‘buffalo’ (Hk ‹lenãnswa›, D ‹länánzwa›, Mc pl. ‹lena^{n}zó^{ε}k$^{i‘}$›)

This replacement of older *i* with *a* in nouns is in striking contrast to the development of word-initial short *i* in **verbs**, where *i* is still retained in the 20th century; for example, for the stem *elwee-* ‘say so’, note the *i*-initial imperative in (19a) and the third person singular independent in (19b). Similarly, from the stem *ešite·he-*- ‘think so’, note the modern imperative in (20a) and the conditional in (20b); see also (11).

(19) a. *ilweelo* ‘say so!’ (LB ‹ir8ero›, D ‹ilwälo›)
b. *ilweewa* ‘he says so’ (P ‹ir8e8a›, D ‹ilwawa›)

(20) a. *išiteeheelo* ‘think so!’ (D ‹icitähälo›)
b. *išiteeheeyiikwe* ‘if you (pl.) think so’ (D ‹ĭcĭtähäĭkwä›)

Initial Proto-Algonquian *iHk and *išp clusters

The most labile word-initial short vowels in Illinois are those deriving from word-initial Proto-Algonquian *iHk and *išp clusters. There are two lines of development in Illinois for such sequences: one for nouns, and a somewhat more elaborate treatment for verbs. I will discuss these vowels in nouns first, before expanding on this to demonstrate their development in verbs.

In the oldest Illinois records, nouns with *iHk and *išp clusters appear with initial *i* (written ‹e› or ‹i›), which in the later Illinois records shifts to *a*. Often this co-occurs with the shifts of *sk* > *hk* and *sp* > *hp*, which were taking place in the language at the same time (see Costa 2024). By the 1790s onward, this initial vowel is deleted from nouns across the board. For example, from the Proto-Algonquian word for 'door' (21), the oldest Illinois records are *i*-initial (21a), while a later, more innovative dialect of Illinois has *a*-initial forms and also shows the shift of *sk* to *hk* characteristic of the modern language (21b). By the early 1800s this initial vowel is deleted in all records (21c).

(21) a. *i̲skwaanteemi* 'door' (Gr/LB ‹esc8antemi›, ‹isc8antemi›)
b. *a̲hkwaanteemi* 'door' (Gr/LB ‹ac8antemi›, P ‹ak8antemi›)
c. *kwaanteemi* 'door' (Tr ‹kwondamēē›, Mc ‹kwā́ndemi›)
d. < PA *iškwa·nte·mi 'door' (Goddard 2002:54)

Occasionally the total deletion of these initial vowels is already found in the Illinois records, especially in LeBoullenger's dictionary. Thus, from the Proto-Algonquian word for 'fire' (22), the most conservative Illinois dialects have *i*-initial forms (22a), while more innovative Illinois dialects show initial *sk* (22b), which is in turn transitional to the modern forms, which obligatorily delete the initial syllable and sibilant entirely (22c).

(22) a. *i̲skoteewi* 'fire' (Gr/P/LB ‹isc8te8i›)
b. *s̲kóteewi* 'fire' (LB ‹sc8te8i›)
c. *kóteewi* 'fire' (V ‹kohteoué›, Hk ‹gutewi›, Tr ‹kōātawaa›)
d. < PA *iškote·wi (Bloomfield 1946:105)

In the oldest records, nouns with initial *iHk- usually preserve this initial vowel as Illinois *e* (< PA *e) when it follows person prefixes, as in the three variant forms for 'my fire' in (23).

(23) a. *nite̲skoteeyomi* 'my fire' (P/LB ‹nitesc8teï8mi›)
b. *nite̲skoteewi* 'my fire' (LB ‹nitesc8te8i›)
c. *nite̲hkoteewi* 'my fire' (P ‹nitek8te8i›)

However, sometimes the word-initial *a* of the later Illinois forms is generalized from the simplex form to possessed forms by analogy. For example, for Illinois 'his door' (24) one sees archaic forms retaining expected *e* (24a), but also an innovative dialect variant with stem-initial *a* (24b). The latter form shows not only the paradigmatic leveling of the stem-initial vowel, but also, again, the shift of *sk* to *hk*:[13]

(24) a. *ateskwàanteemi* 'his door' (Gr ‹atesc8antemi›)
b. *atahkwaanteemi* 'his door' (Gr ‹atac8antemi›)

More common than nouns deriving from word-initial Proto-Algonquian *iHk and *išp clusters are verbs and adverbs with these sequences. There are several initials in Proto-Algonquian that exemplify a pattern in Illinois whereby word-initial Proto-Algonquian *iHk and *išp clusters appear as *isk* and *isp* in the oldest layers of Illinois (25a, 26a, 27a), sometimes *ihp* (27b), with initial *a* in some later Illinois records (25b), with a deleted vowel and initial *sC* in the latest Illinois records (25c, 26b), finally arriving at plain initial *k* and *p* obligatorily in the 19th century and occasionally even in Illinois (25d, 26c, 27c). After person prefixes, these stems appear with inherited stem-initial *e* (26d,e) and in dependent forms with long *ii* when undergoing initial change (26g, 27d).[14] Illinois forms from the Proto-Algonquian initial *išp- 'high' (25–27) exemplify all these patterns:

(25) a. *ispeminki* 'up, above' (R ‹ispemenghi›, Gr/LB/P ‹espeminghi›)
b. *aspeminki* 'up, above' (LB ‹aspeminghi›)
c. *spéminki* 'up, above' (Gr/LB ‹speminghi›)
d. *péminki* 'up, above' (Tr ‹paamīngee›, Gt ‹pắmingi›, Mc ‹pemíñgi›)
e. < PA *išpemenki 'up above' (Bloomfield 1946:88)

(26) a. *ispesiwa* 'he is high, tall' (Gr/P ‹ispessi8a›, LB ‹ispesi8a›)
b. *spésiwa* 'he is high, tall' (P ‹spessi8a›)
c. *pésiwa* 'he is high, tall' (LB ‹pesi8o›, D ‹pắssiwa›)
d. *nintehpisi* 'I am tall' (LB ‹nintêpisi›, D ‹n'däpĭsĭ›)
e. *kitehpisi* 'you are tall' (LB ‹kitepisi›)
f. < PA *išpesiwa (3sg.), *netešpesi (1sg.), *ketešpesi (2sg.)
g. *iispiiki~iihpiiki* 'it is tall' (Gr ‹ispiki›, ‹ippiki›, Gt ‹îhpiki›)

(27) a. *i̲spatinwi* 'it is a high hill, steep' (Gr/LB ‹ispaten8i›, LB ‹espaten8i›)
b. *i̲hpatinwi* 'it is a high hill, steep' (LB ‹ipaten8i›)
c. *pátinwi* 'it is a high hill, steep' (LB ‹paten8i›)
d. *i̲i̲hpatenki* 'it is a high hill, steep' (LB ‹ipatenghi›, V ‹ifpatingué›, D ‹ĭppatắngĭ›)
e. < PA II stem *išpaten- 'it is a high hill'

Other Proto-Algonquian initials that demonstrate similar developments for word-initial short vowels are *iškw- 'left over, set aside', *išk- 'tired, with difficulty', *irk- 'evaporate, dry out', and *iθkwe·- 'woman'. Example (28) demonstrates these patterns for PA *iškw- 'left over, set aside', with (28a) showing archaic word-initial *i*, post-prefixal *e* (28b,c), reanalyzed stem-initial *a* (28d), and forms taking initial change with long *ii* (28e).

(28) a. *i̲skwihaawa* 'he is spared' (Gr ‹isc8iha8a›)
b. *nite̲skahpwaa* 'I leave him from eating' (Gr ‹nitescap8a›)
c. *nite̲hkahpwaa* 'I leave him from eating' (LB ‹nintecap8o›)
d. *nita̲hkwihaa* 'I spare him, do not kill him' (Gr ‹nitac8iha›)
e. *i̲i̲hkahpwaaci* 'he leaves him from eating' (Gt ‹íkpotch›, D ‹ĭkpwatc›)
f. cf. Meskwaki *aškwihe·wa* 'he leaves him, spares him'

The following forms deriving from PA *išk- 'tired, with difficulty' show the same patterns: archaic initial *i* preserved in (29a), *e* preserved after person prefixes (29b-d), and long *ii* from initial change (28e,f).

(29) a. *i̲skahosiwa* 'he is tired of being tied up' (Gr ‹isca8si8a›)
b. *ninte̲skapi* 'I am tired of sitting' (Gr ‹nitescapi›)
c. *ninte̲hkapi* 'I am tired of sitting' (LB ‹nintêcapi›, D ‹n'däkapĭ›)
d. *ninte̲skireehsee* 'I have trouble breathing' (Gr/P ‹niteskiresse›)
e. *i̲i̲hkihkireehseeta* 'he has trouble breathing' (LB ‹ikikiresseta›)
f. *i̲i̲hkileehseeta* 'he sighs'[15] (D ‹ĭ́kĭlắssät›)
g. cf. Ojibwe *ishkabi* and Meskwaki *aškapiwa* 'he is tired of sitting'

There happen to be no attested examples of PA *irk- 'evaporate, dry out' being reflected as initial *i*, as the earliest records already have initial *a* (30a,b). The initial change vowel for this verb is still *ii* (30c).

(30)	a. *ahkiteewi*	'it evaporates, the water dries out'	(Gr/P/LB ‹akite8i›)
	b. *ahkisiwa*	'he evaporates, boils out'	(Gr ‹akisi8a›)[16]
	c. *iihkihsaaki*	'it (water) goes down, recedes, ebbs'	(Gt ‹íksaki›)
	d. cf. Ojibwe *iskate* 'it (water) goes down, dries up'		

Similarly, the common PA initial *iθkwe·- 'woman' is almost never reflected with initial *i*, but rather with *a* word-initially (31a) in Illinois and with an entirely deleted initial syllable in the modern language (31b).[17] After person prefixes, archaic *e* is still found in the oldest layers (31c), but this is commonly shifted to *a* in later Illinois (31d,e):

(31)	a. *ahkweehsa*	'young unmarried woman'	(Gr/LB ‹ac8essa›)
	b. *kweehsa*	'young unmarried woman'	(Hk ‹quechsa›, Mc ‹kwé'sa'›)
	c. *nintehkweehsima*	'my sister-in-law (husband's sister)'	(Gr ‹nitec8essima›)
	d. *nintahkweehsima*	'my sister-in-law (husband's sister)'	(Gr ‹nitac8essima›, LB ‹nitac8essema›)
	e. *nintahkweehsi*	'I am a young girl, a virgin'	(P/LB ‹nitac8essi›)
	f. cf. Plains Cree *iskwe·s* 'teenage girl, little girl', Kickapoo *ihkweeha* 'young woman'		

The verb 'drown', also from the PA initial *išk- 'tired, with difficulty', follows all these same patterns as well, except that its vowel in initial change unexpectedly always appears as *ee* rather than the *ii* seen with all other Miami-Illinois verbs from this initial (32g,h). Examples (32a,b) show the archaic forms of this word with initial *i*; (32c) shows a more innovative form with the initial vowel reduced to *a*; and (32d) shows forms with this vowel deleted entirely, once even in Illinois. Example (32e) shows expected archaic post-prefixal *e*, while (32f) shows a more innovative Illinois form where this *e* has been analogically leveled to *a*.

(32) a. *iskaraamowa* 'he drowns' (LB ‹escaram88o›)
b. *ihkaraamowa* 'he drowns' (LB ‹êcaram8o›)
c. *ahkaraamowa* 'he drowns' (LB ‹âcaram8o›)
d. *káraamowa* 'he drowns' (LB ‹caram8a›, Gt ‹kálamua›)
e. *ninteskaraamwi* 'I drown' (LB ‹nitescaram8i›)
f. *nintahkaraamwi* 'I drown' (LB ‹nintacaram8e›, Gt ‹nindaxkálamwi›)
g. *eeskaraamwita* 'he drowns' (LB ‹escaram8ita›)
h. *eehkaraamwita* 'he drowns' (LB ‹ehcarem8ita›, Tr ‹aahkōlumweet›, Gt ‹äxkálamwit›)
i. < PA *iškaθa·mo-; cf. Ojibwe *ishkanaamo* 'I breathe with difficulty, fatigue.' and Meskwaki *aškana·mowa* 'he runs out of breath, smothers'

This pattern of stem-initial short vowel vocalism is not limited to verbs with initial PA *i, but has also been analogically extended to a few initials deriving from Proto-Algonquian *aHk-. The most common initial restructured this way in Illinois is PA *ašk- 'raw' (33); in the oldest layers of the language, verbs with this initial take unchanged initial *i* (33a), post-prefixal *e* (33d), and changed *ii* (33e). By normal sound laws these stems then later reacquire *a* in word-initial position in later Illinois (33b), which occasionally deletes in innovative Illinois dialects (33c).

(33) a. *iskirwa* 'he is raw' (Gr/P ‹iskir8a›, LB ‹iskir8o›)
b. *askinwi* 'it is raw' (P/LB ‹askin8i›)
c. *skinwi* 'it is raw' (LB ‹skin8i›)
d. *niteskitaan* 'I eat it raw' (Gr ‹niteskitan›)
e. *iiskinki~iihkinki* 'it is raw' (Gr/P/LB ‹iskinghi›, Gt ‹íxkingi›)
f. cf. Ojibwe *ashkini* (AI), *ashkin* (II) 'he/it is raw'

The initial seen in Illinois *askimotayi* 'bag, pocket' probably derives from PA *ašk- 'raw' as well. In the oldest records it shows *ask-* (34a), later *ahk-* (34b) and *sk-* (34c), and late Illinois/modern *k-* (34d). It also consistently appears with initial *e* after person prefixes (34e,f).

(34) a. *askimotayi* 'bag, pocket' (Gr ‹askim8taï›, ‹askim8taie›)
b. *ahkimotayi* 'bag, pocket' (LB ‹akim8tai›)
c. *skímotayi* 'bag, pocket' (Gr ‹skim8taï›, P ‹skim8tai›)
d. *kímotayi* 'bag, pocket' (LB ‹kim8tae›, WP ‹kemotiʋ›)
e. *niteskimotayi* 'my bag, pocket' (LB/P ‹niteskim8tai›)
f. *nintehkimotayi* 'my bag, pocket' (Gt ‹nindäkimutáyi›)
g. cf. Potawatomi *škəmot* 'bag' and *wdəškmodak* 'in his bag'

One Proto-Algonquian noun with word-initial *o- has been pulled into this noun class as well, 'chief's attendant' (35). This word consistently shows initial *i* in Illinois (35a-c), *e* after person prefixes (35e), and always deletes this vowel word-initially in the modern language (35d).[18]

(35) a. *iskaapeewa* 'chief's attendant' (Gr ‹iscape8a›)
b. *ihkaapeewa* 'chief's attendant' (Gr ‹icape8a›)
c. *iskaapia* 'chief's attendant' (Gr ‹escapia›)
d. *kaapia* 'chief's attendant' (Tr ‹kāūpeeau›, Gt ‹kápia›)
e. *niteskaapeeyoma* 'my chief's attendant' (Gr ‹nitescapeï8ma›)
f. PA *oška·pe·wa 'chief's attendant' (Goddard 2002:52; Costa 2003:158)

An interesting fact about the reanalysis of this noun as i-initial is that even though PA *oška·pe·wa literally means 'young man', from an initial *ošk- 'young, new', verb forms with this same initial always retain expected inherited *wisk-* (36a) and changed *weesk-* (36b) in Illinois, and modern Miami-Illinois *we(e)hk-* (36c). This strongly suggests that the meaning of *iskaapeewa* had semantically diverged from verbs with this initial so much that speakers no longer considered it etymologically related.

(36) a. *wiskinwi* 'it is new, fresh' (Gr ‹8iskin8i›)
b. *weeskinki* 'it is new, fresh' (LB/P ‹8eskinghi›)
c. *weehkiinaakwahki* 'it is new, looks new' (Th ‹uehkinakokeh›)
d. cf. Ojibwe *oshkiinaagwad* 'it looks new'

The etymologically mysterious Miami-Illinois word for 'old man' probably fits into this same pattern: From a presumed (but unattested) pre-Illinois *iskiyošiwa, it appears as with initial *i* (37a) or *sk* (37b,c) in the oldest records, eventually settling as modern *kíyoš(i)a* (37d). However, in all time periods it still takes *a* after person prefixes (37e,f) and long *ii* in initial change (37g).[19]

(37)			
	a. *iskiyošia*	'old man'	(LB ‹eski8chiha›)
	b. *skíyošiwa*	'old man'	(Gr ‹ski8chi8a›, LB ‹ski8chi8a›)
	c. *skíyošia*	'old man'	(LB ‹schki8chia›)
	d. *kíyoš(i)a*	'old man'	(E ‹kioushiah›, V ‹kéocha›, Mc ‹kī́yo'caⁿ›)
	e. *nintaskiyošiwi*	'I am an old man.'	(Gr ‹nit'aski8chi8i›)
	f. *kitahkiyošioma*	'your old man, husband'	(Gt ‹kitáxkiyushóma›)
	g. *iihkiyošiwita*	'He is an old man.'	(D ‹ikeocéwĭt›)

Conclusion

Perhaps the most remarkable thing about the development of initial short vowels in Miami-Illinois is how all stages and combinations of the sound changes of initial *i* > *a* > *Ø* and *sC* > *hC* are found in the Illinois dictionaries, often within the same lexeme. As an example, in Largillier's circa-1700 dictionary, he attests the maximally archaic *iskwaanteemi* 'door' alongside newer *ahkwaanteemi*; and for possessed 'his door', he attests both archaic *ateskwaanteemi* and innovative *atahkwaanteemi* (see (21) and (24) above). Similarly, for the PA initial *išp- 'high, tall', in LeBoullenger's dictionary alone one finds archaic *ispatinwi*, later *ihpatinwi* with reduction of *sp* to *hp*, and eventual *pátinwi*, with complete deletion of the word-initial *Vs-* sequence (see (27)).

Moreover, there are other major sound changes that were also underway in Illinois during the early 18th century, and for which doublets are also found in the sources: for example, the extensive variation between word-initial *r* and *n* seen especially often in the Pinet dictionary (Costa 2005), as well as the numerous doublets of nouns varying between older word-final *-iwa*, *-iiwa* and *-eewa* versus newer *-ia* (see Costa 2003:157–163) seen commonly in all Jesuit sources.

There is also significant lexical variation in the Illinois sources, notably among the plural reflexive and emphatic pronouns (see Costa 2008:138–139). For example, for the third person plural emphatic pronoun 'they/them', the Râle prayerbook has archaic *awiirawa* while LeBoullenger has *awiiroowa*; for the second person plural pronoun, Râle and Pinet both have *kiirawa*, while LeBoullenger has both *kiirawa* and *kiiroowa*. Likewise, for the third person plural reflexive pronoun 'themselves', Râle has both *awiiyoowaawi* and *awiiyawaawi*, while LeBoullenger has *awiiyoowaawi* and *awiiyawaawa*.

This level of variation, with archaic, semi-innovative, and even more innovative forms found side by side, is found in all the Illinois manuscripts, and with hundreds of words. This indicates that none of the Illinois manuscripts represents a single, unified dialect, but rather a farrago of various and sundry dialect forms, strongly implying that the missionaries did their work in communities that were already dialectally, and presumably tribally, mixed. Evidently, by the beginning of the 18th century, the Illinois communities with whom the missionaries lived already contained people from various Illinois subtribes speaking different subdialects, quite possibly as a result of refugees from tribes reduced by warfare consolidating into larger villages. In addition to what this tells us about the conditions of the Illinois-speaking peoples in the early 18th century, it also reconfirms that the term 'Illinois' does not represent the name of a single dialect of Miami-Illinois, but merely a particular early time period of the language.

NOTES

1. Proto-Algonquian reconstructions are given here in the system laid out in Goddard (1994). Thus, older PA *l is given as *r, *we is reconstructed as *o, and word-initial *i is written for older *e. Proto-Algonquian *sk and *rk replace Bloomfield's (1946) *xk and *çk, respectively. Reconstructions from earlier sources have been converted to this transcription system. In this paper, 'Illinois' is used as cover term for data from any of the Miami-Illinois Jesuit manuscripts from the late 17th and early 18th centuries.

   The following abbreviations are used in this paper: AI = animate intransitive; BB = Benjamin Barton's (1798) Miami vocabulary, D = Jacob Dunn's (no date) notes on Miami-Illinois, E = the 'Elements' vocabulary of Miami-Illinois and Ojibwe (Shea 2005), Gr = the Gravier/Largillier Illinois-French dictionary (Largillier (no date)), Gt = Albert Gatschet's notes on Miami-Illinois (Gatschet (no date)), Hk = Heckewelder's 1792 vocabulary of Miami-Illinois (Heckewelder (no date)), II = inanimate intransitive, LB = LeBoullenger's (no date) French-Illinois dictionary, Mc = Truman Michelson's (1916) Peoria notes, P = Pinet's (no date) French-Illinois dictionary, PA = Proto-Algonquian; pl. = plural; R = Sébastien Râle's (1908) late-17th-century Illinois Prayer Book; sg. = 'singular'; Th = Thornton's (1802) Miami vocabulary; Tr = Trowbridge's (1824–25) Miami notes; and

V = Volney's (1857) 1790's Miami wordlist.

2. This is reminiscent of similar sound changes in Meskwaki sporadically taking initial Proto-Algonquian *o and *i to *a* (Goddard 2002). Contact may be indicated.
3. More examples can be found in Costa (2003).
4. Pinet also attests this verb with long *oo* generalized throughout: Note his *nitoohši* 'I take a husband' (P ‹nit8chi›) and *oohšiwa* 'she takes a husband' (P ‹8chi8a›).
5. *oošihsaa-* 'fall down' is another example of long *oo* being generalized to a verb stem; compare Dunn's *nintoošihsaa* 'I fall down' (‹n'dócĭssa›) and *kitoošihsaa* 'you fall down' (‹kitócĭssa›) as well as the corresponding dependent forms *oošihsaani* (‹ócĭssánĭ›) and *oošihsaayani* (‹ócĭssayanĭ›; cf. Menominee *ose·hsen* 'he lies in place, lies ready, lies down, goes to bed').
6. This is the regular pattern still found in Shawnee: compare *hosto* 'he makes it' with *noosto* 'I make it' and *koostonaawa* 'you (pl.) make it'. The second person prefix *ki-* presumably contracts with *we* to give *koo-* in Illinois as well, but no examples have yet been found.
7. Cf. Menominee *ona·skenata·w* 'he fills, loads stuffs him/it'. A similar form is also attested by Gatschet in the isolated relic *noošihsaa* 'I fall down' (Gt ‹nű^{n}žissa›), from the AI stem *oošihsaa-*.
8. Glossed by Largillier as 'il n y a pas de place pour vous tous'; cf. Menominee *ona·skenεw* 'he is filled, loaded, stuffed'.
9. This unexpected development of this initial is also shared by Meskwaki and Kickapoo: cf. Meskwaki *ano·hwe·wa* 'he points at him' (Goddard 2002:62) and Kickapoo *anoohikani* 'forefinger' (Jones, no date).
10. In modern Miami-Illinois, this noun has been reshaped as apparent *alaholencaakani*, as shown by the Gatschet's *atalaholencaakani* 'his index finger' (‹talahulénzhakani›) and Dunn's *nintalaholencaakani* 'my index finger' (‹n'dálaholắndjakánĭ›), both Wea dialect forms.
11. The species this designates is uncertain; Largillier glosses it 'grosses prunes', and LB gives it as 'grosses prunes de bon goust'.
12. See also Costa (2022b:27).
13. These forms for 'his door' appear in the noun + noun compounds *ateskwaanteemi ahpikayimaawi* (Gr ‹atesc8antemipigaïma8i›, ‹atesc8antemi pigaima8i›) and *atahkwaanteemi ahpikayi* (Gr ‹atac8antemi pigaï›), all glossed as 'sa derniere coste'. (Cf. Miami-Illinois *ahpikayi* = '(his) rib'.) Ives Goddard has suggested that these forms represent "a metaphor based on the appearance of the rib cage of an animal lying on its back after the skin and meat have been removed. The lower ribs frame the 'entrance' to

the rib cage" (personal communication 2022).

14. The usual vowel of initial change in Miami-Illinois is *ee*.
15. Note the semantic shift this verb stem has undergone in the modern language.
16. The AI of this verb is attested in Largillier's sentence *ahkisiwa pireewa* 'le coq brusle dans la chaudiere le bouillon estant consume' (‹akisi8a pire8a›).
17. The only known example of this initial retaining word-initial *i* in Illinois is the verbal noun *ihkweewioni*, glossed as 'sodomie' (Gr/LB ‹ic8ei8ni›; cf. Meskwaki *ihkwe·wiweni* 'womanhood').
18. Largillier glosses this term 'faiseur de chaudiere'. For a full discussion of the semantics of this word, see Costa (2022a:445).
19. This noun is conceivably related to Ojibwe *akiwenzii* 'old man', though if so, the phonological discrepancies between the two are unexplained.

REFERENCES

Barton, Benjamin Smith. 1798. *New Views of the Origin of the Tribes and Nations of America*, 2nd edn. Philadelphia: Printed for the author by John Bioren.

Bloomfield, Leonard. 1946. Algonquian. *Linguistic Structures of Native America*, ed. by Harry Hoijer et al., pp. 85–129. New York: Viking Fund Publications in Anthropology 6.

Costa, David J. 2003. *The Miami-Illinois Language*. Lincoln: University of Nebraska Press.

Costa, David J. 2005. The St-Jérôme Dictionary of Miami-Illinois. *Papers of the 36th Algonquian Conference*, ed. by H. C. Wolfart, pp. 107–133. Winnipeg: University of Manitoba.

Costa, David J. 2008. New Notes on Miami-Illinois. *Papers of the 39th Algonquian Conference*, ed. by Karl S. Hele & Regna Darnell, pp. 123–165. London, ON: University of Western Ontario.

Costa, David J. 2022a. *As Long as the Earth Endures: Annotated Miami-Illinois Texts*. Lincoln: University of Nebraska Press.

Costa, David J. 2022b. Prenouns and Noun Compounding in Miami-Illinois. *Papers of the 51st Algonquian Conference*, ed. by Monica Macaulay & Margaret Noodin, pp. 19–39. East Lansing: Michigan State University Press.

Costa, David J. 2024. *sk* and *sp* in Illinois. *Papers of the 53rd Algonquian Conference*, ed. by Inge Genee, Monica Macaulay & Margaret Noodin. East Lansing: Michigan State University Press, pp. 75–90.

Dunn, Jacob P. [no date] Various Notes on Miami. Manuscripts at the Indiana State Library Indianapolis.

Gatschet, Albert. [no date] Vocabulary and Text. (Three original Miami and Peoria field notebooks.) Manuscript #236, National Anthropological Archives Smithsonian Museum Support Center, Suitland, MD.

Goddard, Ives. 1973. Delaware Kinship Terminology. *Studies in Linguistics* 23: 39–56.

Goddard, Ives. 1982. The Historical Phonology of Munsee. *International Journal of American Linguistics* 48:16–48.

Goddard, Ives. 1994. The West-to-East Cline in Algonquian Dialectology. *Actes du 25e Congrès des Algonquinistes*, ed. by William Cowan, pp. 187–211. Ottawa: Carleton University.

Goddard, Ives. 2002. Explaining the Double Reflexes of Word-Initial High Short Vowels in Fox. *Diachronica* 19:1, 43–80.

Goddard, Ives. 2003. Heckewelder's 1792 Vocabulary from Ohio: A Possible Attestation of Mascouten. *Papers of the 34th Algonquian Conference*, ed. by H.C. Wolfart, pp. 165–191. Winnipeg: University of Manitoba.

Heckewelder, John. [no date] Vocabulary of the Shawanese Language taken down by means of a White Woman who had been 20 Years a Prisoner with that Nation. Manuscript 3670, American Philosophical Society, Philadelphia.

Jones, William. [no date] Fieldnotes on Mexican Kickapoo. Manuscript 3650, National Anthropological Archives, Smithsonian Museum Support Center, Suitland, MD.

Largillier, Jacques S.J. [no date] (circa 1700). Illinois-French Dictionary. Manuscript in Watkinson Library, Trinity College, Hartford, CT.

LeBoullenger, Antoine-Robert, S. J. [no date] (circa 1725). French and Miami-Illinois Dictionary. Manuscript at the John Carter Brown Library, Brown University, Providence, RI.

Miami Tribe of Oklahoma. 2017. Miami-Illinois Indigenous Languages Digital Archive (ILDA). https://mc.miamioh.edu/ilda-myaamia.

Michelson, Truman. 1916. Notes on Peoria. Manuscript #2721, National Anthropological Archives Smithsonian Museum Support Center, Suitland, MD.

Pinet, Pierre-François. [no date] (circa 1702). French-Miami-Illinois dictionary. Manuscript at the Archives des Jésuites au Canada, Montréal, QC.

Râle, Sébastien. 1908. *Facsimile of Père Marquette's Illinois Prayer Book: It's* [sic] *History by the Owner, Colonel J. L. Hubert Neilson, M.D.* Quebec: Quebec Literary & Historical Society. [misattributed to Claude Allouez]

Shea, John Gilmary (ed.). 2005. *Elements of a Miami-Illinois Grammar*. Bristol, Pennsylvania: Evolution Publishing. American Language Reprints, vol. 34.

Thornton, William. 1802. Vocabulary of the Miami Language taken at the City of Washington. Original manuscript at the American Philosophical Society, Philadelphia.

Trowbridge, Charles. 1824–5. Notes on the Miami. Manuscripts at the Burton Historical Collection, Detroit Public Library, Detroit, MI.

Volney, Constantin F. C. de. 1857 [1790s]. *Œuvres Completes de Volney*. Paris: Chez Firmin Didot Frères, Fils et Cie.

Digitizing, Translating, and Standardizing Pr. Albert Lacombe's *Dictionnaire de la langue des Cris*

Daniel Dacanay and Antti Arppe

A general interest in the lexicographic documentation of the Cree language has existed since at least the beginning of the 18th century.[1] For instance, early translated Cree glossaries, such as those of Henry Kelsey and Thomas Bowrey (1710) and James Isham (1743), generally contained lists of (at most) several hundred words and phrases, with a strong focus on terms relating to the then-profitable fur trade (Tremblay 2005). Relatively simplistic wordlists such as these remained the chief written European sources on the Cree language until the mid-19th century, when, within the span of ten years, two major bilingual dictionaries were published, seemingly independently of one another. The first of these was the *Dictionary of the Cree Language as Spoken by the Indians of the Hudson's Bay Company's Territories*, compiled by the Anglican missionary Revd. Edwin Arthur Watkins in 1865, containing approximately 13,500 entries spanning several dialects of Cree concentrated in the vicinity of James Bay (chiefly corresponding to the modern dialectal divisions of Swampy Cree, Moose Cree, and East Cree (or James Bay Cree)), as well as occasional entries in Saulteaux and Ojibwe that Watkins considered "mingled with those in common use" (Watkins 1865:v). The focus of this paper, however, is to be the second of these two early dictionaries, namely, Pr. Albert Lacombe's *Dictionnaire de la langue des Cris.*

The Lacombe Dictionary

Lacombe's dictionary, compiled over the course of "more than twenty years" of missionary work among various indigenous groups in the "missions of Saskatchiwan [sic]" (Lacombe 1874:vii), is a bilingual document, consisting of approximately 11,400 Cree entries with French translations and slightly fewer than 9,000 French entries with Cree translations, with considerable lexical overlap between the two. In addition to this, it contains an extensive grammar, and is interspersed with translated example sentences and ethnographic notes throughout. Much like Watkins's dictionary before it, the Lacombe dictionary was designed with the specific intention of training Christian missionaries to "communicate with [the] savages" so as to "spread among the errant tribes the lights of civilisation" (Lacombe 1874: unnumbered preface page). In this capacity, much of the dictionary's content, particularly its example sentences, carries definite proselytic tones (see the DISCUSSION section), and the entries contain a disproportionate number of terms relating to theology and liturgy. Nonetheless, the Lacombe dictionary constitutes the first major French dictionary of Cree, as well as the first major dictionary (and still the only French dictionary) of the dialect of Plains Cree, or *nêhiyawêwin.*

The contents of the dictionary are formatted in much the same way as most dictionaries of the time, with two columns of entries per page, with each column headed by the first three letters of the entries within it. Each entry consists minimally of a headword, a part-of-speech tag, and a definition, in that order. The exact means by which Lacombe determined the part of speech for each entry is unclear; however, it appears that for most entries, the part of speech of the Cree headword is made to correspond with the part of speech of the translated definition word in French. Additionally, although Lacombe uses over 20 different acronyms and abbreviations as part-of-speech tags, he only defines 13 of them in the dictionary preface, making it unclear what many of these tags indicate.

Immediately following the headword, most entries also have their relevant plural suffix(es) listed; for most verbs, this plural suffix is the suffix used for third person plural agreement. For transitive verbs (particularly VTAs, transitive verbs with an animate subject and animate object), Lacombe instead includes a list of other potential derivational endings for the relevant verb stem (the most common being TCHIKEW (*-cikêw*, with 1,075 occurrences), TAM or TTAM (*-tam*, 718), HIWEW (*-hiwêw*, 326), and TTAW (*-htâw*, 322)). These suffixes, as with the headword itself, are rendered in majuscule. The definition, by contrast, is rendered in minuscule, as are any example sentences included within the definition. The definitions themselves demonstrate little inter-entry formatting consistency, with some resembling truncated bullet points and others being nearly page-long paragraphs. However, nominal Cree headwords are almost always given in the singular, and verbal headwords are virtually always presented in the third person singular Independent form. Finally, Lacombe makes liberal use of the shorthand *idem.* to indicate that the meaning of an entry is identical to the meaning of the previous entry (with the exception of any grammatical information communicated using the part-of-speech tags). In total, 1,175 entries (or roughly 10.3% of all entries in the dictionary) are glossed as *idem*. An illustrative sample of several entries, taken from page 353 of the Lacombe dictionary, is presented here[2]:

> « ISKANAPIHEW, (v. a.) TTAW, HIWEW, TCHIKEW, il arrête sa marche pour se reposer un jour ou plusieurs
> « ISKITCHEW, ok, (a. a.) le cœur lui fait défaut, le cœur lui tombe, il a une douleur au cœur
> « ISKIKEPIW, ok, (a. a.) il est lassé dans tous ses membres
> « ISKAKUTTEW, a, (a. in.) ça finit par tomber, parceque ça y a été trop longtemps attaché
> « ISKAKUTTIN, wa, (a. in.) idem
> « ISKIPEW, ok, a, (v. im.) l'eau monte. On dirait: n't'iskipân, l'eau monte là où je suis; e.g., kakiyaw ayisiyiniwok ki iskipewok, tous les hommes furent submergés; ekuspi misiwe ki iskipew askiy, alors toute la Terre fut couverte d'eau

Given its foundational status in Cree lexicography, the Lacombe dictionary consists almost entirely of novel recorded vocabulary; that is to say, virtually every entry in the Lacombe dictionary was recorded directly from first-language consultants by Lacombe himself, with minimal reliance on secondary data. Not only this, but owing to its being written during a period of time in which the vast majority of Plains Cree people spoke their language natively and as their predominant means of communication, the Lacombe dictionary provides a picture of the Cree language during its demographic "golden age," in contrast to dictionaries compiled in more recent years, which have largely reflected Plains Cree in its modern state as a minority language that is seldom used in most social settings and domains, and for which the lexical richness among most contemporary speakers has suffered as a result. In comparison to the entirely novel lexical stock of the Lacombe, most later Plains Cree dictionaries have relied heavily on the contents of existing lexicographic works to inform their choice of entries, with the Lacombe dictionary itself naturally being chief among these sources. In this way, the contents of the Lacombe dictionary serve as a common lexico-genetic link for much of the extant lexicographic documentation of Plains Cree; for instance, Wolvengrey's *nêhiyawêwin: itwêwina* (Cree: Words) (2011), LeClaire and Cardinal's *Alberta Elders Cree Dictionary* (2002), and Pr. Gérard Beaudet's *Cree-English, English-Cree Dictionary* (1995) all list the Lacombe dictionary as a lexical source.

However, despite this foundational status, the Lacombe dictionary remains broadly inaccessible to a large majority of the modern Plains Cree-speaking population on account of two primary factors, namely, the lack of accurately transcribed digitizations of its content and the fact that its translated definitions are written entirely in French, a language spoken by only ~6.2% of the total population in Alberta and Saskatchewan (2% natively and 4.2% simply reporting "Knowledge of French" (Statistics Canada 2019a; Statistics Canada 2019b)), the provinces in which the majority of the Plains Cree-speaking population resides. In fact, the Lacombe dictionary was initially brought to our attention for precisely this reason; in summer of 2016, one of the Cree-speaking consultants participating in the audio recordings for the Spoken Dictionary of Maskwacîs Cree (https://speech-db.altlab.app/maskwacis/entries), named *kîsikâw*, requested that the dictionary, which he had acquired and shown to us, be digitized and translated so as to be better available to potential contemporary users. As such, this paper discusses the initial steps in the creation of a digitized translation of the *Dictionnaire de la langue des Cris*, as well as provisional attempts to adapt its spelling conventions to those of the modern Standard Roman Orthography (Okimāsis and Wolvengrey 2008), so as to make it more accessible to contemporary Cree speakers familiar with this orthography, to allow its contents to be parseable by computational models trained using the Standard Roman Orthography, and to allow its integration into existing online Cree lexical databases. In doing this, we also discuss the challenges posed in adapting the dictionary's content for integration into these contemporary lexical resources, as well as the necessary avenues of development for the dictionary's use as both a practical tool and a historical document by modern Plains Cree speaker communities.

Digitization

Although no full digitization of the Lacombe dictionary exists, it would be inaccurate to state that the dictionary's contents are entirely unavailable in a digital setting. There exist high-quality, freely available online image scans of the Lacombe dictionary (such as those of the Bibliotheque et Archives Nationales du Québec (BANQ), available using the BANQ website at the following link: https://numerique.banq.qc.ca/patrimoine/details/52327/3994014), as well as digitized plain text versions produced using optical character recognition (OCR). However, useful though they may be, these resources are still inadequate for the use of the dictionary as a large-scale online lexical resource for a variety of reasons; the image scanned versions, despite their quality, are not searchable, and the OCR digitizations, although complete in scope, are unreliable in terms of their quality.

Existing OCR Scans

Several existing OCR scans of the Lacombe dictionary exist online; this investigation will discuss those available through the University of Alberta's Bruce Peel Collection, the John Carter Brown Library, Oxford University, and the Library of Congress. Despite all originating from (theoretically) identical source material, these four OCR scans differ widely in their accuracy to the original text, particularly concerning the Cree headwords. The general differences in quality between these four OCR versions may be demonstrated by examining how each of the four models transcribed the entry for the Cree word *âstwâwin*, glossed by Lacombe (who does not mark the initial long vowel) as follows:

> « ASTWÂWIN, a, (n. f.) réserve de provisions.

The Peel Collection OCR (http://peel.library.ualberta.ca/bibliography/708.html) is virtually unreadable, inserting spaces and omitting length markers in the Cree headword, mistranscribing the French gloss, replacing the guillemet («) with <u>, and misinterpreting the part of speech tagging as running text:

> u ASTWA WIN, a, To, Cl résérue & M provisions.

The Oxford University scan (https://hdl.handle.net/2027/hvd.hx79ui) is a slight improvement, correctly transcribing the vowel length diacritic on the second <A>, but still erroneously inserting a space in the middle of the headword. The French translation, however, is truncated to the point of near illegibility:

> « ASTWÂ WIN, a, (n. f.) ré provisions.

The John Carter Brown scan (https://brown.primo.exlibrisgroup.com/permalink) is the only one of the four to properly transcribe the Cree headword (at least, to the standards of Lacombe's orthography); however, it still omits a portion of the French translation:

> « ASTWÂWIN, a, (n. f.) réserve \ provisions.

The Library of Congress scan (https://lccn.loc.gov/02003610) is the highest quality of the four, and correctly transcribes and formats the French gloss and part-of-speech tags. However, the transcription of the Cree headword is missing its length diacritic:

> « ASTWAWIN, a, (n. f.) réserve de provisions.

Given errors such as these, which are consistent (and occur in roughly the same degree) across each scanned version, the use of an existing OCR scan of the Lacombe as the basis for an English translation would likely save little time in the overall translation process, as manual annotation would be required throughout the dictionary's contents to correct for transcription errors in Cree headwords, even with the highest quality existing OCR models. This is likely at least partially the result of the bilingual nature of the text, which freely alternates between Cree and French prose with little overt textual separation; any OCR model intended to transcribe this content would need therefore not only to be able to accurately transcribe both French and (an idiosyncratic spelling system for) Cree, but also to be able to distinguish between the two on a word-to-word basis. Initial attempts at producing an original OCR version of the Lacombe using Tesseract and the BANQ image scans were unpromising and showed much the same errors as the already-described scans. However, further research remains to be performed to determine the ideal means to approach OCR on bilingual Cree texts such as the Lacombe. This will principally concern determining whether higher quality transcriptions may be obtained by training a novel OCR model specifically for the text, using an existing French model and then applying a novel Cree model on the result to identify Cree words, or by running an existing French model and a novel Cree model in parallel. Such investigations are left to future research.

Manual Transcription and Translation

Given the lack of success of previous and current attempts at OCR, the decision was made to transcribe and translate the dictionary's contents manually. This decision was also influenced by concerns over quality of translation, which (based on preliminary trials) could not be guaranteed on a large scale using freely available machine translation software such as Google Translate or DeepL (https://www.deepl.com). Additionally, the previously made decision to manually transcribe the dictionary mandated that each individual entry be reviewed by an annotator regardless, mitigating the additional labor necessary for a manual translation. For the sake of both saving time and avoiding redundancy, it was decided that only the 384-page Cree–French section of the dictionary's contents was to be translated, with the 274-page French–Cree section being, for the moment, ignored. This decision was also motivated by lexicographic factors, as the Cree–French section, which provides descriptions and definitions of Cree words themselves, better fits contemporary, descriptive standards for linguistic practice than the French–Cree section, which seeks to rationalize French words in a Cree context. This being said, the translation and transcription of the French–Cree section may still prove useful, and is to be the subject of potential future work.

The full process of transcription and translation took about 18 days of work by a single annotator (the first author), averaging approximately 110 entries per hour. In total, this translation yielded 11,411 entries, a plurality of which (4,543) are already present in contemporary dictionary sources. This transcribed, translated version is available online at https://lacombe.altlab.dev.

Orthographic Revisions

The aforementioned transcription and translation process resulted in a full version of the Lacombe dictionary's Cree–French section with the Cree words written in Lacombe's orthography and the French glosses for those words translated into

English. Although still useful as a historical text, such a digitization remains limited from a practical lexicographic perspective on account of its outdated orthography. This is largely a concern for reasons of searchability, as, without a consistent spelling system, reliably searching for any given entry inevitably becomes a matter of trial and error, particularly when searching databases consisting of several distinct lexicographic sources. Although Lacombe's spelling system bears a strong resemblance to the modern Standard Roman Orthography (SRO), it remains divergent in various respects, such as its inclusion of voiced consonants, its use of <U> to represent some (but not all) unstressed vowels, its use of French-like digraphs and trigraphs such as <TJ> and <TCH> to represent the SRO character <c> (compare, for example, Lacombe's entries WATJIY ('mountain') and WATCHISTUN ('nest') (Lacombe 1874) with the SRO-rendered *waciy* ('hill, mountain') and *wacistwan* ('nest') (Wolvengrey 2011)), and its occasional (but inconsistent) use of double consonants to represent pre-aspiration, as well as other individual idiosyncrasies. Not only this, but the spelling of individual Cree words in the Lacombe dictionary, particularly with respect to diacritics, is subject to occasional error, as Lacombe himself acknowledges in the introductory pages of the work:

> "Il est très probable qu'on rencontrera dans ce second Dictionnaire certains mots écrits avec une telle quantité, et dans le premier avec une autre quantité. Cela peut venir de la part des imprimeurs, qui ignorant entièrement cette langue, ont pu prendre une voyelle pour une autre, et malgré tout le soin, qui a été apporté, pour la correction des *épreuves*, on ne devra pas s'étonner que dans ce premier travail, il se soit glissé bien des fautes." (Lacombe 1874)
>
> "It is very likely that one shall encounter in this second dictionary certain words written in one way, and in the first [dictionary] in a different way. This may come on behalf of the printers, who, entirely ignorant of the language, may have taken one vowel for another, and in spite of the greatest possible care to ensure the correctness of the proof sheets, one should not be surprised in this first edition to see the inclusion of some errors." (Lacombe 1874)

Given the broadly inconsistent nature of the orthographic irregularities throughout the Lacombe, it was quickly determined that it would be infeasible to regularize the dictionary's content using only find-and-replace methods using regular expressions or a finite state based transcriptor; rather, the anthropogenic idiosyncrasies of the

Lacombe were again regularized by manual annotation. Additionally, part-of-speech markings for entries, which in the original Lacombe dictionary were seemingly based largely on French parts of speech, were altered to fit modern Cree inflectional subclasses (identical to those used in the existing Cree dictionary *nêhiyawêwin: itwêwina* (Wolvengrey 2011)), with these tags being assigned based on the judgment of the first author. The resultant revised text was formatted to represent a three-way distinction between entries: namely, those that are present in other, contemporary digital dictionaries such as *nêhiyawêwin: itwêwina*, those that are derivationally analyzable but not present in any current dictionary, and those that are derivationally unanalyzable (that is, the first author was not able to confidently determine the morphological makeup of the word using available Cree lexical resources). Entries present in other dictionaries were rendered in SRO and given modern part of speech tagging. Entries that were derivationally analyzable but not present in other dictionaries were rendered in SRO and given modern part of speech tagging, but were marked with an asterisk. These entries were marked distinctly from entries present in other, modern dictionaries for reasons of attestation; while entries included both in Lacombe and in other, modern dictionaries can be presumed to still be in use by contemporary Cree speakers (given that they were also recorded by modern lexicographers), entries solely attested in Lacombe cannot necessarily be guaranteed to still be in use, given that they were recorded nearly 150 years in the past and have not been recorded since. This distinct marking is therefore intended to aid in the later process of reviewing the dictionary's contents with contemporary native speakers (see the DISCUSSION section); in the eventual fully standardized version, these asterisk markers therefore will be redundant, and will be made invisible to the end user. Entries that were derivationally unanalyzable could not be standardized (as the SRO overtly represents morphological information such as morpheme boundaries), and were thus left in their original orthography and with their original part-of-speech tags:

« SÂKIKUTEW, ok, (v. n.) he shows his nose
« SÂKISKWEW, ok, (v. n.) he shows his head
« SÂKITAWEHAM, wok, (v. n.) he arrives at the mouth of the river or the lake in a canoe
« *sâkikotêw, ok, (VAI-1) he shows his nose
« sâkiskwêw, ok, (VAI-1) he shows his head
« SÂKITAWEHAM, wok, (v. n.) he arrives at the mouth of the river or the lake in a canoe

Similarly to the nonstandardized version of the text, the orthographically standardized Lacombe digitization will be available online using an identical interface to the aforementioned https://lacome.altlab.dev.

Discussion

The end results of this investigation are twofold. First, it has yielded both the first fully digitized and manually verified text version of the Cree lexicon of the Lacombe dictionary and the first English translation of the contents of that dictionary. Second, it has provided an initial, albeit incomplete, attempt at the standardization of the Lacombe dictionary to the modern SRO. The immediate practical uses for these resources are manifold, ranging from increasing the size of existing lexical repositories for Plains Cree (such as the University of Alberta-run online dictionary *itwêwina* (itwewina.altlab.app)) by at least 4,917 entries (possibly more, given that the example sentences have yet to be accounted for in this count), to providing easy access to historical Cree vocabulary not recorded in contemporary dictionaries, in addition to the general value of the Lacombe dictionary as a historical document. Not only this, but the translated Lacombe is also a valuable source of parallel running text, given the large number of translated example sentences present in the glosses of its entries. Although an exact figure is not known (on account of these example sentences not being explicitly marked in the text), these example sentences likely constitute at least several thousand tokens of Plains Cree text.

Limitations of the Lacombe Dictionary

Despite its many uses, the currently translated and transcribed Lacombe dictionary is far from complete, and represents only an initial benchmark in the full digitization process. Perhaps its most obvious deficiency at present is its omission of the entirety of the French–Cree section, which, although highly repetitious of the Cree–French section, nonetheless contains thousands of tokens and translations of Cree words, many of which are doubtless novel to currently digitized lexical sources. Furthermore, Lacombe's extensive grammatical notes and field observations, including many that document grammatical features now lost in Plains Cree (such as the dubitative verb paradigm, which is largely undescribed in English language sources), remain untranscribed and untranslated, as do his lengthy introductory segments. Additionally, although the example sentences found throughout the entries of the Cree–French section have been transcribed, they have still yet to be orthographically standardized, reducing their searchability (particularly in cases wherein the headword of the entry was also not yet standardizable). Finally, before making use of its contents alongside those of more contemporary lexical resources, it remains necessary (due to the substantial diachronic gap between the early 21st and late 19th century) to review the entries in the Lacombe dictionary with contemporary native speakers (particularly the entries not present in any other, modern dictionaries, as previously discussed). This serves two purposes, being both to identify and explicitly mark archaic or obsolete vocabulary, allowing us to display such vocabulary in online lexical resources with obvious tagging to indicate that it is 'historical' or 'archaic', and to confirm that the definitions that Lacombe provides for certain entries are synchronically valid.

The consultation of native speakers concerning the contents of the Lacombe is not, however, to be limited to the process of semantic validation. Rather, community engagement is also necessary to determine which aspects of the dictionary's contents are congruous with the modern sociocultural sensibilities of Cree speakers and community members. This is of particular relevance given the dictionary's origins as a tool intended to ease the proselytization and conversion of the "savage" inhabitants of the Western Prairies (Lacombe 1874:343). Although relatively sympathetic to Indigenous perspectives for its time, the Lacombe dictionary nonetheless frequently lapses into moralistic tirades against the "superstitions of the savages," employing example sentences such as *kwatakittâwin kitchi iskutek namawiya kita kisipan* ("the suffering (in Hell) will have no end"), and using terms such as 'jongleur' (a French term literally meaning 'juggler', but carrying definite charlatanical connotations) to refer to Indigenous medicine men. Rather than adopting the revisionist and historically dismissive approach of simply deleting such entries from the dictionary entirely, it is the opinion of the authors that decisions of "suitable" and "unsuitable" content should be left to native speakers and community members. From a practical perspective, this would entail a parallel process of determining which entries, example sentences, and notes should not be presented in generally available online versions of the dictionary at the same time as these entries and example sentences are reviewed by native speakers for their linguistic contents. This would result in two online versions of the translated Lacombe dictionary, the first being a "revisionist" (or "modernized") version with standardized modern orthography, archaic vocabulary either overtly tagged or omitted by default, and definitions modified with community oversight, and the second being a "non-revisionist" version, with Lacombe's original orthography, definitions, and notes (for practical purposes, essentially identical to the online version linked throughout the paper). As such, in proceeding with the digitization and standardization of the Lacombe dictionary, direct community engagement becomes a matter of practical necessity and priority; indeed, it should be recalled that this project was initiated following a request by a Cree speaker and community member in the first place.

Conclusion

Owing to the incomplete and impractical nature of existing digital versions of Pr. Albert Lacombe's *Dictionnaire de la langue des Cris*, the following investigation has produced a digitized, plain-text version of the approximately 11,400 Cree–French entries present therein, with the French glosses translated into English. Additionally, preliminary orthographic standardizations have been performed on the Cree headwords of the dictionary to modernize their spelling to the contemporary SRO, although a large portion of these headwords have yet to be derivationally analyzed, and thus cannot be confidently orthographically revised. Similar revisions have been performed on the part-of-speech tags present for each entry. Although usable and freely available in its present state, the current digitized version of the Lacombe is strictly provisional, with plans to fully translate the French–Cree section and the grammatical notes and field observations, and to complete the currently partial orthographic standardizations being prioritized. Additionally, prior to its incorporation into existing digital repositories of Cree vocabulary, we plan to run review sessions of the dictionary entries with native speakers and community members, both to identify and appropriately tag archaic vocabulary and to moderate and mitigate some of the more intrusive influences of the dictionary's initial intended purpose as a missionary tool.

NOTES

1. We would like to acknowledge Sharon Farnel and Sarah Severson of the University of Alberta Library for directing us to the existing OCR versions of the Lacombe dictionary, as well as *kîsikâw* for his role in catalyzing the digitization process as a whole. We also

thank Jolene Poulin, who is responsible for the Web version of the Lacombe dictionary linked throughout the paper, using the morphodict platform (https://github.com/UAlbertaALTLab/morphodict) developed by the Alberta Language Technology Lab (ALTLab).

2. The guillemet («) was inserted by Lacombe before each entry, presumably as a delimiter.

REFERENCES

Beaudet, Gérard O.M.I. 1995. *Cree-English English-Cree Dictionary*. Winnipeg: Wuerz Publishing Ltd.

Kelsey, Henry, and Thomas Bowery. 1710. *A Dictionary of the Hudson's-Bay Indian Language*. London: s.n.

Isham, James. 1743. *Observations on Hudsons Bay*. Unpublished manuscript.

Lacombe, Albert O.M.I. 1874. *Dictionnaire de la langue des Cris*. Montréal: C. O. Beauchemin et Valois.

LeClaire, Nancy, and George Cardinal. 2002. *Alberta Elders' Cree Dictionary/alberta ohci kehtehayak nehiyaw otwestamâkewasinahikan*. Edmonton: University of Alberta Press.

Okimāsis, Jean, and Arok Wolvengrey. 2008. *How to Spell it in Cree: The Standard Roman Orthography*. Regina, SK: Miywâsin Ink.

Statistics Canada. 2019a. The French Language in Alberta, 2001 to 2016: Facts and Figures. https://www150.statcan.gc.ca/n1/pub/89-657-x/89-657-x2019016-eng.htm.

Statistics Canada. 2019b. The French Language in Saskatchewan, 2001 to 2016: Facts and Figures. https://www150.statcan.gc.ca/n1/pub/89-657-x/89-657-x2019015-eng.htm.

Tremblay, Manon. 2005. Les dictionnaires de la langue crie : histoire et regard critique. MA thesis, Université de Montréal.

Watkins, Edwin Arthur. 1865. *Dictionary of the Cree Language, As Spoken by the Indians of the Hudson's Bay Company's Territories*, London: Society for Promoting Christian Knowledge.

Wolvengrey, Arok. 2011. *Cree: Words*. Regina, SK: University of Regina Press.

The Syntax of Meskwaki Adverbs

A Preliminary Survey

Amy Dahlstrom

In earlier work on Meskwaki word order (e.g., Dahlstrom 1993) I have proposed a template with positions for topic and focus, a position for particles expressing negation, and positions for the verb and its arguments: oblique, subject, object, second object, and complement clauses.[1]

(1) [$_{S'}$ TOPIC [$_{S}$ NEG FOCUS* OBLIQUE V XP*]]
{SUBJ, OBJ, OBJ2, COMP}

Omitted from this template is a class of words found extremely frequently in Meskwaki and other Algonquian languages: **ADVERBS**.

Other work on Algonquian has included adverbs within a similar word order template: for example, Lewis (2015) on Potawatomi, which is reproduced in Lockwood (2017:161):

(2) Potawatomi template (boldface added); Lewis (2015)
TOPIC NEG **ADV** {ARGFOCUS, OBL} V {SUBJ, OBJ, OBJ2, OBL}

In this paper I consider how adverbs fit in to the overall picture of Meskwaki word order. The adverb position identified for Potawatomi by Lewis in (2) is found in Meskwaki as well, but other positions are also possible, as shown in the following.[2] The source of data drawn upon for this paper is approximately 600 pages of narrative texts written in the early 20th century in the Great Lakes syllabary by monolingual Meskwaki speakers; these texts are now stored at the archives of the Smithsonian Institution.

Although this paper is only a preliminary report on the syntax of adverbs, some generalizations can be made regarding the interaction of adverbs and other elements of Meskwaki word order. I will first define the class of data that I am labeling as adverbs, then distinguish three classes of adverbs (discourse, propositional, and predicate) and investigate how these three classes interact with the other elements in the word order template in (1). It will be seen that most adverbs appear to the left of the verb, though some observations can be made regarding the motivations for placing adverbs to the right of the verb. Moreover, the behavior of adverbs strengthens the case for revising the template in (1) to include an internal topic position within the clause, as well as the clause-external topic position shown in (1).

What Counts as an Adverb?

It is first necessary to clarify what is meant by the term "adverb" in this investigation. By adverb I mean a syntactically independent word functioning as a modifier of a verb or of a clause. Let us first consider the requirement that the adverb be syntactically independent.

Syntactically Independent

It is clear that not all Meskwaki phenomena translated by adverbs in English should be counted as adverbs in Meskwaki. For example, many Meskwaki preverbs or initials correspond to elements in English expressed by adverbs. I am not including such preverbs and initials here because they are not syntactically independent words. Consider the initial or preverb expressing 'extremely'.

(3) 'extremely': *ki·ša·kot-* [verb initial] / *ki·ša·koči–* [preverb]

In forms like (4), where *ki·ša·kot-* is realized as an initial, it is clear that it is part of the verb and a linguist would be unlikely to be tempted to count it as an adverb in Meskwaki:[3]

(4) **ki·ša·kotekwa·mwa**
ki·ša·kotekwa·m-wa
extremely.sleep-3.IND
'He/she sleeps soundly.'

However, in forms like (5), where the same element expressing 'extremely' is realized as a preverb, the situation is perhaps less clear.

(5) ke**ki·ša·koč**imeko–menwamo·nekona·naki!
ke-**ki·ša·koči**–=meko –menwamo·n-ekona·naki
2-extremely–=EMPH –feed.well-3P>21.IND
'They gave us a very good feast!' W192

My assumption in this paper is that a preverb like the one in (5) is also not an adverb for the purposes of the present word order investigation. Rather, it is part of a compound verb, as can be seen by the location of the second person inflectional prefix *ke-* to the left of the preverb.

Other elements that correspond to English adverbs might be expressed by second position enclitics in Meskwaki: for example, *=a·pehe* 'usually', *=kohi* 'certainly', or *=ye·toke* 'apparently'.

(6) pe·hkimeka·**pehe** kekwi·nokwi·nomenepwa.
pe·hki=meko=a·**pehe** ke-kwi·no-kwi·nom-enepwa
really=EMPH=usually 2-REDUP-long.for-1>2P.IND
'I have really been longing to see you.' W196

(7) ni·na**kohi** neta·čimoha·waki.
ni·na=**kohi** ne-a·čimoh-a·waki
I=certainly 1-instruct-1>3P.IND
'I myself instructed them.' W187

(8) o·nimekoye·toke no·hkomesa e·ha·hkwe·či.
o·ni=meko=ye·toke ne-o·hkomes-a e·h-a·hkwe·-či
and.then=EMPH=apparently 1-grandmother-SG AOR-be.angry-3.AOR
'And now I guess my grandmother is angry.' W76

Again, enclitics such the ones in (6)–(8) are excluded from consideration here because their word order position is determined by the rules of cliticization, not by the more general rules applying to adverbs in the word order template.

Modifier

The criterion of syntactic independence therefore entails that adverbs in Meskwaki are a subset of the part of speech labeled "particle" by Bloomfield (cf. 1946:94 inter alia). A particle in Algonquian languages is a word that is not inflected, taking neither the nominal paradigm of inflection nor any of the verbal paradigms of inflection. It is important to realize that while all adverbs in Meskwaki are particles, the reverse is not true: Not all particles are adverbs.[4] For the purposes of the current investigation, we want simply to distinguish particles that are modifiers (the adverbs) from those that are arguments and from those that are themselves predicates.

Particles That Are Arguments

Some words in Meskwaki that are classified morphologically as particles (because they are not inflected) may function as arguments of a verb. Such particles are oblique arguments, which in Meskwaki typically occur immediately before the verb.[5] Obliques are further classified by the semantic role they bear: for example, stationary location, goal of motion, source of motion, manner, and so on, and the verb subcategorized for an oblique argument is typically morphologically marked for the type of oblique. For example, in (9) the initial morpheme *tan-* on the verb stem indicates that the verb requires an oblique argument expressing stationary location; the particle *sa·kiči* 'outside' immediately to the left of the verb satisfies the requirement of a stationary location oblique.

(9) **sa·kiči** e·hki·wi–tano·te·či.
sa·kiči e·h-ki·wi–tano·te·-či
outside AOR-around–crawl.there-3.AOR
'He was crawling around outside.' W26

The verb in (10), on the other hand, requires an oblique expressing goal of motion (indexed by the stem-initial morpheme *in-*), and the particle *waninawe* 'in all directions' satisfies that requirement.

(10) **waninawe** e·hinohino·te·pahoniči.
waninawe e·h-inoh-ino·te·paho-niči
in.all.directions AOR-REDUP-race.thither.crawling-3′.AOR
'They darted off in all directions.' W51

Example (11) further illustrates a particle functioning as an oblique argument. Here the verb requires an oblique expressing manner (indexed by the preverb *iši-* 'thus') and the oblique argument is expressed by the particle *meškwi·kite·we* 'annoyingly':

(11) **meškwi·kite·we**meko e·hiši–kečika·niki.
meškwi·kite·we=meko e·h-iši–kečika·-niki
annoyingly=EMPH AOR-thus-drip.out-0′.AOR
'It was dripping out in a very annoying way.' W41

To sum up this section, particles such as *sa·kiči* 'outside', *waninawe* 'in all directions', and *meškwi·kite·we* 'annoyingly' do *not* function as adverbs in Meskwaki since they are oblique arguments of the verb, not an optional modifier.

Particles That Are Predicates

Besides the class of particles that function as arguments, exemplified in the previous section, another class of particles must be excluded from consideration in our investigation of adverbs: particles that themselves function as predicates, being subcategorized for a complement clause.[6] For example, in (12) the particle *tawa·nahi* 'I wish' is the main predicate of the sentence, subcategorized for a subordinate clause containing a verb inflected in the subjunctive paradigm indicating what the speaker wishes for.

(12) **tawa·nahi** mahkwa·či mehtose·neni·wi·wa·te no·šisemaki.
tawa·nahi [mahkwa·či mehtose·neni·wi-wa·te ne-o·šisem-aki]
I.wish quietly live-3P.SUBJNCT 1-grandchild-PL
'May my grandsons live quiet lives.' W535

Likewise, the combination of particles *a·kwi kana·kwa* 'it's impossible' is a predicate, taking a clause containing a verb inflected in the future aorist conjunct as its argument:

(13) **a·kwi kana·kwa** wi·hpetekeška·niki
a·kwi kana·kwa [wi·h-petekeška·-niki]
not possible FUT-go.back-0′.AOR
'It is impossible to go back.' W28

A further example may be seen in (14), where the particle *ke·nema·pi* 'I don't know' is subcategorized for a clause containing a verb inflected as an interrogative participle, which expresses what the speaker does not know.

(14) **ke·nema·pi** mana a·ya·pa·hte·ha e·šite·he·kwe·ni.
ke·nema·pi [mana a·ya·pa·hte·h-a IC-išite·he·-kwe·ni]
I.don't.know this.ANIM A-SG IC-think.thus-3.INTERR.PART.OBL
'I don't know what Ayapahteha here thinks.' W236

It is important to exclude predicates such as those in (12)–(14) from our examination of adverbs. For example, we do not want to analyze (12) as exhibiting two *adverbs* before the verb *mehtose·neni·wi·wa·te* 'live'; rather, there is a main clause predicate *tawa·nahi* 'I wish' and within the lower clause there is one adverb *mahkwa·či* 'quietly' preceding the verb.

Types of Adverbs

There are a number of proposals for a taxonomy of adverbs in the linguistic literature, many of which are too fine-grained for our purposes here. I will, however, make a distinction between three types, which I will call DISCOURSE ADVERBS, PROPOSITIONAL ADVERBS, and PREDICATE ADVERBS. The latter two, propositional adverbs and predicate adverbs, correspond to the more familiar terms of "S-adverbs" and "VP-adverbs" (cf. Oxford 2008, McCawley 1988, inter alia) but I want to avoid making claims about the syntactic constituent structure here so I will use the more semantically based terms of proposition and predicate.

(15) Types of adverbs

a. DISCOURSE ADVERBS (*našawaye* 'long ago', *aškači* 'after a while', *kapo·twe* 'at some point', *ke·keya·hi* 'finally' . . .)

b. PROPOSITIONAL ADVERBS [= S-adverb, cf. Oxford 2008, McCawley 1988 inter alia] (*ke·htena* 'truly', *me·mešihka* 'perhaps', *ma·mahka·či* 'necessarily', *wa·wosa·hi* 'unsurprisingly' . . .)

c. PREDICATE ADVERBS [= VP-adverb, cf. Oxford 2008, McCawley 1988, inter alia] (*mahkwa·či* 'quietly', *opye·ni* 'slowly', *sese·si* 'hurriedly', *wa·nato·hka* 'unconcernedly' . . .)

Discourse adverbs are oriented toward the discourse structure or episode structure of a narrative. That is, in telling a story a narrator uses discourse adverbs to establish the time of the story at the beginning (*našawaye* 'long ago'), to indicate that some time has passed (*aškači* 'after a while') or that the next action occurs at a particular point (*kapo·twe* 'at some point'), or to indicate action that occurs after a given stretch of time (*ke·keya·hi* 'finally'). Propositional adverbs modify the whole clause: For example, *wa·wosa·hi* 'unsurprisingly' expresses that the entire proposition is not surprising. Predicate adverbs, on the other hand, such as *mahkwa·či* 'quietly', modify just the verb, not the entire clause.

Unmarked Position for Adverbs Is to the Left of the Verb

For all three adverb types, their unmarked position is to the left of the verb. (Examples to the right of the verb are discussed in the following.) Consider these examples of clauses consisting only of an adverb and a verb:

(16) DISCOURSE ADVERB

aškači e·ha·čimoniči.

aškači e·h-a·čimo-niči

a.while.later AOR-narrate-3′.AOR

'A while later he [obviative] spoke.' W239

(17) PROPOSITIONAL ADVERB

ke·htenameko e·hwi·kaniki.

ke·htena=meko e·h-wi·kan-niki

truly=EMPH AOR-taste.good-0′.AOR

'They truly tasted very good.' W45

(18) PREDICATE ADVERB

mahkwa·či e·hkano·neči,

mahkwa·či e·h-kano·n-eči

quietly AOR-speak.to-X>3.AOR

'When they are spoken to quietly,' W526

Example (16) contains a discourse adverb *aškači* 'a while later'; (17) contains a propositional adverb *ke·htena* 'truly'; (18) contains a predicate adverb *mahkwa·či* 'quietly'. All three types of adverb appear to the left of the verb. However, since these examples contain only a single adverb and a verb, we do not yet know how the different types of adverbs interact with other elements of the clause, or what the ordering might be if more than one adverb is employed.

Ordering of More than One Adverb

It is possible for a clause in Meskwaki to contain more than one adverb. In such cases, what conditions the relative order of the adverbs?

The first observation we can make is that discourse adverbs precede other adverbs, as seen in (19) and (20):

(19) **ke·keya·hmeko wa·wosa·hi** e·hpemi–nowi·či.
DISCOURSE-ADV PROP-ADV V
ke·keya·hi=meko **wa·wosa·hi** e·h-pemi–nowi·-či
finally=EMPH unsurprisingly AOR-along–go.out-3.AOR
'Eventually, she naturally went outside.' W72

(20) **aškači na·hkači** e·hwe·pi–a·čimoniči.
DISCOURSE-ADV PRED-ADV V
aškači **na·hkači** e·h-we·pi–a·čimo-niči
after.a.while again AOR-begin–narrate-3′.AOR
'A while later she began to speak again.' W113

In (19) the discourse adverb *ke·keya·hi* 'finally' precedes the propositional adverb *wa·wosa·hi* 'unsurprisingly', and in (20) the discourse adverb *aškači* 'after a while' precedes the predicate adverb *na·hkači* 'again'.

Propositional adverbs precede predicate adverbs, as can be seen in (21):

(21) **ke·htenameka·pehe mahkwa·či** kano·šiwe·waki.
PROP-ADV PRED-ADV V
ke·htena=meko=a·pehe **mahkwa·či** kano·šiwe·-waki
truly=EMPH=usually quietly speak.to.people-3P.IND
'Surely they answer very quietly indeed.' W526

In (21) the first adverb, *ke·htena* 'truly', is a propositional adverb, while the following adverb, *mahkwa·či* 'quietly', belongs to the predicate type.

We can also observe that more than one predicate adverb may occur in a single clause:

(22) **e·škamimeko čača·tepi** e·hne·moniči.
PRED-ADV PRED-ADV V
e·škami=meko **čača·tepi** e·h-ne·mo-niči
gradually=EMPH in.regular.succession AOR-breathe-3′.AOR
'and gradually he was breathing regularly.' W174

In (22) both *e·škami* 'gradually' and *čača·tepi* 'in regular succession' belong to the predicate adverb class.

Position of Adverbs Relative to Other Elements on the Word Order Template

We have so far established that the unmarked position for adverbs is to the left of the verb, and seen that discourse adverbs appear before other types of adverbs, and that propositional adverbs appear before predicate adverbs. We will now consider where adverbs appear relative to the other elements of Meskwaki syntax that appear in positions to the left of the verb. The word order template of (1) is repeated here:

(1) [$_{S'}$ TOPIC [$_{S}$ NEG FOCUS* OBLIQUE V XP*]]
{SUBJ, OBJ, OBJ2, COMP}

In the discussion that follows I will consider each of the elements to the left of the verb—topic, negative particles, focus, and oblique—and investigate where adverbs of the three different types appear relative to each.

Topic

Overt topic constituents are frequently followed by an adverb. This is true for all three adverbial types. For example, in (23) the independent pronoun *wi·nwa·wa* 'they' functioning as a topic is followed by a discourse adverb *kapo·twe* 'at some point':

(23) o·ni wi·nwa·wa **kapo·twe** e·hnenohta·ti·hiwa·či.

	TOP	DISCOURSE-ADV	V
o·ni	wi·nwa·wa	**kapo·twe**	e·h-nenohta·ti·hi-wa·či
and.then	they	at.some.point	AOR-understand.e.o.DIM-3P.AOR

'And then as for them [the little boys], at some point they understood each other.' W35

Example (24) demonstrates that an overt topic, *mana ki·hka·nena·na* 'this friend of ours (inclusive)', may be followed by a propositional adverb, *ke·htena* 'truly':

(24) "nahi, mana ki·hka·nena·na **ke·htena**meko te·pwe·wa e·nowe·či.

	TOP		PROP-ADV	V
nahi,	mana	ke-i·hka·n-ena·n-a	**ke·htena**=meko	te·pwe·-wa
well,	this.ANIM	2-friend-21-SG	truly=EMPH	speak.the.truth-3.IND

IC-inowe·-či.
IC-talk.so-3.PART.OBL
'Well, as for this friend of ours, he is truly right in what he said.' W464

Example (25) demonstrates that an overt topic, *owi·hka·nani* 'his friend', may also be followed by a predicate adverb, *wa·nato·hka* 'unconcernedly'.

(25) **owi·hka·nanike·hi wa·nato·hkameko e·hkehči–nepa·niči.**
TOP PRED-ADV V
o-i·hka·n-ani=ke·hi wa·nato·hka=meko e·h-kehči–nepa·-niči
3-friend-OBV=moreover unconcernedly=EMPH AOR-greatly–sleep-3'.AOR
'As for his friend, he was peacefully sound asleep.' W495

However, besides the clear examples in (23)–(25) of overt topics followed by an adverb, there are additional cases where an adverb is followed by an NP that seems to be functioning as a topic element. In both (26) and (27) the name of the culture hero, Wisahkeha, follows an adverb (a discourse adverb in (26); a propositional adverb in (27)).

(26) **kapo·twe wi·sahke·ha e·hpwa·wi–kaški–po·nwe·kesiči,**
DISCOURSE-ADV TOP V
kapo·twe wi·sahke·h-a e·h-pwa·wi–kaški–po·nwe·kesi-či
at.some.point W-SG AOR-not–able–stop.crying-3.AOR
'At some point Wisahkeha was not able to stop crying,' W12

(27) **ke·htenake·hmeko wi·sahke·ha e·hkehči–mahkate·wi·či.**
PROP-ADV TOP V
ke·htena=ke·hi=meko wi·sahke·h-a e·h-kehči–mahkate·wi·-či
truly=moreover=EMPH W-SG AOR-greatly–fast-3.AOR
'And Wisahkeha truly fasted very seriously.' W226

Example (28), with a predicate adverb preceding an NP, is nearly a minimal pair with (25):

(28) **wa·natohka**meko osi·me·hani e·hkehči–nepa·niči.
PRED-ADV TOP V
wa·natohka=meko o-si·me·h-ani e·h-kehči–nepa·-niči
unconcernedly=EMPH 3-y.sib.DIM-OBV AOR-greatly–sleep-3′.AOR
'His younger brother was peacefully sound asleep.' W317

The NP following an adverb in (26)–(28) seems to be functioning as a topic, using the definition of topic as what the following comment is about: The following lines of text after (27), for example, continue talking about Wisahkeha and the powers he gains through fasting. Moreover, the putative internal topic NPs in (26)–(28) are clearly not focus elements, nor are they oblique arguments of the verb, the only other two possibilities for NP elements in the word order template of (1). Given this word order pattern, I will return to a suggestion made in Dahlstrom (2004), that there is both an external topic position and an internal topic position, as shown in the revised template in (29):

(29) [$_{S'}$ EXTERNAL-TOPIC [$_{S}$ INTERNAL-TOPIC NEG FOCUS* OBLIQUE V XP*]]
{SUBJ, OBJ, O2, COMP}

Dahlstrom (2004) used clitic placement, among other arguments, to distinguish between the two topic positions, where the external topic is outside the clause proper while the internal topic is the first possible position within the smaller clause unit. The adverbs seen in examples (23)–(28) occur in between the external topic position and the internal topic position, providing an additional diagnostic for distinguishing the two.

Negative

We now turn to the next element within the word order template, the negative position. The interaction of the three types of adverbs with negative elements is more limited than their interaction with topics. For one thing, the set of discourse adverbs employed in narration is unlikely to be followed by an independent negative particle. Verbs in narrative contexts are inflected in the aorist conjunct, which is negated by the preverb *pwa·wi-* 'not', not by an independent particle (cf. (26)). I have found no examples of a discourse adverb followed by an independent negative particle.

The propositional class of adverbs, on the other hand, do appear to the left of a negative word, as seen in (30):

(30) ke·htenameko a·kwi me·h–mi·nakečini ma·haki kemehtose·neni·mena·naki.

PROP-ADV	NEG	V	OBJ
ke·htena=meko	a·kwi	me·hi–mi·n-akečini	ma·haki
truly=EMPH	not	yet–give-1P>3.NEG	these.ANIM

ke-mehtose·neni·m-ena·n-aki
2-person-21-PL
'It is true that we have not yet given it to our people.' W469

However, it is also possible to find a propositional adverb following a negative word:

(31) a·kwike·hi **ke·htena** wi·hkosa·či.

NEG	PROP-ADV	V
a·kwi=ke·hi	**ke·htena**	wi·h-kos-a·či
not=moreover	truly	FUT-fear-3>3′.AOR

'He wasn't truly afraid of them.' W353

The propositional adverbs appear to have scope over a clause, just as the negative words do. Either order is possible for these scope-taking elements:

(32) it.is.true > not [. . .]
not > it.is.true [. . .]

Adverbs modifying predicates, on the other hand, follow the negative element and are in the scope of negation, as seen in (33):

(33) a·kwi **pi·neši** nahkomakini.

NEG	PRED-ADV	V
a·kwi	**pi·neši**	nahkom-akini
not	of.own.accord	accept.by.speech-1>3.NEG

'I didn't say yes to him just because I wanted to.' W135

In (33) the adverb *pi·neši* 'of one's own accord' is part of what is negated by the particle *a·kwi* 'not'.

Focus

A number of different elements may appear in the position labeled "focus," including contrastive focus, quantifiers, answers to question-word questions, and surprising information. A propositional adverb can appear after an element in focus:

(34) wi·nameko **ke·htena** ki·šihto·wa.
FOCUS PROP-ADV V
wi·na=meko **ke·htena** ki·šiht-o·wa
he=EMPH truly complete-3>0.IND
'He surely made it.' (contrastive focus) W329

And a predicate adverb can appear before an element in focus, as in (35):

(35) **opye·ni**meko a·neta e·hwi·seniwa·či
PRED-ADV FOCUS V
opye·ni=meko a·neta e·h-wi·seni-wa·či
slowly=EMPH some AOR-eat-3P.AOR
'Some others ate very slowly' W260 [*a·neta* 'some' in focus position]

Oblique

All three types of adverbs appear to the left of the Oblique position, as seen in (36) with a discourse adverb, (37) with a propositional adverb, and (38) with a predicate adverb:

(36) **ke·keya·h**meko o·šisemeki e·ha·wa·či.
DISCOURSE-ADV OBLIQUE V
ke·keya·hi=meko o-o·šisem-eki e·h-a·-wa·či
finally=EMPH 3-grandchild-LOC AOR-go-3P.AOR
'Finally they went over to her grandson's place.' W347

(37) o·**ke·htena** i·ni e·šite·he·wane·ni,

PROP-ADV	OBLIQUE	V
o·=**ke·htena**	i·ni	IC-išite·he·-wane·ni
oh,=truly	that	IC-think.thus-2.CH.INTERR

'Oh, if you truly think that way,' W212

(38) **sese·simeko** i·ya·hi e·hpya·či.

PRED-ADV	OBLIQUE	V
sese·si=meko	i·ya·hi	e·h-pya·-či
hurriedly=EMPH	yonder	AOR-come-3.AOR

'He arrived over yonder very quickly.' W506

It is possible, but rare, to find an adverb following an oblique. Here is one example:

(39) i·ni **ke·htena** e·nowe·kwe·hiki

OBLIQUE	PROP-ADV	V
i·ni	**ke·htena**	IC-inowe·-kwe·hiki
that	truly	IC-talk.so-3P.CH.INTERR

'If they truly said that' W157

(Notice that (39) is a near-minimal pair with (37): Both contain verbs inflected in the changed interrogative expressing 'if'.)

Since in Meskwaki there is a strong preference for an oblique argument to immediately precede the verb, it is not surprising that we find adverbs nearly always preceding an oblique, not following it.

Adverbs Appearing to the Right of the Verb

As stated above, the unmarked position for an adverb of any type is to the left of the verb. It is possible, however, to find adverbs appearing to the right of the verb. This seems to be similar to the phenomenon of preverbs appearing on their own to the right of the verb (cf. Thomason 2016): In other words, the speaker or writer is deliberately choosing a marked position for an element that ordinarily occurs to the left of the verb. Although I do not have an analysis for all instances of adverbs appearing to the right of a verb, there are two constructions that favor adverbs in this position.

When a Direct Quote Occupies the Oblique Position

The first construction is when a direct quote occupies the oblique position of the quoting verb. In such environments, a predicate adverb modifying the quoting verb often appears to the right, as can be seen in (40) and (41):

(40) "hao," e·hineči **mahkwa·či.**
"hao," e·h-in-eči **mahkwa·či**
all.right AOR-say.thus.to-3>3′.AOR quietly
'"All right," he was told quietly.' W512

(41) "mehto·čini·hka mehtekwapeno·ha!" e·hiči **wa·natohka** neniwa.
"mehto·či=ni·hka mehtekwapeno·h-a!" e·h-i-či **wa·natohka**
like=MAN'S.EXPL wood.baby-SG AOR-say.thus-3.AOR unconcernedly

neniw-a
man-SG
'"Gosh, it's like a wood-baby [walking-stick insect]!" said the man calmly.' W66

A likely motivation for putting the adverb after the verb in such constructions is that it disambiguates the scope of the adverb: It is clearly modifying the quoting verb and is not part of the direct quote.

Chiasmus

Another construction which accounts for some of the adverbs found to the right of the verb is a chiastic construction. That is, an adverb used in the previous line to the left of the verb is repeated in the following line, but in the following line it appears to the right of the verb. Examples (42) and (43) illustrate this pattern, both using the propositional adverb *ke·htena* 'truly':[7]

(42) **ke·htena** i·ni išite·he·ye·kwe, ki·hmenwawipwa **ke·htena.**
ke·htena i·ni išite·he·-ye·kwe
truly that think.thus-2P.SUBJNCT

ke-i·h-menwawi-pwa **ke·htena**
2-FUT-do.well-2P.IND truly
'If you truly think that way,
you will truly do well.' W404

(43) i·ni **ke·htena** e·nowe·kwe·hiki, nete·pwe·htawa·wakimekoho **ke·htena.**
i·ni **ke·htena** IC-inowe·-kwe·hiki
that truly IC-talk.so-3P.CH.INTERR

ne-te·pwe·htaw-a·waki=mekoho **ke·htena**
1-believe-1>3P.IND=EMPH truly
'If they truly said that, I surely believe them.' W157

As can be seen in (42) and (43), the chiastic pattern provides some stylistic variation in the word order of the two clauses: instead of repeating the adverb *ke·htena* 'truly' in the same position in the second clause, the adverb is moved to the right of the verb.

Conclusion

An extremely rough summary of what we have seen in this paper is shown in (44), amending the word order template given in (29) to include adverb positions:

(44) [$_{S'}$ EXT-TOP [$_{S}$ ADV INT-TOP ADV NEG ADV FOCUS* ADV OBL ADV V ADV XP* ADV]]
{SUBJ, OBJ, O2, COMP}

In other words, adverbs have been found preceding or following all the elements of the word order template. The more fine-grained observations made above are best expressed as local constraints, such as the preference for discourse adverbs to precede propositional adverbs, which in turn precede predicate adverbs. Another example of a local constraint or preference is the interaction between independent negative particles and the three types of adverbs: No examples of a discourse adverb preceding an independent negative particle were found in my corpus of examples taken from third person narrative texts, because verbs in narrative contexts are negated with a negative preverb, not with an independent negative particle. The propositional type of adverb may either precede or follow an independent negative particle, producing a scope difference, while predicate adverbs occur to the right of an independent negative particle. As a final comment on the template in (44), let me point out again that the appearance of any kind of adverb occurring after an oblique argument and before the verb is quite rare: Oblique arguments are typically immediately to the left of the verb.

The template in (44) also lists two possible positions for adverbs to occur to the right of the verb: either immediately after the verb, optionally followed by one or more arguments of the verb, or at the extreme right edge of the clause. As stated above, the appearance of an adverb in either position to the right of the verb is marked; two constructions favoring post-verbal adverbs were described above (avoiding ambiguity with a direct quotation preceding the verb, and chiasmus) but more remains to be discovered regarding the appearance of adverbs to the right of the verb.

NOTES

1. Thanks to Will Oxford, Peter Grishin, Lucy Thomason, Monica Macaulay, and other audience members for useful comments; thanks as well to the two anonymous readers for very helpful suggestions. In the template in (1) the * indicates that more than one element of that type may appear.
2. Lockwood (2017:171) points out that other adverb positions are possible in Potawatomi as well.
3. Abbreviations: 1 = first person singular, 1P = first person exclusive plural, 2 = second person singular, 2P = second person plural, 21 = first person inclusive plural, 3 = third person singular, 3P = third person plural, 3′ = third person animate obviative, 0 = inanimate, 0′ = inanimate obviative, ADV = adverb, ANIM = animate, AOR = aorist prefix; aorist conjunct inflection, CH.INTERR = changed interrogative, COMP = complement clause, DIM = diminutive, EMPH = emphatic, e.o. = each other, EXPL = expletive, EXT-TOP = external topic, FUT = future, IC = Initial Change (ablaut rule), IND = independent indicative, INT-TOP = internal topic, INTERR.PART = interrogative participle, LOC = locative, MAN('S) = a word or morpheme used by men but not women, NEG = negative inflection,

OBJ = (first) object, O2, OBJ2 = second object, OBL = oblique head of relative clause, OBV = obviative, PART = conjunct participle, PL = plural, PRED = predicate, PROP = propositional, REDUP = reduplication, SG = singular, SUBJ = subject, SUBJNCT = subjunctive, TOP = topic, V = verb, X = unspecified subject, XP = phrasal category, y.sib = younger sibling. Subject and object features in verb inflection are separated by > and are followed by identification of the verbal paradigm. The head of a relative clause is identified following the label PART (participle). En dashes indicate the boundary between a preverb and a verb stem; if material (e.g., an enclitic or an independent constituent) intervenes between the preverb and the verb stem, an en dash appears on both the preverb and the verb stem. Vowel length is marked by a raised dot. Examples cited as W are from Kiyana (1913).

4. For an exhaustive investigation of types of Algonquian particles see Oxford (2008), on Innu-aimun, and for Meskwaki, see Goddard (2023:357–370). Valentine (2001:138–147) also gives a comprehensive overview of adverbs in Nishnaabemwin.
5. Not all obliques are expressed by particles: some obliques are nouns bearing locative case, and others are subordinate clauses.
6. See Kasper and Lewis (2022) for examples of such predicates in Potawatomi.
7. The first clause of (43) is a repetition of example (39), which demonstrated that an adverb may follow an oblique argument.

REFERENCES

Bloomfield, Leonard. 1946. Algonquian. *Linguistic Structures of Native America*, ed. by Harry Hoijer et al., pp. 85–129. Viking Fund Publications in Anthropology 6. New York: Wenner-Gren Foundation for Anthropological Research.

Dahlstrom, Amy. 1993. The Syntax of Discourse Functions in Fox. *Berkeley Linguistics Society 19. Special Session on Syntactic Issues in Native American Languages*, ed. by David A. Peterson, pp. 11–21. Berkeley, CA: Berkeley Linguistics Society.

Dahlstrom, Amy. 2004. External and Internal Topics in Meskwaki. Paper read at the 36th Algonquian Conference, University of Wisconsin, Madison.

Goddard, Ives. 2023. *A Grammar of Meskwaki*. Petoskey, MI: Mundart Press.

Kiyana, Alfred. 1913. wisakea osani okyeni osimeani okomeseani. [Wisahkeha, His Father, His Mother, His Younger Brother, His Grandmother.] Unpublished manuscript, 2958-a, National Anthropological Archives, Smithsonian Institution, Washington, DC.

Kasper, Corinne, and Robert E. Lewis, Jr. (2022). The Potawatomi Complementizer System. Paper read at the 54th Algonquian Conference, University of Colorado, Boulder.

Lewis, Robert E., Jr. 2015. Determining that Potawatomi Word Order is Pragmatically Conditioned. Paper read at the 47th Algonquian Conference, University of Manitoba, Winnipeg.

Lockwood, Hunter. 2017. How the Potawatomi Language Lives: A Grammar of Potawatomi. PhD thesis, University of Wisconsin–Madison.

McCawley, James D. 1988. *The Syntactic Phenomena of English*, vol. 2. Chicago: University of Chicago Press.

Oxford, Will. 2008. *A Grammatical Study of Innu-Aimun Particles.* Winnipeg: Algonquian and Iroquoian Linguistics.

Thomason, Lucy. 2016. Meskwaki Postposed Preverbs. Paper read at the 48th Algonquian Conference, University of Wisconsin, Milwaukee.

Valentine, J. Randolph. 2001. *Nishnaabemewin Reference Grammar.* Toronto: University of Toronto Press.

Arguments for Multiple Positions of Relative Roots in Passamaquoddy, Penobscot, Meskwaki, and East Cree

Ying Gong

This paper investigates three verb-internal morphemes (Oxford 2019) in Algonquian languages known as "relative roots" in the Algonquianist literature: reflexes of Proto-Algonquian *taθ-, *eθ-, and *went-. Relative roots typically occur either in the stem-initial position or to the left of the verb stem as a preverb. In (1), for example, the stem *-očiwen* is formed from the initial *oč-* and the final *-iwen-*; *oč-* is a reflex of the relative root *went- in its stem-initial form, whereas *-iwen-* is a verb final meaning 'carry'. In (2), on the other hand, the reflex of the relative root *taθ- is realized as a preverb in the form of *taši-* and combines with a full verb stem (Dahlstrom 2014).[1]

(1) menes-eki eh-očiwen-ekoči.
island-LOC AOR-carry.from-3'>3.CJ
'It carried him from the island.' (Meskwaki; Dahlstrom 2014:60)

(2) ayohi ke-ih-taši-witamaw-ene.
here 2-FUT-at-explain-1>2.IND
'I will explain it to you here.' (Meskwaki; Dahlstrom 2014:59)

In both cases, a non-core argument not subcategorized for by the verb is added to the sentence and is indexed on the verbal complex by a relative root. The locative argument *meneseki* 'island' is taken as the spatial source of the carrying event in (1) and the argument *ayohi* 'here' is understood as the general location where the event of explaining will take place in (2). This paper uses the terminology following Bruening (2004) and Dahlstrom (2014) in which the argument associated with a relative root is referred to as an "oblique argument." Others such as Rhodes (2010) and Branigan and Brittain (2016) call such arguments "relative root complements" and distinguish them from true obliques, which are viewed as adjuncts in Dahlstrom (2014) (i.e., arguments that are not associated with any overt morpheme in the syntax).

The relative roots may also have a corresponding free-standing form, which is often treated as a preposition-like particle (Bruening 2001). As shown in (3), the Passamaquoddy relative root *oloq-* 'that way, in that direction' occurs either as a preverb or as a separate word in the form of *oloqiw*, where the final *-w* is identified as marking the syntactic category of particle by Bruening (2001).

(3) 't-**oloq**-aph-a-l **oloqi-w** qospem-ok.
3-**that.way**-track-DIR-OBV **that.way**-PTCL lake-LOC
'She tracked him toward the lake.' (Passamaquoddy; Bruening 2001:169)

In this paper, while the discussion is mostly around preverbal relative roots, there are cases where the stem-initial and the free-standing uses of the relative roots are also involved, especially in the discussion on the rationale use of *went-.

Relative Roots and Applicatives

Previous studies on relative roots often focus on their argument-associated uses and suggest that the relative roots, in a certain sense, "license" the oblique argument. Bruening (2001) suggests that the oblique argument forms a constituent with its associated relative root and is added to the argument structure of the verb in Passamaquoddy. Dahlstrom (2014) argues for the same in Meskwaki; she suggests that relative roots subcategorize for an oblique argument and specify the thematic role of it. The kind of licensing relation between a relative root and its associated argument is, however, unique, as pointed out by Rhodes (2006): The associated arguments present distinct properties from objects and other adjunct obliques that are (obligatorily or optionally) licensed by the verb with respect to several morphosyntax and syntax patterns in Algonquian, including verb agreement, obviative marking, change of grammatical relations, and so on.

Algonquian relative roots are reminiscent of the applicatives in Bantu languages and many other languages, such as Winnebago, Tagalog, and others, wherein an oblique or non-core argument is added to the argument structure of the verb via certain morphemes recognized as applicatives.[2] Applicatives can be divided into two types, namely, thematic applicatives and (athematic) licensing applicatives. With thematic applicatives, it is commonly assumed that the thematic role of the applied argument is assigned by the applicative. Hence, different thematic roles are often associated with different forms of applicatives. In some languages like isiXhosa, however, the same form of the applicative is associated with applied arguments of various thematic roles. If the thematic role is always assigned by the applicative, then all applicative constructions in such languages are predicted to have multiple interpretations. Yet the thematic role of the applied argument is often understood unambiguously and often depends on the meaning of the verb (Jerro 2016). This empirical fact leads to the proposal of the licensing applicative, which only serves to syntactically license the applied argument without assigning a thematic role (Paul and Whitman 2010; Georgala 2012; Nie 2020; Myler and Mali 2021a).

Another feature of the licensing applicative is that it does not always introduce an additional argument. The licensing applicative may function to raise an applied argument introduced by other applicatives (such as the raising applicative proposed by Paul and Whitman (2010) for Mandarin and Nie (2020) for Tagalog). In some other cases, the licensing applicative may function to restrict the interpretation of an argument. Marten (2003) reports that in Swahili, the applicative can be used to index a pragmatically salient information status of the object without introducing a new argument.

Relative roots appear to share properties of both types of applicatives. On the one hand, similar to thematic applicatives, different relative roots are associated with different thematic roles (see (1) and (2)). On the other hand, the same relative root can be associated with oblique arguments of various thematic types, and the very same relative root may have athematic uses (similar to licensing applicatives). (The availability of each use of the relative roots varies slightly across the language family.) For instance, the oblique argument licensed by *eθ- can be interpreted as expressing goal of motion in some cases (with motion verbs) as in (4), and as expressing manner in other cases (with non-motion verbs) as in (5).

(4) gii=izh-yaa-w ishpimisagw-ing.
PST=to-go-3.SBJ upstairs-LOC
'S/he went (to) upstairs.' (Ojibwe; Rhodes 2010:317)

(5) mâmâhch chiki ishi-nâkun.
different FUT.3 thus-appear.0.IND
'It(inan.) will look different.' (East Cree; Branigan and Brittain 2016:6)

Meanwhile, in addition to its locative use in (2), *taθ- can be used to express the progressive aspect without adding any additional argument to the sentence, as shown in (6):

(6) eh-ayeši-keh-mani aškotewi-taši-aniwešeniki.
AOR-still-but-now fire-PROG-burn.vigorously
'But the fire was still going strong.' (Meswaki; Dahlstrom 1996:137)

Proposal

The similarities between relative roots and applicatives motivate an applicative-like analysis of relative roots. In this paper, I pursue this road and provide a unified analysis of the relative roots that can account for both their valency-increasing uses and their other syntactic functions. In particular, I identify both a lower and a higher position where the relative roots can merge similar to the Low/High and SuperHigh positions of applicatives following Pylkkänen (2008), Myler and Mali (2021a), and others. The relative roots may have their position at the edge of vP, taking an oblique argument as their complement; this accounts for their non-sentential thematic uses. On the other hand, the aspectual and sentential uses are tied to a rather high position above VoiceP, in contradistinction to the lower vP-level position of the relative roots. To keep in line with the tradition in the applicative literature, the vP-level relative roots are referred to as the High Relative Roots (RR_{high}s) and the above-Voice relative roots as the SuperHigh Relative Roots ($RR_{superhigh}$s).

(7) $RR_{superhigh}$ > Voice > RR_{high} > v
{aspectual; sentential} {thematic}

To account for the various (non-sentential) thematic uses of the same relative root, I suggest further that the interpretation of a High relative root is determined by the semantic class of the verb (e.g., motion vs. non-motion), akin to Kratzer's (1996) treatment of various interpretations of Voice, as exemplified below with the High *eθ- for its goal and manner uses.

(8) a. $[\![\text{*e}\theta\text{-}]\!] = \lambda x.\, \lambda e_s.\, \textsc{goal}(e, x)$ /__(motion event)

b. $[\![\text{*e}\theta\text{-}]\!] = \lambda x.\, \lambda e_s.\, \textsc{manner}(e, x)$ /__(non-motion event)

Here I use the GOAL and MANNER functions in the semantic entries as shorthand for the purpose of illustration. Notice that the first argument that this relative root takes should be type-neutral (at least for the manner use) since the oblique argument expressing manner can be various syntactic categories, including clauses, adverbs, NPs, and so on, or even implicit (Dahlstrom 2014). A similar account can be given to the High *went-, which, in addition to having the path-related source use, is found to be associated with path-unrelated roles such as instrumentals in languages like Plains Cree (Cook 2008) or benefactives in Eastern Algonquian languages (Quinn personal communication). But such uses are almost entirely associated with *went- in its free-standing adposition form.

The proposed analysis straightforwardly accounts for (i) the aspectual use of the relative roots (e.g., *taθ- for progressive), as well as two other properties that are underexplored in the literature, including that (ii) relative roots with a sentential interpretation (e.g., the rationale *went- and the sentential complementizer *eθ-) prefer a left-peripheral position, and (iii) multiple relative roots can stack together within one verbal complex. In the remainder of this paper, I go through the properties of the relative roots one by one and demonstrate how the proposed analysis accounts for them. Before we delve into the details of the analysis, it is important to note that this study is based on published examples only, focusing on data from four languages, namely, Passamaquoddy, Penobscot, Meskwaki, and East Cree. It does not assert the universality of these properties in the whole language family, and variations are indeed expected. The textual sources used in this paper mainly come from Dahlstrom (1996, 2014, 2015) for Meskwaki, Bruening (2001, 2004, 2006) for Passamaquoddy, Quinn (2017) for Penobscot, and Branigan and Brittain (2016) for East Cree. The paper also incorporates examples from Objiwe (Rhodes 2006, 2010) and Plains Cree (Cook 2008).

Athematic Uses of SuperHigh RRs

Compare the Meskwaki examples shown next, repeated from (2) and (6). While the relative root *taθ- functions as the introducer of the general location in (9a), *taθ- is used to mark the progressive aspect in (9b). The same morpheme *taši-* is attached to the verb stem *aniwešeniki* 'vigorously burn', yet there is no general location being added to the sentence. Instead, the sentence is reported to have a progressive reading that "the fire is (was) burning" (Dahlstrom 1996).

(9) a. Ayohi ke-ih-taši-witamaw-ene.
here 2-FUT-at-explain-1>2.IND
'I will explain it to you here.' (Meskwaki; Dahlstrom 2014:59)

b. Eh-ayeši-keh-mani aškotewi-taši-aniwešeniki.
AOR-still-but-now fire-PROG-burn.vigorously
'But the fire was still going strong.' (Meskwaki; Dahlstrom 1996:137)

Shown next is another pair of examples of the two uses of *(en)taθ- in Passamaquoddy. While the occurrence of *etoli-* in (10a) is associated with the locative use, the occurrence of *totoli-* in (10b) gives rise to a progressive reading.

(10) a. etoli-mskuw-at nicalku-l utene-k.
IC.at-find-3.CJ 3.uncle-OBV town-LOC
'He found his uncle in the town.' (Passamaquoddy; Bruening 2001:169)

b. Mecote totoli-ye Lula utapakonum.
still PROG-move Lula 3.car
'Lawrence's car is still running.' (Passamaquoddy; Francis et al. 2008)

In addition to Meskwaki and Passamaquoddy, this dual function of *taθ- is found across the language family—at least among Eastern Algonquian languages, including Penobscot and Mikmaq (Quinn 2017), as well as Ojibwe.

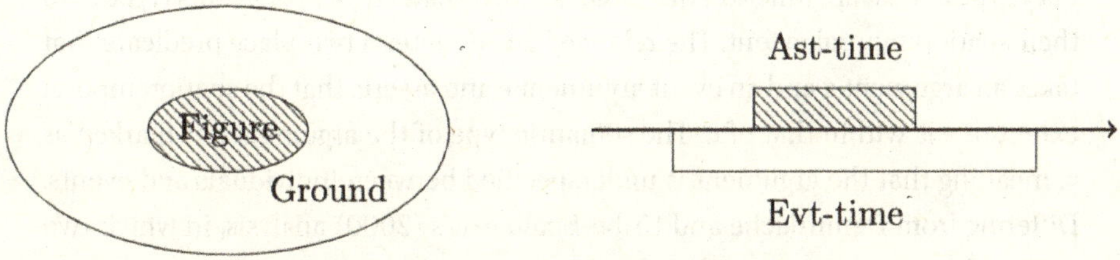

FIGURE 1. Illustration of the within relation in a spatial and temporal sense

It is not rare cross-linguistically that items functioning as locative adpositions are also used in expressing the progressive aspect in the language (e.g., Mandarin *zài*, Tunisian Arabic *fī*, Basque *-n*, Dutch *aan*, etc.). Demirdache and Uribe-Etxebarria (2000) posit that syntactic aspects can be understood as a type of relative relations that are calculated in the same way as calculating the relative relation between the FIGURE and the GROUND. For instance, the English locative preposition *in* in a sentence like *the cat is in the box* denotes a WITHIN relation in the spatial sense: The spatial stretch of the figure (e.g., *the cat*) is contained within the spatial stretch of the ground (e.g., *the box*), as illustrated by the picture on the left in Figure 1.

Similarly, the progressive aspect can be understood as a WITHIN relation in the temporal realm. As shown in Figure 1 on the right, the assertion time, namely, the time for which an assertion is made (Klein 1995), can be viewed as the temporal figure that is contained within the event time, which can be understood as the temporal ground. Hence, the progressive interpretation in a sentence like *John is reading a book* is derived from the sense that the time interval visible to the semantic interpretation (i.e., the assertion time) is a subpart of the event of John reading a book that includes neither its initial nor its final endpoint (Demirdache and Uribe-Etxebarria 2000).

Given the analogy between the spatial and temporal WITHIN relation, a similar treatment can be implemented to the two uses of *taθ-. I propose a unified semantics of *taθ-, as in (11).

(11) $[\![\text{*ta}\theta\text{-}]\!] = \lambda \alpha_{\sigma} . \lambda e_{s} . \mu_{\text{ext}}(e) \subseteq \mu_{\text{ext}}(\alpha)$

Let μ_{ext} be a measure function that relates individuals (type e) or events (type s) to their spatiotemporal extent. The relative *taθ- denotes a two-place predicate that takes an argument α and an event argument e and asserts that the spatiotemporal extent of e is within that of α. The semantic type of the argument α is marked as σ, meaning that the argument is underspecified between individuals and events. Differing from Demirdache and Uribe-Etxebarria's (2000) analysis, in which two temporal arguments are introduced in the syntax as the external argument of Aspect Phrases, in this study, the temporal relation is calculated using the μ_{ext} function.

The general location of the event is expressed in the sense that the spatiotemporal extent of the event is within the spatiotemporal extent of the place. The derivation of (9a) is illustrated in Figure 2. When the locative argument of type e appears, *taθ- combines with the argument via Function Application, taking it as the (locative) ground. The resulting event predicate further combines with the event predicate denoted by vP through Predicate Modification. Sentence (9a)

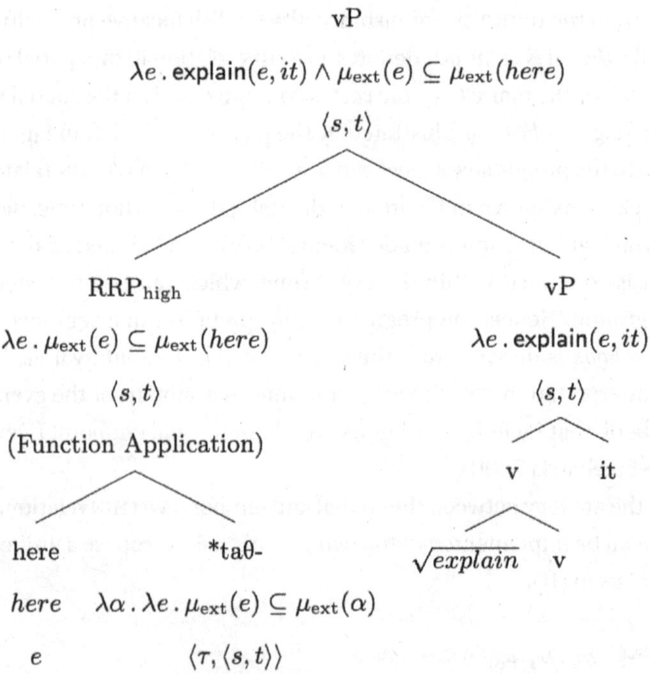

FIGURE 2. Syntax trees for relevant examples

can be hence interpreted as follows: There is an event of explaining such that the agent is "I," the theme is "it," and the spatiotemporal extent of the event is within the spatiotemporal extent of "here."

The progressive use of *taθ- can be accounted for in a similar fashion but with *taθ- composing with the event predicate (type <*e*, *t*>) denoted at the VoiceP directly. This composition can be done via a single process similar to Restriction plus a following Existential Closure (Diesing 1992, Chung and Ladusaw 2004). The derivation of the progressive sentence in (9b) is given in Figure 3. Notice that while in the locative use the understood ground is a certain place, for the progressive use it is the (spatio)temporal extent of an event that contributes to the (temporal) ground. Here, the event predicate of type <*s*, *t*> can compose with *taθ- (type <*σ*, <*s*, *t*>>) in

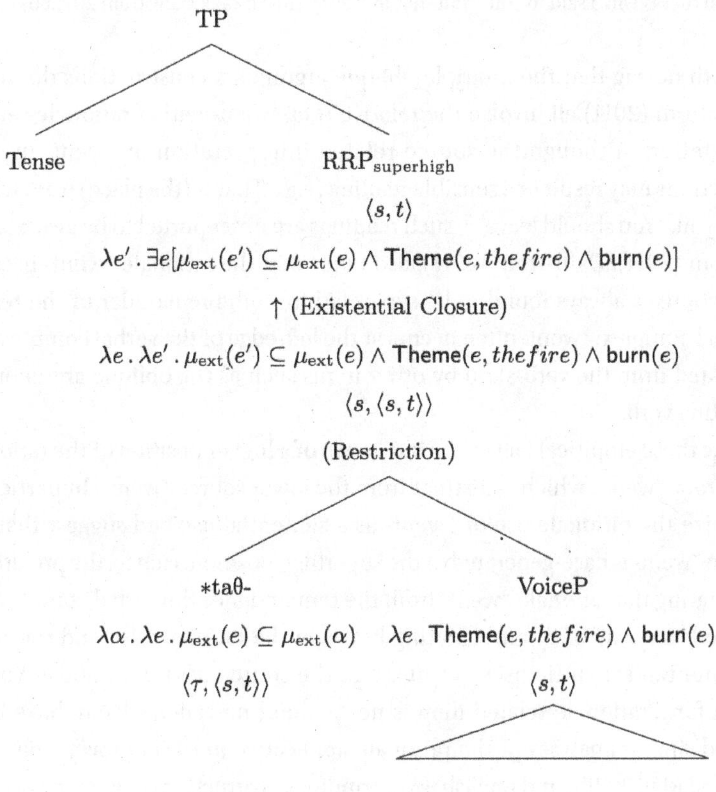

FIGURE 3. Syntax trees for relevant examples

the same vein as bare NPs (type <*e, t*>) composing with transitive verbs (type <*e*, <*e, t*>>). In this way, it gives at the top node of the SuperHigh Relative Root Phrase ($RRP_{superhigh}$) a set of events for which the spatiotemporal extent is contained by the fire-burning event described by the verb, giving rise to the progressive reading.[3]

Sentential RRs at Left-Periphery

Dahlstrom (2014) discusses constructions where multiple oblique arguments occur (either overtly or covertly) like the following:

(12) ini=čahi weči- 'ke-ih-nakwa'-inenani
that=so IC.from- 2-FUT-leave.2.IND-say.(thus).to.1>2.PART/OBL.HEAD
'So that is why I said to you, "You should leave."' (Meskwaki; Dahlstrom 2014:66)

It is worth noting that the multiple oblique arguments constructions discussed by Dahlstrom (2014) all involve the relative root *went- with a rationale-related interpretation. Although the source-related interpretation of *went- in such constructions may result in a sensible reading (e.g., 'That is (the place) from where I said to you, "You should leave"'), such readings are not reported to be available by Dahlstrom (2014). Dahlstrom (2014) also notes that the rationale *went- in these constructions is always found to be separated from the remainder of the rest of the verbal complex: *went- often occurs at the left-edge of the verbal complex and is separated from the verb-stem by other items such as the oblique argument of the quoting verb.

I take these empirical facts to be indicative of a higher position of the rationale relative root *went-, which is distinct from the lower source *went-. In particular, I recognize the rationale use of *went- as a sentential use and suggest that the rationale *went- is base-generated in the superhigh position. Hence, the preference for separating the rationale *went- from the remainder of the verbal complex can be viewed as a way of disambiguating between the rationale use and the other non-sentential semantic uses *went- (e.g., the source use). This above VoiceP position for a rationale-related item is not without precedent. There have been proposed similar analyses of the rationale applicative in isiXhosa *why*-questions (Myler and Mali 2021b) and English *why*-stripping constructions (e.g., *John ate natto. Why natto*?) (Yoshida et al. 2013).

The data from East Cree provide another argument for the left-peripheral position of the rationale *went-. Consider the following examples:

(13) a. Julie nit-isi-nihkâsun.
Julie 1-thus-be.named.3.IND
'My name is Julie.' (East Cree; Branigan and Brittain 2016:6)

b. mâmâhch chiki ishi-nâkun.
Different FUT.3 thus-appear.0.IND
'It(inan.) will look different.' (East Cree; Branigan and Brittain 2016:6)

In both examples, the oblique argument associated with the manner relative root *isi-/ishi-*, namely, *Julie* in (13a) and *mâmâhch* 'different' in (13b), occurs to the left of the verbal complex. Moreover, in (13b), the oblique argument and the verbal complex are intervened by the tense morpheme *chiki* 'FUT.3'.

However, when an additional relative root occurs, namely, the rationale *went-, the manner oblique argument appears to occur postverbally instead of preverbally. As shown in (14), the manner oblique argument *hotdogs* is placed at the end of the sentence, despite the fact that (14) involves the free-standing form of the relative root (i.e., *wâhchi*).

(14) châkwân wâhchi ishi-nihkâtâ-hch û-hî hotdogs?
what from thus-be.named-0.PL.CJ DEM-0.PL hotdogs
'Why are these called *hotdogs*?' (East Cree; Branigan and Brittain 2016:12)

Branigan and Brittain (2016) also report that *hotdogs* is not just preferred in a postverbal position, but in fact it is disallowed in preverbal positions, including the pre-*wh* position as in (15a) and the pre-*wâhchi* position as in (15b).

(15) a. *hotdogs châkwân wâhchi ishi-nihkâtâ-hch û-hî?
b. *châkwân hotdogs wâhchi ishi-nihkâtâ-hch û-hî? (East Cree; Branigan and Brittain 2016:12)

From a descriptive perspective, the distinct behaviors of the manner oblique arguments in (13) and (14) allow for the following generalizations: (i) non-sentential oblique arguments are allowed in both preverbal and postverbal positions, (ii) a preverbal non-sentential oblique argument and its associated relative root can be interrupted by certain morphemes, and (iii) the intervening morpheme cannot be sentential relative roots like the rationale *wâhchi*.

This pattern can be accounted for straightforwardly with the assumption that the rationale *went- occupies a superhigh position. In particular, assume that the rationale relative root *wâhchi*, together with its associated *wh*-phrase, is at the superhigh position, whereas *hotdogs* is base-generated lower under the RRP_{high} projected by the manner relative root *ishi-*. As the *wh*-phrase would move to Spec-CP from the specifier position of the $RRP_{superhigh}$, it follows that *hotdogs* cannot be fronted to any position above *wâhchi*, for such a higher position would be occupied by the *wh*-phrase or the trace it leaves, as shown in Figure 4. In other words, the ungrammaticality of (15a) and (15b) is precisely because fronting a lower NP to a position preceding the superhigh rationale relative root is disallowed.

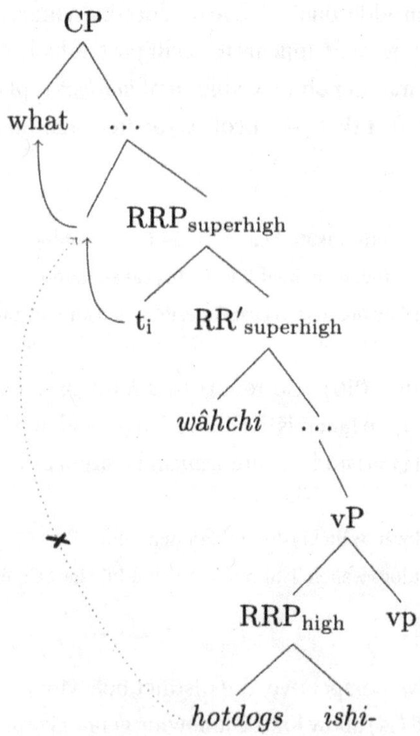

FIGURE 4. Syntax trees for relevant examples

The proposed analysis only bans non-sentential oblique arguments from preceding the sentential relative root in interrogative sentences. It does not rule out cases where the oblique argument occurs in a preverbal position that is after the sentential relative root. However, it was suggested by an audience member at the 54th Algonquian Conference that such an order is actually unacceptable in East Cree, as shown in (16).

(16) *châkwân wâhchi hotdogs ishi-nihkâtâ-hch û-hî?

The ungrammaticality of (16), however, does not provide a negative argument against the proposed analysis. In fact, there is room to doubt whether the ungrammaticality in (16) as well as in (15) is due to the fact that the rationale relative root in such cases is used in its free-standing form. Hence, if there exists a rule banning non-sentential oblique arguments from occurring preverbally in the presence of a free-standing relative root in East Cree, it follows that the surface order in (15) and (16) should be bad. It is worth noting that such a word order was suggested to be permissible in Meskwaki and Passamaquoddy by some other audience members at the conference, providing evidence in favor of this account. The ungrammaticality of (16) then may exemplify an instance of language variation between East Cree and Meskwaki/Passamaquoddy.

On the other hand, this analysis does not posit the same restrictions on non-interrogative sentences: Without the *wh*-phrase occupying the preverbal positions, the non-sentential oblique argument should be allowed to land in such positions. Hence, a more flexible order between a non-sentential oblique argument and the rationale *went- is expected in non-interrogative sentences. Regardless of language variations, this prediction is borne out in Meskwaki. Compare (17) with example (12), repeated here in (18).

(17) ini 'hawo' **weči-** in-aki.
that all.right IC.**from-** say.(thus).to-1>3.PART/OBL.HEAD
'That is why I said, "All right," to him.' (Meskwaki; Dahlstrom 2014:66)

(18) ini=čahi **weči-** ke-ih-nakwa'-inenani
that=so IC.**from-** 2-FUT-leave.2.IND-say.(thus).to.1>2.PART/OBL.HEAD
'So that is why I said to you, "You should leave."' (Meskwaki; Dahlstrom 2014:66)

These two examples both involve a "non-sentential" oblique argument—the direct quote in both cases—that is selected by the verb (Dahlstrom 2014). This shows that the non-sentential oblique argument can occur either preverbally before the rationale *went-, being separated from the verbal complex as in (17) or as part of the verbal complex after the rationale relative root as in (18).

Stacked RRs

Another potential piece of evidence for the SuperHigh Relative Roots comes from cases where multiple relative roots are found within the same verbal complex. Consider the Penobscot example in (19) where two relative roots are stacked together to the left of the verb stem *kəlosəya* 'speak'—one being *went-, in its reflex *weci-*, and the other being *eθ-, in its reflex *ali-*. The sentence is interpreted as meaning "that is why I speak thus" where *went- receives a rationale interpretation and *eθ- receives a manner interpretation.

(19) Ni **weci-ali-kəlosəya.**
that IC.**from-thus-speak**.1.CJ
'That is why I speak thus.' (Penobscot; Quinn 2017:13)

In Penobscot, the relative *went- has the basic source-related use, as shown in (20a), and *eθ- can function as the sentential complement marker, similar to the English complementizer *that*, as in (20b) (Quinn 2017).

(20) a. tɑn **wéč-ohs-an?**
which IC.**from-walk**-2.CJ
'Where do you walk from?' (Penobscot; Quinn 2017:18)

b. nə-wew-élətam-ən **eli-kámɑč-wəssak-alɑməy-an.**
1-know-by.mind-N IC.**that-very-bitter-be.hungry-2.CJ**
'I know that you are very distressingly hungry.' (Penobscot; Quinn 2017:11)

If the sentential uses of the relative roots are not associated with a higher position, it is then predicted that (19) should have a reading where the outer *went- is associated with the source use and the inner *eθ- with the sentential, complementizer use (e.g., 'that I speak from (some place)'). Contrary to fact, such a reading is unavailable (Quinn personal communication). The proposed analysis provides a straightforward explanation for the lack of the 'that... from' interpretation in (19): It is impossible to move the source *went-, which is base-generated in the high position to a position higher than the sentential *eθ- in the superhigh position.

In fact, the "that . . . from" interpretation is likely to be associated with the reversed *eθ-*went- order, as illustrated by the following example. I use a question mark in parentheses to indicate that the grammaticality of the example is not confirmed by native speakers.

(21) (?)eli-'ci-kolusi n-ikon-uk.
that-from-speak.1.CJ 1-house-LOC
'That I speak from our house.' (Passamaquoddy; constructed example courtesy Conor Quinn, personal communication)

If it turns out to be true that different orders of the relative roots are associated with a different interpretation, as suggested by (19) and (21), this will provide a convincing argument for the proposed analysis.

Concluding Remarks

This study has investigated three relative roots in a group of Algonquian languages, aiming to gain some understanding of their syntax and semantics. It has been argued that there are at least two possible positions where the relative roots can merge: a superhigh position above VoiceP, responsible for the aspectual and sentential uses (e.g., the progressive use of *taθ-, the rationale use of *went-), and a vP-level high position associated with the basic thematic uses (e.g., the locative use of *taθ-, the source use of *went-, and the goal/manner use of *eθ-).

The proposed analysis makes several predictions that require further confirmation. First, this analysis suggests that the aspectual and sentential uses are linked to the superhigh position above VoiceP. This predicts that relative roots with such uses should not be realized as initials. Counterexamples to this prediction, where an initial relative root receives an aspectual or sentential interpretation, will challenge the analysis.

Second, the analysis predicts that multiple relative roots constructions should be productive, although only a very limited number of such examples are found in the textual sources this study covers. It is also worth noting that this analysis only rules out interpretations where the outer relative root receives a non-sentential interpretation but the inner one receives an aspectual/sentential interpretation. The analysis does not posit any restriction on stacking the same relative root, as long as each occurrence of the relative root is associated with a different use (e.g., one aspectual/sentential and one thematic). In addition, the analysis does not rule out cases where three or more non-sentential thematic relative roots are stacked in the same verbal complex. I leave it to future research to examine this prediction and explore how the final spell-out may interact with other linguistic rules, such as Haplology and the Obligatory Contour Principle effect.

This study also has some limitations. First, it only focuses on a small set of relative roots and some of their uses. Many other identified relative roots, including those associated with degrees and amounts as discussed in Dahlstrom (2015), are not covered. On the other hand, many other observed uses of the three relative roots are not discussed in this paper. For example, Quinn (2017) suggests that *eθ- and *went-, in addition to *taθ-, also have aspectual uses, although such aspectual uses are mostly restricted to the motion-verb aspect. Bruening (2004, 2006) reports that in Passamaquoddy, a "dummy" relative root, often the *eθ-, is obligatorily added to the matrix verb in *wh*-constructions that inquire about the oblique argument of the embedded verb. The "dummy" relative root may function to license the long-distance movement of the embedded *wh*-phrase (Bruening 2004), or it may be the spell-out of the higher copy of the relative root (Bruening 2006). Either way, the "dummy" relative root does not serve to introduce any additional argument or to express grammatical aspects. Future research could expand the scope of this study by how the proposed analysis can be extended to account for a larger set of relative roots and their uses that are not included in this paper.

Second, the analysis relies on the hierarchy positions of relative roots to disambiguate their aspectual/sentential and non-sentential thematic interpretations. This dependence on syntax may pose challenges when extending a similar analysis to other Algonquian languages that exhibit significantly different syntactic features. An audience member at the 54th Algonquian conference suggested that the proposed analysis could be framed alternatively in terms of different scope takings instead of hierarchy positions. Future investigations might explore this alternative framework to deepen our understanding of relative roots across the language family.

NOTES

1. List of Abbreviations: 0 = inanimate (in verb agreement), 3′ = obviative, AOR = aorist (prefix), CJ = conjunct, DEM = demonstrative, FUT = future, IC = initial change (ablaut), IND = independent indicative, LOC = locative, OBV = obviative third person, OBL = oblique, PST = past, PART = participle, PTCL = particle, PL = plural, SG = singular, ">" separates subject and object features. Verbs in relative clauses are inflected in the participle paradigm and bear an additional suffix agreeing with the head of the relative clause, indicated after a slash.
2. Rhodes (2006) recognizes a type of construction as "applicative constructions" where the applicative suffix *-amaw* is obligatorily used to introduce beneficiaries or recipients. Notice that in what Rhodes (2006) calls Algonquian applicative constructions, the original grammatical relation is changed: The original object shows the syntax of a secondary object, whereas the applied argument surfaces as the primary object and shows full verbal agreement (hence beneficiaries and recipients are added as the primary object, i.e., a core argument). In contrast, in relative root constructions, the new argument is not indexed by agreement on the verb, leaving the original grammatical relation unchanged. Hence, while I propose an applicative-like analysis of relative roots, I assume that the Algonquian relative root construction and the Algonquian applicative construction are two distinct constructions with few interactions.
3. One reviewer wonders whether a lexical ambiguous account where the high and superhigh *taθ- have different but related semantics is possible, especially given that the high *taθ- is likely to be of type <e, <s, t>> in most cases and the superhigh *taθ- of type <s, <s, t>>. A lexical ambiguous account indeed works just fine as a unified semantics account here. I am unaware of any evidence necessitating the unified account. I defer to other independent evidence for this issue.

REFERENCES

Branigan, Phil, and Julie Brittain. 2016. East Cree RR Complements as Criterial Sisters. Unpublished manuscript, Memorial University.

Bruening, Benjamin. 2001. Syntax at the Edge: Cross-Clausal Phenomena and the Syntax of Passamaquoddy. PhD thesis, Massachusetts Institute of Technology.

Bruening, Benjamin. 2004. Two Types of Wh-scope Marking in Passamaquoddy. *Natural Language & Linguistic Theory* 22:229–305.

Bruening, Benjamin. 2006. Differences between the Wh-Scope-Marking and Wh-Copy Constructions in Passamaquoddy. *Linguistic Inquiry* 37(1):25–49.

Chung, Sandra, and William Ladusaw. 2004. *Restriction and Saturation*. Cambridge, MA: MIT Press.

Cook, Clare Elizabeth. 2008. The Syntax and Semantics of Clause-typing in Plains Cree. PhD thesis, University of British Columbia.

Dahlstrom, Amy. 1996. Narrative Structure of a Fox Text. *nikotwâsik iskwâhtêm, pâkihtêpayih! Studies in Honour of H.C. Wolfart*, ed. by J. D. Nichols and A. C. Ogg, pp. 113–162. Algonquian and Iroquoian Memoir 13. Winnipeg: Algonquian and Iroquoian Linguistics.

Dahlstrom, Amy. 2014. Multiple Oblique Arguments in Meskwaki. *Papers of the 42nd Algonquian Conference 2010*, ed. by J. Randolph Valentine and Monica Macaulay, pp. 56–68. Albany: State University of New York Press.

Dahlstrom, Amy. 2015. Meskwaki Comparatives: A First Look. *Papers of the 43rd Algonquian Conference 2011*, ed. by Monica Macaulay and J. Randolph Valentin, pp. 15–27. Albany: State University of New York Press.

Demirdache, Hamida, and Myriam Uribe-Etxebarria. 2000. The Primitives of Temporal Relations. *Step by Step: Essays on Minimalist Syntax in Honor of Howard Lasnik*, ed. by Roger Martin, David Michaels, and Juan Uriagereka, pp. 157–186. Cambridge, MA: MIT Press.

Diesing, Molly. 1992. *Indefinites*. Cambridge, MA: MIT Press.

Francis, David A., Robert M. Leavitt, and Margaret Apt. 2008. *Peskotomuhkati Wolastoqewi Latuwewakon: A Passamaquoddy-Maliseet Dictionary*. Orono: University of Maine Press, Fredericton, NB: Goose Lane Editions.

Georgala, Efthymia. 2012. Applicatives in Their Structural and Thematic Function: A Minimalist Account of Multitransitivity. PhD thesis, Cornell University.

Jerro, Kyle Joseph. 2016. The Syntax and Semantics of Applicative Morphology in Bantu. PhD thesis, University of Texas at Austin.

Klein, Wolfgang. 1995. A Time Relational Analysis of Russian Aspect. *Language* 71(4):669–695.

Marten, Lutz. 2003. The Dynamics of Bantu Applied Verbs: An Analysis at the Syntaxpragmatics Interface. *Actes du 3e Congrès Mondial de Linguistique Africaine Lomé 2000*, ed. by Kézié K. Lébikaza, pp. 207–221. Köln: Köppe.

Myler, Neil, and Zoliswa O. Mali. 2021a. Accounting for the Mirror Principle and Its Exceptions in Causative-applicative Interactions: The Case of isiXhosa. Talk given at 50 ans de Linguistique al'UQAM.

Myler, Neil, and Zoliswa O. Mali. 2021b. Two Places for Causees in Productive isiXhosa Morphological Causatives. *Syntax* 24(1):1–43.

Nie, Yining. 2020. Licensing Arguments. PhD thesis, New York University.

Oxford, Will. 2019. Algonquian Languages. *The Routledge Handbook of North American*

Languages, ed. by Daniel Siddiqi, Michael Barrie, Carrie Gillon, Jason Haugen, and Eric Mathieu, pp. 504–523. New York: Routledge.

Paul, Waltraud, and John Whitman. 2010. Applicative Structure and Mandarin Ditransitives. *Linguistik Aktuell/Linguistics Today*, ed. by Maia Duguine, Susana Huidobro, and Nerea Madariaga, vol. 158, pp. 261–282. Amsterdam: John Benjamins Publishing.

Pylkkänen, Liina. 2008. *Introducing Arguments*. Cambridge, MA: MIT Press.

Quinn, Conor McDonough. 2017. Path and Aspect in Northeastern-Area Algonquian. Talk presented at Society for the Study of the Indigenous Languages of the Americas, University of Texas at Austin.

Rhodes, Richard Alan. 2006. *Clause Structure, Core Arguments, and the Algonquian Relative Root Construction.* Winnipeg: Voices of Rupert's Land.

Rhodes, Richard Alan. 2010. Relative Root Complement: A Unique Grammatical Relation in Algonquian Syntax. *Rara and Rarissima*, ed. by Jan Wohlgemuth and Michael Cysouw, pp. 305–324. Berlin: De Gruyter Mouton.

Yoshida, Masaya, Chizuru Nakao and Ivan Ortega-Santos. 2013. The Syntax of Why-stripping. Manuscript, Northwestern University.

Subordinative Long-Distance Agreement in Passamaquoddy-Wolastoqey and the Syntax of the Inverse

Peter Grishin

A central issue in Algonquian morphosyntax is the INVERSE QUESTION:[1]

(1) **The Inverse Question:**
Does morphological inverse marking correlate with some syntactic process of inversion—the primary object gaining syntactic prominence over the actor?

In other words, is morphological inverse marking tied to a voice construction akin to Austronesian object voice that promotes the primary object, while not necessarily demoting the actor (Oxford 2018)?

In Algonquian, morphological inverse marking appears in two kinds of contexts, which Oxford (2023) calls the SAP (speech act participant) INVERSE and the THIRD PERSON INVERSE. The SAP inverse involves scenarios with third persons—animate (3), inanimate (0), or unspecified (X)—acting on speech act participants (first or second person, SAP). I illustrate here with Passamaquoddy-Wolastoqey (Eastern Algonquian):[2]

(2) a. n-tokom-**oq**
1-hit.TA-INV
'She hit me.' (3→1)
b. n-tokom-**oku**-n
1-hit.TA-INV-N
'It hit me.' (0→1)
c. n-tokom-**ok**
1-hit.TA-INV.X
'I was hit (by someone).' (X→1)

The third person inverse involves scenarios with a semantically/pragmatically less prominent (in some sense) third person acting on another third person—obviative (3') on proximate (3), or inanimate on third person animate:

(3) a. '-tokom-**oku**-l
3-hit.TA-INV-3'SG
'She (OBV) hit her (PROX).' (3'→3)
b. '-tokom-**oku**-n
3-hit.TA-INV-N
'It hit her.' (0→3)

How does inverse morphology connect to the syntax? Here, I focus on this question for the independent order, which features both SAP and third person inverses in the vast majority of Algonquian languages (in contrast to the conjunct, which demonstrates great variation; Oxford 2022).

In this paper I compare three possible answers to this question:[3]

(4) a. **Yes:** morphological inversion indicates syntactic inversion.
(e.g., Rhodes 1976, 1994; Bruening 2001, 2009)
b. **No:** morphological inversion doesn't indicate syntactic inversion.
(e.g., Dahlstrom 1991; Lochbihler 2012)
c. **3 Only:** the SAP inverse is purely morphological, whereas the third person inverse involves syntactic inversion.
(Oxford 2023)

Here, I provide an argument for 3 Only, using a long-distance agreement (LDA) construction in Passamaquoddy-Wolastoqey involving subordinative complements to the TA+O verbs *'pawatomuwan* 'want s.o. to do s.t.' and *'kisehtuwan* 'make s.o. do s.t.', which I call SUBORDINATIVE LDA (see also Dahlstrom (2023) on TA+O LDA in Meskwaki). Some illustrative examples appear next:

(5) a. Makolit **'-pawatomuw-a-n** ['-qasqi-li-n Piyel-ol sepawonu].
Margaret **3-want.TA+O-3OBJ-N** 3-run.AI-3'-N Peter-3'SG tomorrow
'Margaret wants Peter to run tomorrow.' (EM, RP)

b. **N-kisehtuw-a-ne-n** [Can 't-olintu-n].
1-make.TA+O-3OBJ-N-1PL John 3-sing.AI-N
'We made John sing.' (GP, RP)

The core observation I make is that the matrix verb *'pawatomuwan* or *'kisehtuwan* can generally only agree with the embedded actor—even in the SAP inverse. There's one crucial exception: When the embedded verb is third person inverse, the matrix verb can then in fact agree with the embedded object. To analyze this pattern, I propose that subordinative LDA can only target the most syntactically prominent embedded argument, generally always the actor. Only the third person inverse can change these prominence relations, resulting in LDA with the embedded object. I intentionally remain vague about how exactly to formalize the notion of "syntactic prominence," as different syntactic models implement it in different ways, and nothing I say here crucially depends on one's preferred syntactic model.

Before we proceed further, I wish to provide some clarificatory notes on my assumptions about the syntactic structure of this construction.[4] First, observe that the target of subordinative LDA can either be clearly inside the subordinative clause (5a), ambiguous in its position (5b), or clearly in the matrix clause (6):

(6) Ma=te weni-l Sapet **'-pawatomuw-a-wi-n**
NEG=EMPH who-3'SG Elizabeth **3-want.TA+O-3OBJ-NEG-N**

['-peciya-li-n sepawonuk].
3-come.AI-3'-N tomorrow
'Elizabeth doesn't want anyone to come tomorrow.' (EM)

For consistency, I bracket ambiguous LDA targets as part of the subordinative clause, but this is purely a typographical choice—whether those nominals are really part of the embedded clause is not a crucial part of this paper. As far as I am aware, the agreement behavior we see in this construction is the same no matter where the LDA target is located—in the embedded clause, ambiguous in its position, or in the matrix clause (see also Grishin 2023a). Most commonly, the LDA target will be in an ambiguous position at the left edge of the embedded clause.

There are (at least) three possible analyses of subordinative LDA, which we can call TRUE LDA, RAISING TO OBJECT, and MATRIX THEMATIC OBJECT:

(7) a. **True LDA:** the matrix verb agrees *into* the embedded clause, across a clause boundary (e.g., Bruening (2001) on LDA into independent indicative and conjunct complements). If the LDA target appears in the matrix clause, this is due to an independently available syntactic process that can displace phrases across clause boundaries.[5]

b. **Raising to object:** The LDA target starts out in the embedded clause, then *raises* into the matrix clause—only then does the matrix verb agree with it. If the LDA target surfaces in the embedded clause, this is because this raising process can be *covert* (Deal 2017; Grishin 2023a).

c. **Matrix thematic object:** The LDA target originates in the matrix clause as a thematic object of the matrix verb (LeSourd 2019). It is simply coindexed with some (potentially null) argument in the embedded clause.

Here, I do not adjudicate between any of these three analyses.[6] The argument I make goes through no matter which analysis one prefers. The relevant point is that there's some syntactic process sensitive to syntactic prominence—whether it's true LDA, raising to object, or whatever mechanism constrains coindexation possibilities under the matrix thematic object analysis—and it's this sensitivity that allows us to diagnose a syntactic difference between the SAP and third person inverses. I use the term "long-distance agreement" in a purely descriptive way (perhaps slightly abusing terminology) to simply refer to the fact that the matrix verb has indexed some argument whose referent is also an argument of the embedded verb, however this state of affairs should be formally derived.

This paper is organized as follows. I first provide background on the subordinative mode, then briefly discuss another, better-studied LDA construction involving independent and conjunct clauses (Bruening 2001; LeSourd 2019). Then we examine the behavior of subordinative LDA, first establishing its baseline agreement and obviation properties with intransitive complements, before examining different transitive scenarios. I end by discussing the consequences of subordinative LDA for the syntax of the inverse.

Background

Passamaquoddy-Wolastoqey is an Eastern Algonquian language currently spoken by about a few hundred speakers in eastern Maine and New Brunswick, the vast majority of whom are older than 60 years. There are two dialects: Passamaquoddy, spoken in current-day eastern Maine, and Wolastoqey (also known as Maliseet), spoken in current-day New Brunswick. The data for this paper come from ongoing work with four Passamaquoddy-Wolastoqey speakers, started in 2020 and carried out mostly over Zoom: two Passamaquoddy speakers, Grace Paul (GP) and Margaret Apt (MA), and two Wolastoqey speakers, Edwina Mitchell (EM) and Roger Paul (RP).

Subordinative Mode

The distinction between independent and conjunct orders is well known in Algonquian, with the independent order being generally characteristic of main clauses, and the conjunct being generally characteristic of embedded clauses and *wh* questions (e.g., Brittain 2001; Richards 2004; Cook 2014; Grishin 2023b). A third clause type is found in the Eastern languages, which innovated a submode of the independent called the SUBORDINATIVE.[7] Morphologically, it is a "submode" of the independent, since it uses the same morphology characteristic of the independent (the same distribution of inverse marking, the same prefixes and central suffixes, the same allomorphs of negation), though the precise distribution of these morphemes differs. Syntactically, the use of the subordinative seems to vary across Eastern languages, though in general it's characteristic of some subset of subordinate clauses; see discussion by Goddard (1979, 1983, 2020, 2021) on Delaware, Quinn (2004, 2007) on Penobscot, and Grishin (2023b) on Passamaquoddy-Wolastoqey. Here, I focus on the use of the subordinative with *'pawatomon* 'want' and *'kisehtun* 'make'.

Morphologically, the subordinative differs from the independent indicative in two main ways. The first is that the subordinative systematically lacks peripheral suffixes on the right edge of the verb:

(8) a. pileyawi-w-ol

be.new.II-0-0PL

'They (INAN) are new.' (independent indicative)

b. pileyawi-w

be.new.II-0

'It/they (INAN) is/are new.' (subordinative)

In the independent indicative, the peripheral suffix indexes the number and animacy of the subject of the *pileyawiw* 'be new' (8a). But in the subordinative (8b), there is no peripheral suffix, rendering the form ambiguous for the number of the subject.

The second difference is that if there is at least one animate argument of a subordinative verb, the N formative -(*o*)*n*(*e*) must appear (see Goddard 2007 on formative suffixes):

(9) a. n-conehl-a-nnu-k

1-stop.TA-3OBJ-1PL-3PL

'We stop them.' (independent indicative)

b. n-conehl-a-ne-n

1-stop.TA-3OBJ-N-1PL

'We stop her/them.' (subordinative)

The independent indicative form in (9a) features the peripheral suffix -*k* indexing the (proximate) plural object, and no formative (or a null formative from Proto-Algonquian **-w*). In contrast, the subordinative form in (9b) lacks the peripheral suffix, resulting in an ambiguity in the number of the object, and has the N formative.

Standard LDA

There is a better-studied LDA construction in Passamaquoddy-Wolastoqey involving independent indicative and conjunct complements to verbs like *'kosiciyal* 'know' and *wewitahamal* 'remember' (Bruening 2001; LeSourd 2019), which I'll call STANDARD LDA. Like several other Algonquian languages—Innu (Branigan and MacKenzie 2002), Blackfoot (Bliss 2013), Meskwaki (Dahlstrom n.d.), and Kitigan Zibi Algonquin (Lochbihler and Mathieu 2016)—standard LDA allows for agreement with *any* argument in the embedded clause—a "free LDA" pattern (Fry and Hamilton 2016):

(10) a. **N-wewitaham-a-k** [$_{IND}$ ma=te Ø-nomiy-a-wi-yik
1-remember.TA-3OBJ-3PL NEG=EMPH 1-see.TA-3OBJ-NEG-3PL

mawsuwinu-wok Kehlis-k].
person-3PL Calais-LOC
'I remember that I didn't see people in Calais.' (Bruening 2001:259)

b. **N-kosiciy-a-k** [$_{CJ}$ eli Piyel litahasi-t [$_{CJ}$ eli
1-know.TA-3OBJ-3PL IC.C Peter think.AI-3CJ IC.C

kis-ankum-i-hti-t nikt ehpic-ik posonuti-yil]].
PFV-sell.TA+O-1OBJ-3PL-3CJ that.3PL woman-3PL basket-0PL
'I know that Peter thinks that those women sold me the baskets.' (LeSourd 2019:360)

In contrast, subordinative LDA has a different locality profile: a *restricted* LDA pattern. While there are other languages with restricted LDA, like Odawa (Rhodes 1994) and Mi'gmaq (Hamilton 2018), these involve conjunct complements, which have a different distribution of inverse marking than the independent. As the subordinative is a submode of the independent, Passamaquoddy-Wolastoqey subordinative LDA is thus more relevant to the question of how inverse marking in the independent correlates with syntactic inversion.

The Data

There are two properties of subordinative LDA we'll need to pay attention to: (i) which argument the matrix verb indexes and (ii) the proximate/obviative status of embedded third person arguments.

The Basics

I focus on verbs meaning 'want' and 'make', which appear in several forms. With 'want', we either have TI *'pawatomon*, TA *'pawalal*, or TA+O *'pawatomuwan* (which can all optionally begin with *puwa-* instead of *pawa-*):

(11) a. Piyel **'-pawatom-on** [stahqon-ol yut oloqiw Ø-maceki-li-n].
Peter **3-want.TI-N** tree-3'SG here toward 3-grow.AI-3'-N
'Peter **wants (TI)** a tree to grow here.' (GP, MA)

b. Piyel **'-pawal-a-l** [stahqon-ol yut oloqiw Ø-maceki-li-n].
Peter **3-want.TA-3OBJ-3'SG** tree-3'SG here toward 3-grow.AI-3'-N
'Peter **wants (TA)** a tree to grow here.' (GP)

c. Piyel **'-pawatomuw-a-n** [stahqon-ol yut oloqiw Ø-maceki-li-n].
Peter **3-want.TA+O-3OBJ-N** tree-3'SG here toward 3-grow.AI-3'-N
'Peter **wants (TA+O)** a tree to grow here.' (GP, MA)

The TA version of 'want', *'pawalal*, is constructed by switching out the TI final *-tom* for the TA final *-l*. I leave aside this verb here, as it seems to have a slightly different semantics than the others, and consultants often reject its use except in specific contexts yet to be properly understood.

For 'make', we either have TI *'kisehtun* or TA+O *'kisehtuwan* (though note that TI *'kisehtun* seems to only be possible if there is no legitimate animate LDA target):

(12) a. Motewolon **'-kisehtu-n** [wisoki= psan-Ø].
motewolon **3-make.TI-N** very= snow.II-0
'The motewolon **made (TI)** it snow a lot.' (EM)

b. Mali **'-kisehtuw-a-n** [Tumaw-ol Ø-macaha-li-n].
Mary **3-make.TA+O-3OBJ-N** Thomas-3'SG 3-leave.AI-3'-N
'Mary **made (TA+O)** Thomas leave.' (EM, RP)

Note that the TA+O verbs are transparently derivationally related to the TI verbs by the addition of the applicative suffix –(*u*)*w*. In addition to subordinative complements, these verbs can also take nominal objects of the appropriate animacy.[8]

It is the TA+O verbs *'pawatomuwan* and *'kisehtuwan* that concern us, as it is they that participate in the relevant LDA construction, agreeing with an argument in the embedded clause:

(13) a. Sapet **'-pawatomuw-a-n** ['-tomhuwa-li-n pesku-wol Ø-nican-ol
Elizabeth **3-want.TA+O-3OBJ-N** 3-win.AI-3'-N one-3'SG 3-child-3'SG

sepawonu].
tomorrow
'Elizabeth wants one of her children to win tomorrow.' (EM)

b. **N-kisehta-ku-n** kisuhs [n-piskiqehpusi-n].
1-make.TA+O-INV-N sun 1-blink.AI-N
'The sun made me blink.' (GP, RP)

As can be seen by comparing the LDA examples above with the plain ditransitive ones below, subordinative LDA involves the same agreement morphology associated with primary objects of ditransitives (the recipient):

(14) a. **N-kisihtuw-a-n-ol** n-itapi-yik nisonu-l posonuti-yil.
1-make.TA+O-3OBJ-N-0PL 1-friend-3PL two.INAN-0PL basket-0PL
'I made my friends two baskets.' (EM, RP)

b. N-itap **n-kisihta-ku-n-ol** posonuti-yil.
1-friend **1-make.TA+O-INV-N-0PL** basket-0PL
'My friend made me some baskets.' (EM, RP)

Similar restrictions hold on subordinative LDA as ditransitive verbs. The primary object of ditransitive verbs must be grammatically animate, and subordinative LDA can only occur with grammatically animate arguments. Additionally, agreement with primary objects of direct ditransitive verbs only tracks person (not number or obviation)—the same is true of subordinative LDA.

Subordinative LDA also impacts obviation: If there's subordinative LDA with a third person animate, then it must be part of the same obviation domain (proximate span) as the matrix clause. Generally, obviation is "reset" across clause boundaries in Passamaquoddy-Wolastoqey, and speakers are very happy (and usually prefer) to have multiple proximates, as long as there's a clause boundary separating them (see (10b) above for another example):

(15) a. **Piyel** litahasu-Ø [kci= wewisosku-Ø **psuwis**].
Peter.PROX think.AI-3 great=be.nosy.AI-3 **cat.PROX**
'**Peter (PROX)** thinks that **the cat (PROX)** is very nosy.' (GP)

b. **Roger** '-kocicihtu-n [eli **nutsihpiluwet**
Roger.PROX 3-know.TI-N IC.C **doctor.PROX**

kikih-i-nokot].
heal.TA-1OBJ-3:1PL.CJ
'**Roger (PROX)** knows that **the doctor (PROX)** will heal us.' (GP, MA)

Under subordinative LDA, this is no longer possible if an embedded third person is indexed by the matrix verb and there is already a proximate in the matrix clause:[9]

(16) a. Roger '-pawatomuw-a-n [**Asawis-ol** 't-olintu-li-n].
Roger.PROX 3-want.TA+O-3OBJ-N **John-3'SG** 3-sing.AI-3'-N
'Roger (PROX) wants **John (OBV)** to sing.' (EM, RP)

b. *Roger '-pawatomuw-a-n [**Asawis** 't-olintu-n].
Roger.PROX 3-want.TA+O-3OBJ-N **John.PROX** 3-sing.AI-N
Intended: 'Roger (PROX) wants **John (PROX)** to sing.' (EM, RP)

Note that only third persons indexed by the matrix verb are part of the same obviation domain as matrix third persons, as evidenced by the following contrast:

(17) a. **Roger** n-puwatoma-ku-n [nt-olintuwew-a-n **Asawis**].
Roger.PROX 1-want.TA+O-INV-N 1-sing.to.TA-3OBJ-N **John.PROX**
'**Roger (PROX)** wants me to sing to **John (PROX)**. (EM, RP)

b. ***Roger** n-puwatoma-ku-n [nt-olintuwew-a-n **Asawis-ol**].
Roger.PROX 1-want.TA+O-INV-N 1-sing.to.TA-3OBJ-N **John-3'SG**
Intended: '**Roger (PROX)** wants me to sing to **John (OBV)**. (EM, RP)

Here, as *npuwatomakun* 'he wants me to do it' doesn't agree with *Asawis* 'John', speakers greatly disprefer making *Asawis* 'John' obviative.

With that background in place, I move on to examples involving embedded transitive verbs.

SAP→SAP

Let's start with SAP→SAP scenarios, which are neither direct nor inverse (Hockett 1992; Macaulay 2009). In these cases, you only get LDA with the embedded actor, and you cannot get LDA with the embedded object:

(18) 1→2: LDA with 1 actor only
a. Sapet **n-pawatoma-ku-n** ['-kinolu-l-on].
Elizabeth **1-want.TA+O-INV-N** 2-praise.TA-2OBJ-N
'Elizabeth wants me to praise you.' (RP)
b. *Sapet **k-pawatoma-ku-n** ['-kinolu-l-on].
Elizabeth **2-want.TA+O-INV-N** 2-praise.TA-2OBJ-N
Intended: 'Elizabeth wants me to praise you.' (RP)

(19) 1→2: LDA with 1 actor only
a. Roger **n-kisehta-ku-n** [tehpuk k-uskicinu-westuwam-ol-on].
Roger **1-make.TA+O-INV-N** only 2-Indian-speak.to.TA-2OBJ-N
'Roger made me only speak to you in Passamaquoddy.' (EM)
b. *Roger **'-kisehta-ku-n** [tehpuk k-uskicinu-westuwam-ol-on].
Roger **2-make.TA+O-INV-N** only 2-Indian-speak.to.TA-2OBJ-N
Intended: 'Roger made me only speak to you in Passamaquoddy.' (EM)

These examples are particularly striking because the person prefix prefers indexing second persons over first persons, yet here we must have the first person prefix *n-* on the matrix verb, not the second person *k-*.

SAP→3

Similarly, in SAP→3 scenarios, you only get LDA with the embedded actor:

(20) SAP→3: LDA with SAP actor only
a. Roger **n-puwatoma-ku-n** [nt-olintuwew-a-n Asawis].
Roger **1-want.TA+O-INV-N** 1-sing.to.TA-3OBJ-N John
'Roger wants me to sing to John.' (EM, RP)
b. *Roger **'-puwatomuw-a-n** [Husaw-ol nt-olintuwew-a-n].
Roger **3-want.TA+O-3OBJ-N** John-3'SG 1-sing.to.TA-3OBJ-N
Intended: 'Roger wants me to sing to John.' (GP, MA)

(21) SAP→3: LDA with SAP actor only

a. Roger **n-kisehta-ku-ne-n** [n-uskicinu-westuwam-a-ne-n
Roger **1-make.TA+O-INV-N-1PL** 1-Indian-speak.to.TA-3OBJ-N-1PL

wasis-ok].
kid-3PL
'Roger made us speak to the kids in Passamaquoddy.' (EM)

b. *Roger **'-kisehtuw-a-n** [wasis-` n-uskicinu-westuwam-a-ne-n].
Roger **3-make.TA+O -3OBJ-N** kid-3'PL 1-Indian-speak.to.TA-3OBJ-N-1PL
Intended: 'Roger made us speak to the kids in Passamaquoddy.' (EM)

These examples are not particularly surprising, given that SAPs outrank third persons.

3→3'/0 Direct

Turning to 3→3'/0 direct scenarios, it is often difficult to identify which argument you're agreeing with, in particular when the matrix verb is direct, as in this case LDA only tracks person features, not number or obviation. In the case of 3→3' direct, no possible featural difference between embedded actor and object would result in different agreement behavior on the matrix verb.[10]

However, we can employ the behavior of obviation as a proxy for which argument is the LDA target—recall that only arguments indexed by the matrix verb become part of the matrix obviation domain. Paying attention to obviation, we can note that the actor (usually proximate) generally becomes obviative if there's already a matrix proximate:[11]

(22) 3→3': LDA with 3 actor (diagnosed via obviation)

a. Asawis 't-olintuwew-a-l '-temis-ol.
John.PROX 3-sing.to.TA-3OBJ-3'SG 3-dog-3'SG
'John (PROX) sang to his dog (OBV).' (constructed)

b. Roger **'-puwatomuw-a-n** [Asawis-ol 't-olintuwew-a-n
Roger **3-want.TA+O-3OBJ-N** John-3'SG 3-sing.to.TA-3OBJ-N

'-temis-ol].
3-dog-3'SG
'Roger (PROX) wants John (OBV) to sing to his dog (OBV).' (EM)

(23) 3→0: LDA with 3 actor (diagnosed via obviation)

a. Wasis-ok Ø-mici-ni-ya-l mahsusi-yil.
kid-3PL 3-eat.TI-N-3PL-0PL fiddlehead-0PL
'The children (PROX) ate fiddleheads.' (constructed)

b. Tihtiyas **'-puwatomuw-a-n** [wasis-` Ø-mici-ni-ya
Tihtiyas **3-want.TA+O-3OBJ-N** kid-3'PL 3-eat.TI-N-3PL

mahsusi-yil].
fiddlehead-0PL
'Tihtiyas (PROX) wants the children (OBV) to eat fiddleheads.' (EM, RP)

We can conclude that in 3→3 direct scenarios, LDA is with the embedded actor.[12]

SAP Inverse

Now we turn to inverse scenarios, starting with the SAP inverse. Strikingly, here LDA must target the embedded actor, even though the embedded object is higher ranked:

(24) 3→SAP: LDA with 3 actor only

a. Roger **'-pawatomuw-a-n** [Winiw-ol nt-olahyem-ku-ne-n].
Roger **3-want.TA+O-3OBJ-N** Winnie-3'SG 1-play.with.TA-INV-N-1PL
'Roger wants Winnie to play with us.' (MA)

b. *Roger **n-pawatoma-ku-ne-n** [nt-olahyem-ku-ne-n Wini(w-ol)].
Roger **1-want.TA+O-INV-N-1PL** 1-play.with.TA-INV-N-1PL Winnie(-3'SG)
Intended: 'Roger wants Winnie to play with us.' (MA)

(25) 3→SAP: LDA with 3 actor only

a. Roger **'-kisehtuw-a-n** [wasis-` tehpu
Roger **3-make.TA+O-3OBJ-N** kid-3'PL only

n-uskicinu-westuwam-ku-ne-n].
1-Indian-speak.to.TA-INV-N-1PL
'Roger made the kids only speak to us in Passamaquoddy.' (EM)

b. *Roger **n-kisehta-ku-ne-n** [wasis-` tehpu
Roger **1-make.TA+O-INV-N-1PL** kid-3'PL only

n-uskicinu-westuwam-ku-ne-n].
1-Indian-speak.to.TA-INV-N-1PL
Intended: 'Roger made the kids only speak to us in Passamaquoddy.' (EM)[13]

Interestingly, this is even true of inanimate actor scenarios (though only for some speakers; see Grishin 2023b:§2.4.3 for discussion):

(26) 0→SAP: no LDA with SAP object
a. *Sapet **n-pawatoma-ku-n** [kiwhosuwasq n-kikuh-uku-n].
Elizabeth **1-want.TA+O-INV-N** flagroot 1-heal.TA-INV-N
Intended: 'Elizabeth wants flagroot to heal me.' (EM, RP)
b. Sapet '-pawatom-on [kiwhosuwasq n-kikuh-uku-n].
Elizabeth 3-want.TI-N flagroot 1-heal.TA-INV-N
'Elizabeth wants flagroot to heal me.' (EM, RP)

Note that subordinative LDA doesn't target inanimates (as inanimates cannot be primary objects of ditransitives), so we can't get LDA with inanimate *kiwhosuwasq* 'flagroot'. Since we cannot get LDA with the SAP object either, the only possibility for expressing this meaning is to use a non-agreeing TI form *'pawatomon* (26b).

Third Person Inverse

So far, we've only seen subordinative LDA with embedded (animate) actors—so one might think there's a semantically motivated constraint here: Subordinative LDA is only possible with agent/causer roles. The third person inverse falsifies this hypothesis: With an embedded third person inverse, subordinative LDA *can* target the embedded object.

There are two scenarios to discuss: 3'→3 and 0→3. Let's tackle animate actors first. Just like the case of 3→3', we cannot directly tell which argument is the LDA target if the matrix verb is direct.[14] However, we can tell from the behavior of obviation that it's possible to get LDA with the object:

(27) 3'→3: LDA with 3 object (diagnosed via obviation)

a. Wasis-ok Ø-wolikolul-ku-wa-l w-ikuwoss-uwa-l.
kid-3PL 3-praise.TA-INV-3PL-3'SG 3-mother-3PL-3'SG
'The children (PROX) were praised by their mother (OBV). (GP, MA, RP)

b. Piyel **'-pawatomuw-a-n** [wasis-` Ø-wolikolul-ku-ni-ya
Peter **3-want.TA+O-3OBJ-N** kid-3'PL 3-praise.TA-INV-N-3PL

w-ikuwoss-uwa-l].
3-mother-3PL-3'SG
'Peter (PROX) wants the children (OBV) to be praised by their mother (OBV).' (GP, MA, RP)

(28) 3'→3: LDA with 3 object (diagnosed via obviation)

a. Wasis-ok Ø-nomiy-uku-wa-l w-ikuwoss-uwa-l.
kid-3PL 3-see.TA-INV-3PL-3'SG 3-mother-3PL-3'SG
'The children (PROX) were seen by their mother (OBV). (GP, MA, RP)

b. Roger **'-kisehtuw-a-n** [wasis-` Ø-nomiy-uku-ni-ya
Roger **3-make.TA+O-3OBJ-N** kid-3'PL 3-praise.TA-INV-N-3PL

w-ikuwoss-uwa-l].
3-mother-3PL-3'SG
'Roger (PROX) made the children (OBV) to be seen by their mother (OBV).' (GP, MA, RP)

Turning to inanimate actors, (0→3), we see that, in contrast to 0→SAP forms where subordinative LDA was simply impossible (for some speakers), subordinative LDA now *can* target the embedded object.

(29) 0→3: LDA with 3 object

a. Sapet **'-pawatomuw-a-n** [Piyel-ol 't-eksqihka-ku-n
Elizabeth **3-want.TA+O-3OBJ-N** Peter-3'SG 3-make.sneeze.TA-INV-N

tehpiseweya-l].
pepper-0PL
'Elizabeth wants pepper to make Peter sneeze.' (GP, MA, RP)

b. Sapet '-pawatomuw-a-n [kiwhosuwasq '-kikuh-uku-n
Elizabeth **3-want.TA+O-3OBJ-N** flagroot 3-heal.TA-INV-N

Lacaw-ol].
Roger-3'SG
'Elizabeth wants flagroot to heal Roger.' (EM, RP)

(30) 0→3: LDA with 3 object
N-kisehtuw-a-n [wasis '-kiptehka-ku-n n-utapakon].
1-make.TA+O-3OBJ-N kid 3-knock.over.TA-INV-N 1-sled
'I made my sled knock over the child.' (EM)

Thus, the one exception to the actor-only generalization with subordinative LDA is the third person inverse. Therefore, the third person inverse is special in a way that the SAP inverse is not.

Conclusion: Consequences for the Syntax of the Inverse

Crosslinguistically, LDA/raising to object/exceptional case marking is often restricted to the most syntactically prominent (or "highest") argument in the embedded clause (e.g., Bhatt and Keine 2017). The proposal for Passamaquoddy-Wolastoqey subordinative LDA is simple: It is similarly restricted to the highest argument in the embedded clause (unlike standard LDA, which is free).

Under this view, we can conclude the following: In the direct (SAP→3, 3→3'/0), the actor is the most syntactically prominent argument, a conclusion that all views of the syntax of the direct-inverse contrast agree on. Thus, we only get subordinative LDA with the actor in direct scenarios. Additionally, we also confirm that SAP→SAP scenarios are never inverse (Hockett 1992; Macaulay 2009), as the actor is always the most prominent argument.

However, different answers to the inverse question make different predictions about how subordinative LDA should behave in inverse scenarios:

(31) **The Inverse Question:**
Does morphological inverse marking correlate with some syntactic process of inversion—the primary object gaining syntactic prominence over the actor?

(32) a. **Yes** (e.g., Rhodes 1994; Bruening 2009): Since inverse marking always involves syntactic inversion, we should get subordinative LDA with the embedded object in both SAP and third person inverses.

b. **No** (e.g., Dahlstrom 1991): Since inverse marking doesn't involve syntactic inversion, we should get subordinative LDA with the embedded actor in both SAP and third person inverses.

c. **3 only** (Oxford 2023): Since only the third person inverse involves syntactic inversion, we should get subordinative LDA with the embedded actor in the SAP inverse, but the embedded object in the third person inverse.

And, as we've just seen, the data exactly verify 3 Only, and falsify Yes and No.

The contrast between SAP and third person inverse with inanimate actors is especially informative:

(33) a. *Sapet **n-pawatoma-ku-n** [kiwhosuwasq n-kikuh-uku-n].
Elizabeth **1-want.TA+O-INV-N** flagroot 1-heal.TA-INV-N
Intended: 'Elizabeth wants flagroot to heal me.' (EM, RP)

b. Sapet **'-pawatomuw-a-n** [kiwhosuwasq '-kikuh-uku-n
Elizabeth **3-want.TA+O-3OBJ-N** flagroot 3-heal.TA-INV-N

Lacaw-ol].
Roger-3'SG
'Elizabeth wants flagroot to heal Roger.' (EM, RP)

As we cannot get subordinative LDA with grammatical inanimates due to independent restrictions on agreement with recipients in Algonquian, in neither case would we be able to get agreement with the inanimate actor *kiwhosuwasq* 'flagroot'. Thus, if the TA+O form of 'want' has any chance of surviving, it must agree with the embedded object. In the SAP inverse, the third person actor is the most syntactically prominent argument (as there is no syntactic inversion), so the only option for subordinative LDA is the embedded actor. Since the embedded actor in (33a) is grammatically inanimate, that means it's completely impossible to get LDA. However, in the third person inverse, the object becomes the most syntactically prominent argument (since there *is* syntactic inversion), so we *can* get subordinative LDA with the embedded object in (33b). Thus, just as Oxford

(2023) concludes, the SAP inverse is purely morphological, whereas the third person inverse is a voice construction.

NOTES

1. Acknowledgments: *Nkoti-wolasuweltomuwak Margaret Apt, Edwina Mitchell, Grace Paul, naka Roger Paul eli kisokehkimihtit 'tolatuwewakonuwa.* Thank you also to David Pesetsky, Norvin Richards, Will Oxford, the audience at the 54th Algonquian Conference, two anonymous reviewers, and the editors of the *Papers of the Algonquian Conference* for their helpful comments.
2. I use the standard Passamaquoddy orthography, which differs from the IPA in the following ways: /ə/ <o>, /tʃ/ <c>, /kʷ/ <q>, /j/ <y>. Word-initial <'> indicates devoicing of initial obstruents, the historical remnants of word-initial consonants that synchronically are only identifiable via their impact on the voicing of following obstruents. I depart from the standard orthography in using a grave accent ` to indicate a final low pitch accent that marks obviative plural. Throughout, I **bold** LDA verbs and <u>underline</u> the LDA targets. I default to 'she, her' as translations for third person singular, though it should be noted that Algonquian languages do not grammatically distinguish gender. Abbreviations: 1 = first person, 2 = second person, 3 = (proximate) third person, 3' = obviative, 0 = inanimate, AI = animate intransitive, AI+O = animate intransitive with secondary object, C = complementizer, CJ = conjunct, DUB = dubitative preterite, EMPH = emphatic, IC = initial change, II = inanimate intransitive, INAN = inanimate, INV = inverse, LOC = locative, N = N formative, NEG = negative, OBJ = object, OBV = obviative, PFV = perfective, PL = plural, PROX = proximate, SAP = speech act participant (1st or 2nd person), SG = singular, TA = transitive animate, TA+O = transitive animate with secondary object (ditransitive), TI = transitive inanimate, X = unspecified actor, X:Y = X acting on Y.
3. A fourth view is that Algonquian languages vary in terms of how morphological inversion correlates with syntactic inversion (Dahlstrom n.d.; Fry and Hamilton 2016). I don't argue against this view here. If correct, the inverse question applies separately to each language, and this paper is about the right answer in Passamaquoddy-Wolastoqey specifically.
4. I thank an anonymous reviewer for pressing me to clarify my assumptions on these points.
5. Embedded arguments can displace across clause boundaries even in the absence of LDA:

(i) a. Nita nit tuceyi-k, psi=te wen n-pawatom-on ['-peci=
then that.0SG IC.go.by.II-0CJ all=EMPH who 1-want.TI-N 3-come=

iyi-n, '-peciya-n, Ø-naci= kuhpessewi-n, naka '-kuminiyewi-n].
be.at.AI-N 3-come.AI-N 3-go= confess.AI-N and 3-take.communion.AI-N

'When the time has come, I want **everyone** to come and do something—to come for confession, and to take communion.' Charles Laporte, "Norridgewock Massacre" (Teeter and LeSourd 2007:116)

b. N-kotuw-ahq sepawonuk, ma=te **wen** n-pawatom-uw-on
1-want-cook.AI tomorrow NEG=EMPH **who** 1-want.TI-NEG-N

[n-conehl-oku-n].
1-stop.TA-INV-N
'I want to cook tomorrow, I don't want **anyone** to stop me.' (EM)

In (i.a), *psi-te wen* 'everyone' is understood as the subject of the subordinative clause, yet it appears in the matrix clause without triggering any agreement on TI *npawatomon* 'I want'. In (ii.a), *wen* 'who, someone, anyone' is understood as the subject of *nconehlokun* 'stop me', but it appears in the matrix clause, again without triggering any agreement on TI *npawatomuwon* 'I don't want'. Thus, cross-clausal displacement out of subordinative clauses is an independent process not crucially linked to LDA.

6. Though see Grishin (2023a) for arguments for the raising to object derivation of subordinative LDA.
7. Menominee has made the same morphological innovation (Goddard 1974, 1983), but the subordinative look-alike in Menominee is used as a negative mode.
8. As an anonymous reviewer notes, *'kisehtun* 'do, make' generally takes nominal objects that denote events:

(i) ('-)Kisehtu-ne-ss elokim-ol-ok?
2-make.TI-N-DUB IC.order.TA-2OBJ-XCJ
'Did you do what you were told?' (https://pmportal.org/dictionary/olokimal)

Here, the object of *kisehtuness* is *elokimolok* 'what you were told', a headless relative. Occasionally, nominal objects of *'kisehtun* are interpreted as created objects, though usually the TI final *-iht* rather than *-eht* is used for these purposes (*'kisihtun* 'make s.t.').

9. At least in elicitation settings, speakers are relatively happy to leave off obviative markers on nouns in these kinds of cases (similar observations are made by Cook and Mühlbauer

2006 about Plains Cree). However, speakers seem to generally consistently reject incorrect *agreement* for obviation—thus, in (16), what is really absolutely necessary is the obviative suffix *-li* on *'tolintulin* 'he sings (OBV)', indicative that *Asawis(ol)* must really be underlyingly obviative, even if it might lack an obviative suffix.

10. This only applies if the matrix verb (*'pawatomon* 'want' or *'kisehtuwan* 'make') is 3→3' direct. If the matrix verb is third person inverse (3'→3, 0→3) we can clearly identify the number features of the LDA target. I have only recently begun investigating how matrix third person inverse interacts with LDA. With this, it is possible to clearly show that we can agree with the embedded actor in embedded 3→3':

    (i) Mus '-kisehta-ku-n sqot ['-sesolahki= maton-a-n pomawsuwinu-`].
    moose 3-make.TA+O-INV-N fire 3-sudden= attack.TA-3OBJ-N person-3'PL
    'The fire made the moose suddenly attack the people.' (MA)

    Here, the embedded actor *mus* is singular, and the embedded object *pomawsuwinù* 'people' is plural. The matrix verb *'kisehtakun* is inflected for a 0SG actor and 3SG object, indicating LDA with *mus*. I haven't yet gathered the relevant data to show whether it is (im)possible to get LDA with the embedded object in these configurations—I predict it should be impossible.
11. I don't yet have examples of 3→3' direct under *'kisehtuwan* 'make'. I predict it to behave the same as *'pawatomuwan* 'want'.
12. Technically, I haven't shown it's *impossible* to get LDA with the embedded object here. We can't use the obviation diagnostic because the embedded object is already obviative (or it's inanimate, which doesn't contrast obviation in Passamaquody-Wolastoqey). It's also difficult to conclude anything from consultants assenting to having the embedded agent be proximate rather than obviative in elicitation settings due to the methodological issues discussed in endnote 9.
13. Though I suspect it won't make a difference to this judgment, this sentence should be double-checked with proximate plural *wasisok*, given the generalization about obviation and LDA established above.
14. As discussed in footnote 10, we would be able to tell apart LDA with singular versus plural third persons if the matrix verb is third person inverse. So far, initial work with my consultants on these configurations hasn't resulted in reliable judgments, as the combination of two third person inverses appears difficult to parse.

REFERENCES

Bhatt, Rajesh, and Stefan Keine. 2017. Long-Distance Agreement. *The Wiley Blackwell Companion to Syntax*, vol. 4, ed. by Martin Everaert and Henk C. van Riemsdijk, pp. 2291–2321. Hoboken, NJ: Blackwell-Wiley.

Bliss, Heather. 2013. The Blackfoot Configurationality Conspiracy: Parallels and Differences in Clausal and Nominal Structures. PhD thesis, University of British Columbia.

Branigan, Phil, and Marguerite MacKenzie. 2002. Altruism, A'-Movement, and Object Agreement in Innu-aimûn. *Linguistic Inquiry* 33(3):385–407.

Brittain, Julie. 2001. *The Morphosyntax of the Algonquian Conjunct Verb*. New York: Garland Publishing.

Bruening, Benjamin. 2001. Syntax at the Edge: Cross-Clausal Phenomena and the Syntax of Passamaquody. PhD thesis, Massachusetts Institute of Technology.

Bruening, Benjamin. 2009. Algonquian Languages have A-Movement and A-Agreement. *Linguistic Inquiry* 40(3):427–445.

Cook, Clare. 2014. *The Clause-Typing System of Plains Cree: Indexicality, Anaphoricity, and Contrast*. Oxford: Oxford University Press.

Cook, Clare, and Jeff Mühlbauer. 2006. The Behavior of Obviation in Elicitation. *Actes du 37e Congrès des Algonquinistes*, ed. by H. C. Wolfart, pp. 103–129. Winnipeg: University of Manitoba.

Dahlstrom, Amy. 1991. *Plains Cree Morphosyntax*. New York: Garland Publishing.

Dahlstrom, Amy. 2023. Ditransitive Licensing of Long Distance Agreement in Meskwaki. *Papers of the 52nd Algonquian Conference*, ed. by Monica Macaulay and Margaret Noodin, pp. 19–36. East Lansing: Michigan State University Press.

Dahlstrom, Amy. n.d. Meskwaki (Fox) Syntax. Unpublished manuscript, University of Chicago, Chicago, IL. https://lucian.uchicago.edu/blogs/adahlstrom/publications-2/selected-manuscripts/meskwaki-syntax-book.

Deal, Amy Rose. 2017. Covert Hyperraising to Object. *Proceedings of NELS 47*, ed. by Andrew Lamont and Katerina Tetzloff, pp. 257–270. Amherst, MA: GLSA.

Fry, Brandon J., and Michael David Hamilton. 2016. Long-Distance Agreement in Algonquian: Accounting for Syntactic Variation. *Proceedings of CLS 50*, ed. by Ross Burkholder, Carlos Cisneros, Emily R. Coppess, Julian Grove, Emily A. Hanink, Hilary McMahan, Cherry Meyer, Natalia Pavlou, Özge Sarıgül, Adam Roth Singerman, and Anqi Zhang, pp. 159–174. Chicago: Chicago Linguistic Society.

Goddard, Ives. 1974. Remarks on the Algonquian Independent Indicative. *International Journal of American Linguistics* 40(4):317–327.

Goddard, Ives. 1979. *Delaware Verbal Morphology: A Descriptive and Comparative Study*. New

York: Garland Publishing.

Goddard, Ives. 1983. The Eastern Algonquian Subordinative Mode and the Importance of Morphology. *International Journal of American Linguistics* 49(4):351–387.

Goddard, Ives. 2007. Reconstruction and History of the Independent Indicative. *Papers of the 38th Algonquian Conference*, ed. by H. C. Wolfart, pp. 207–271. Winnipeg: University of Manitoba.

Goddard, Ives. 2020. The Paradox of Partial Similarity: Unami Secondary-Object Marking and Other Clones of the N- Endings. *Papers of the 49th Algonquian Conference*, ed. by Monica Macaulay and Margaret Noodin, pp. 99–113. East Lansing: Michigan State University Press.

Goddard, Ives. 2021. *A Grammar of Southern Unami Delaware (Lenape)*. Petosky, MI: Mundart Press.

Grishin, Peter. 2023a. How to Covertly Move: Evidence from Passamaquoddy-Wolastoqey. *Proceedings of NELS 53*, vol. 2, ed. by Suet-Ying Lam and Satoru Ozaki, pp. 1–10. Amherst, MA: GLSA.

Grishin, Peter. 2023b. Lessons from CP in Passamaquoddy and Beyond. PhD thesis, Massachusetts Institute of Technology.

Hamilton, Michael David. 2018. On Ordering and Reordering Arguments in Algonquian. *Papers of the 47th Algonquian Conference*, ed. by Monica Macaulay and Margaret Noodin, pp. 107–128. East Lansing: Michigan State University Press.

Hockett, Charles F. 1992. Direction in the Algonquian Verb: A Correction. *Anthropological Linguistics* 34(1):311–315.

LeSourd, Philip S. 2019. Raising and Long-Distance Agreement in Passamaquoddy: A Unified Analysis. *Journal of Linguistics* 55(2):357–405.

Lochbihler, Bethany. 2012. Aspects of Argument Licensing. PhD thesis, McGill University.

Lochbihler, Bethany, and Éric Mathieu. 2016. Clause Typing and Feature Inheritance of Discourse Features. *Syntax* 19(4):354–391.

Macaulay, Monica. 2009. On Prominence Hierarchies: Evidence from Algonquian. *Linguistic Typology* 13(3):357–389.

Oxford, Will. 2018. What's the Inverse of an Inverse? Transitive Constructions in Algonquian and Austronesian. *Actes du congrès annuel de l'Association Canadienne de linguistique 2018*, ed. by Emily Dmyterko. Canadian Linguistics Society.

Oxford, Will. 2022. Probe Specification and Agreement Variation: Evidence from the Algonquian Inverse. *Linguistic Inquiry* (advance publication). doi:10.1162/ling_a_00478.

Oxford, Will. 2023. A Tale of Two Inverses. *Syntax* 26(3):311–354.

Quinn, Conor. 2004. Head Parametrization at the Multiclausal Level: Clause-Chaining as Episodic Macroevents in Altaic-Area Languages. Paper read at WAFL 2, Boğaziçi University.

Quinn, Conor. 2007. The Eastern Algonquian Subordinative as Event-Argument Dependency. Paper read at the 39th Algonquian Conference, York University.

Rhodes, Richard A. 1976. The Morphosyntax of the Central Ojibwa Verb. PhD thesis, University of Michigan.

Rhodes, Richard A. 1994. Agency, Inversion, and Thematic Alignment in Ojibwe. *Proceedings of the 20th Annual Meeting of the Berkeley Linguistics Society*, ed. by Susanne Gahl, Andy Dolbey, and Christopher Johnson, pp. 431–446. Berkeley, CA: Berkeley Linguistics Society.

Richards, Norvin. 2004. The Syntax of the Conjunct and Independent Orders in Wampanoag. *International Journal of American Linguistics* 70(4):327–368.

Teeter, Karl V., and Philip S. LeSourd. 2007. *Tales from Maliseet Country: The Maliseet Texts of Karl V. Teeter*. Lincoln: University of Nebraska Press.

Patterns of Portmanteau Robustness across Algonquian

Peter Grishin and Will Oxford

This paper examines the robustness of portmanteau agreement morphology in the conjunct inflection of Algonquian verbs.[1] To see what we mean by ROBUSTNESS, compare the Southwestern Ojibwe forms in (1) and the Northern Algonquin forms in (2). The two languages show the same pattern in the animate intransitive (AI) forms in (a), where a simple central suffix indexes the first-person singular subject (*-a:n* '1s'), and in the transitive animate (TA) indicative forms in (b), where a portmanteau central suffix indexes both the first-person singular actor and the third-person object (*-ak/-ik* '1s:3'). The languages differ, however, in the TA modal forms in (c), which are the dubitative counterparts of the indicative forms in (b): In Southwestern Ojibwe, the 1s→3 portmanteau *-ak* is ROBUST, being preserved in the dubitative, but in Northern Algonquin, the 1s→3 portmanteau *-ik* is FRAGILE, failing to appear in the dubitative and being replaced by the same simple 1s suffix *-a:n* that appears in the AI form. This is the phenomenon of interest in this paper: the non-use of a portmanteau suffix in a marked mode even though that portmanteau exists in the language. When does this happen, and why?[2]

(1) Southwestern Ojibwe conjunct forms (Nichols 1980:303, 315)

a. *waniššina:n*	b. *wa:pamak*	c. *waya:pama:wake:n*
waniššin -a:n	wa:pam -Ø -ak	IC.wa:pam -a: -w -**ak** -e:n
lost.AI -1s	see.TA -3OBJ -1s:3	IC.see.TA -3OBJ -W -**1s:3** -DUB
'I am lost.'	'I see **him/her.**'	'I might see **him/her.**'

(2) Northern Algonquin conjunct forms (Brouillard and Dumont-Anichinapeo 1987:73, 98)

a. *takoššina:n*	b. *sa:ki:hik*	c. *sa:ki:ha:wa:ne:n*
takoššin -a:n	sa:ki:h -Ø -ik	sa:ki:h -a: -w -a:n -e:n
arrive.AI -1s	love.TA -3OBJ -1s:3	love.TA -3OBJ -W -1s -DUB
'I arrive.'	'I love **him/her.**'	'I might love him/her.'

The paper is organized as follows. We begin by defining the object of study—portmanteau central suffixes in the conjunct order—distinguishing several reasons why such suffixes may disappear. We then survey the robustness of portmanteau agreement across the family. Based on this survey, we establish three generalizations: (i) Portmanteaux expressing the action of a third person upon a speech-act participant (SAP, i.e., a first or second person), which we will refer to as "3→SAP portmanteaux," are always robust; (ii) no language's delayed imperative/prohibitive modes ("k-modes") are more robust than its dubitative/negative conjunct modes ("w-modes"); and (iii) if a third-person plural central suffix co-occurs with a portmanteau in the conjunct indicative, then that portmanteau is robust in the w-modes. We suggest tentative and incomplete functional explanations for generalizations (i) and (ii), but ultimately we suspect that the right analysis of the three generalizations has to rely on more abstract, formal properties of portmanteau formation. The paper is thus a first step in understanding the mechanisms that underlie portmanteau formation across Algonquian, and lays out the empirical challenge for future research.

Portmanteau Central Suffixes in the Conjunct Order

This section introduces the central suffix slot in the inflection of conjunct verbs, shows how portmanteau central suffixes can be identified, and lists the portmanteau central suffixes that exist in Proto-Algonquian (PA) and the daughter languages.

Conjunct Central Suffixes

The phenomenon of interest in this paper occurs in the CENTRAL SUFFIX slot (Goddard 1969:103; Nichols 1980:189) in the inflection of the conjunct order and the morphologically related dubitative/interrogative, prohibitive, and delayed imperative orders. The position of this suffix is indicated in the template in (3).

(3) Basic inflectional template for conjunct, interrogative, and prohibitive orders

Stem – Theme Sign – Negative/Irrealis – **Central Suffix** – Mode

As illustrated by the Ojibwe forms in (4) (Nichols 1980:316, 329), the central suffix slot hosts agreement markers that express the person and number of either the actor, as in (4a), the primary object, as in (4b), or both arguments simultaneously, as in (4c).

(4) Central agreement indexing actor, primary object, and both (Nichols 1980)

a. *wa:pame:k*

wa:pam -Ø -**e:k**

see.TA -3OBJ -**2p**

'**You.PL** see him/her.'

b. *wa:pamine:k*

wa:pam -in -**e:k**

see.TA -2OBJ -**2p**

'S/he sees **you.PL**'

c. *wa:paminakok*

wa:pam -in -**akokw**

see.TA -2OBJ -**1s:2p**

'**I** see **you.PL**'

In the conjunct indicative forms in (4), the central suffix immediately follows the theme sign, but there are also paradigms in which the theme sign + central suffix sequence is interrupted by a negative/irrealis marker (underlined in (5)):

(5) Ojibwe negative, dubitative, and delayed imperative forms (Nichols 1980:315, 318, 334)

a. *wa:pama:ssiwat*

wa:pam -a: -<u>ssiw</u> -**at**

see.TA -3OBJ -<u>NEG</u> -**2s:3**

'**You** don't see **him/her**.'

b. *waya:pama:wate:n*

IC.wa:pam -a: -<u>w</u> -**at** -e:n

IC.see.TA-3OBJ -<u>W</u> -**2s:3** -DUB

'**You** might see **him/her**.'

c. *kanawa:pama:kkan*

kanawa:pam -a: -<u>kk</u> -**an**

look.at.TA -3OBJ -<u>DEL</u> -**2s**

'(**You**) look at him/her later!'

The negative/irrealis markers that intervene between the theme sign and the central suffix continue PA suffixes with *-*w*-, as in Ojibwe negative -*ssiw* (5a) and dubitative

-w (5b), or PA suffixes with*-(*h*)*k*-, like Ojibwe delayed imperative *-kk* (5c) (Goddard 2006). The functions of these markers vary across the languages. In order to have neutral cover terms, we will refer to paradigms reflecting *-*w*- as "w-modes" and paradigms reflecting *-(*h*)*k*- as "k-modes," regardless of their function.

What Is (and Is Not) Portmanteau Agreement

We make a distinction between SIMPLE CENTRAL SUFFIXES, which express the person, and sometimes also the number, of one argument (e.g., Ojibwe *-a:n* '1s', *-t* '3'), and PORTMANTEAU CENTRAL SUFFIXES, which express the person, and sometimes also the number, of two arguments (e.g., Ojibwe *-ak* '1s:3'). We diagnose a central suffix as indexing two arguments X and Y if the suffix occurs in a form in which X acts on Y, and it has a distinct shape from the simple suffixes for X and Y that appear in AI, TI, and some TA forms. As an illustration of this diagnostic, consider the Unami and Passamaquoddy 2s→3 prohibitive forms in (6) (Goddard 2021:110; Francis and Leavitt 2008:681).

(6) Unami vs. Passamaquoddy 2s→3 TA prohibitive

a. *kpahwiḗ:k:ač*	b. *kpahahkəč*
kpahw -əye: -k -ač	kpah -a -hk -əč
close.TA -3OBJ -K -??	close.TA -3OBJ -K -??
'Don't shut the door on him.' (Unami)	'Don't lock him up.' (Passamaquoddy)

Both forms have a central suffix *-ač/-əč* that occurs only in the prohibitive. From these forms alone, it is unclear whether this is a portmanteau ('2s:3') or a simple suffix ('2s'). To clarify its status, we compare the TA 2s→3 forms in (6) with the corresponding AI 2s forms in (7) (Goddard 2021:110; Francis and Leavitt 2008:650). If the TA suffix differs from the AI 2s suffix, then the TA suffix is a 2s:3 portmanteau; if it is the same as the AI 2s suffix, then it is a simple suffix indexing only the 2s subject.

(7) Unami vs. Passamaquoddy 2s AI prohibitive

a. *šenki:x:ínkhan*	b. *ləssinuhkəč*
šenki:x:in -kh -an	ləssin -uhk -əč
lie.down.AI -K -2s	lie.down.AI -K -2s
'Don't lie down.' (Unami)	'Don't lie down.' (Passamaquoddy)

Strikingly, the languages diverge here. The Unami AI 2s form has a suffix *-an*, which differs from the suffix *-ač* in the TA 2s→3 form. Since *-ač* appears only in the 2s→3 form, it qualifies as a portmanteau. The Passamaquoddy suffix *-əč*, on the other hand, appears in both the TA 2s→3 form and the AI 2s form and must therefore be a simple 2s suffix rather than a 2s→3 portmanteau.

We note here that for the purposes of this paper, we are staying neutral regarding the correct formal analysis of portmanteau suffixes. A suffix like Ojibwe *-ak* '1s:3' could in principle be analyzed either as a true portmanteau that expresses both '1s' and '3' (cf. Goddard 2004:104 for Meskwaki) or as a contextual allomorph of the simple 1s suffix *-a:n*, expressing only '1s' but conditioned by the presence of a third-person object (Nichols 1980:190; cf. Goddard 1969:125 for Delaware, Costa 2003:300 for Miami-Illinois). We suspect that both of these analyses are correct in different cases, but we believe that for purely descriptive purposes, the term "portmanteau" remains appropriate across the board for any suffix whose occurrence is conditioned by the features of two arguments, no matter what the correct formal analysis may ultimately be.

The Set of Portmanteau Central Suffixes

The conjunct order in PA has the set of simple central suffixes in (8) and the set of portmanteau central suffixes in (9) (reconstructions follow Bloomfield 1946:102; Goddard 1969:133).

(8) Simple central suffixes in the PA conjunct order
**-a:n* '1s', **-an* '2s', **-a:nk* '1p', **-ankw* '21', **-e:kw* '2p', **-t* ~ *-k* '3', **-k* '0'

(9) Portmanteau central suffixes in the PA conjunct order
a. TA SAP/X→3 portmanteaux: **-ak* '1s:3', **-at* '2s:3', **-akent* '1p:3', **-ent* 'X:3'[3]
b. TA 3→SAP.PL portmanteaux: **-ament* '3:1p', **-a:kw* '3:2p'[4]
c. TA SAP→SAP portmanteau: **-akokw* '1s:2p'

As indicated in (9), PA has portmanteau central suffixes for certain TA argument combinations in which an SAP or an unspecified person (X) acts upon a third person ("TA SAP/X→3", (9a)), certain TA argument combinations in which a third person acts upon a plural SAP ("TA 3→SAP.PL", (9b)), and one TA argument combination in which an SAP acts upon another SAP ("TA SAP→SAP", (9c)). These are the only argument combinations for which portmanteau suffixes exist. All other TA argument combinations are realized with a simple central suffix indexing only one of the two arguments, and all TI and AI+O forms have a simple central suffix indexing only the actor.

Turning from PA to the daughter languages, Table 1 shows the set of portmanteau central suffixes in PA and their reflexes in each language in our survey. Our survey includes only languages with documented w-mode or k-mode paradigms: Swampy and Moose Cree (Ellis 1971), Atikamekw (Béland 1978), Northern East Cree (Junker and MacKenzie 2010–2014), Southern East Cree (Junker and MacKenzie 2011–2014), Pessamit and Mamit Innu (transcribed by authors based on audio recordings in Baraby and Junker 2011–2020), Sheshatshiu Innu (Clarke 1982), Southwestern Ojibwe (Nichols 1980), Nishnaabemwin (Valentine 2001), Nipissing (Jones 1977),

TABLE 1. Portmanteaux in PA and reflexes in surveyed daughter languages

	1S:2P	1S:3	2S:3	1P:3	X:3	3:1P	3:2P
PA	*-akokw	*-ak	*-at	*-akent	*-ent	*-ament	*-a:kw
Sw./M. Cree	-akok	-ak	-at	-akiht	-iht	-amiht	-a:kw
Atikamekw	-akok	-ak	-at	-akitt	-itt	-amitt	-a:kw
N. East Cree	-ikut	-ik	-it	-ičiht	×	-imiht	×
S. East Cree	-akut	-ak	-at	-ačiht	×	-amiht	-a:kw
Pessamit Innu	-əkut	-ək	-a:t	-əčət	×	-(ə)mət	-a:kw
Mamit Innu	-ikut	-ak	-a:t	-ati:ht	×	-(i)mi:ht	-a:hkw
Shesh. Innu	-akut	-a:k	-at	-ači:t	×	-ami:t	-a:kw
SW Ojibwe	-akokw	-ak	-at	-ankit	-int	(-ankit)	×
Nishnaabemwin	-akokw	-ak	-at	-ankit	-int	(-ankit)	×
Nipissing	-akokw	-ak	-at	-ankit	-int	-amint	-a:kw
Golden Lk. Alg.	-akokw	-akw	-at	-ankit	-int	-amint	-a:k
Northern Alg.	-ikok	-ik	-it	-ikit	×	-emit	×
Meskwaki	-ako:w	-ak	-at	-aket	-et	-amet	-a:kw
Kickapoo	-ako	-ak	-at	-aket	-et	-amet	-a:kw
Miami-Illinois	-akok	-ak	-at	-akint	-ent	-amint	-a:kw
Delaware	×	-ak	-at	×	-ənt	×	×
Massachusett	×	-ak	-at	-akət	-ət	×	×
Penobscot	×	-ok	-at	-okət	-ot	(-akət)	×
Passamaquoddy	×	-uk	-ət	-ukət	-ut	-əmət	-akw
Mi'kmaq	×	-ək	-ət	-əkət	-ut	-amət	×
Cheyenne	×	-o	-ose	×	×	×	×

Golden Lake Algonquin (Aubin 1984, 1989), Northern Algonquin (Brouillard and Dumont-Anichinapeo 1987), Meskwaki (Goddard 1994, 1995), Kickapoo (Voorhis 1974), Miami-Illinois (Costa 2003), Munsee and Unami Delaware (Goddard 1969, 2021), Massachusett (Goddard and Bragdon 1988), Penobscot (Voorhis 1979; Quinn 2015), Passamaquoddy (Francis and Leavitt 2008), Mi'kmaq (Francis and Hewson 2016), and Cheyenne (Goddard 2000; Leman 2011). Several of the languages have a smaller set of portmanteaux than PA due to changes discussed in the next section. Argument combinations for which a particular language lacks a portmanteau are indicated by "×" in the table, and parentheses mark a portmanteau that does not directly reflect the corresponding PA portmanteau.

Portmanteaux involving inclusive first-person plural ("21") are conspicuously absent in PA and most daughter languages. A functional explanation for this gap is suggested by Costa's (2003:305) observation that since the arguments of an Algonquian transitive verb are required to be fully disjoint in reference (Valentine 2001:273), the other argument of a verb with an inclusive 21 argument could only possibly be a third person. A portmanteau for '21:3' or '3:21' would thus convey no more information beyond what is already conveyed by the presence of a simple 21 suffix in a transitive form. The same does not hold for exclusive first-person plural (1p), since the other argument of a verb with an exclusive 1p argument could be either a second or third person, and thus a 1p:3 portmanteau does convey more information than a simple 1p suffix. This rationale may explain why 21 portmanteaux are generally absent, but it does not predict that they should be impossible, and indeed, there is at least one case of an innovated 21 portmanteau in the family: Golden Lake Algonquin extended the use of *-ankit* '1p:3' (< PA **akent* '1p:3') to 21→3 scenarios, and *-amint* '3:1p' (< PA **-ament* '3:1p') to 3→21 scenarios (Aubin 1989). This extension is not simply the loss of the inclusive–exclusive contrast, as the two functions of *-ankit* are distinguished by their robustness in the w-mode: 1p→3 *-ankit* is robust but 21→3 *-ankit* is blocked.

Loss of Portmanteau Central Suffixes

Portmanteau central suffixes can disappear for at least three reasons, the third of which is the primary focus of this paper.

1. Eliminate the portmanteau suffix from the language. In the same way that a word can drop out of the lexicon, a portmanteau suffix can drop out of the grammar entirely. For example, the portmanteau **-akent* '1p:3' has been replaced by the reflex of simple **-a:nk* '1p' in Delaware (Goddard 1969:131) and for some speakers of Passamaquoddy (Francis and Leavitt 2008:668). Similarly, the portmanteau **-a:kw* '3:2p' has been replaced by the reflex of simple **-e:kw* '2p' in Penobscot (Quinn 2015) and most Ojibwe varieties (Costa 2003:385, note 61), and the portmanteau **-akokw* '1s:2p' has been replaced by the reflex of simple **-e:kw* '2p' in Cheyenne, Arapaho, and the Eastern languages. Such changes are easy to model: A particular portmanteau suffix is lost from a language's set of central suffixes and the most featurally similar simple suffix takes up the slack.

2. Make the relevant forms inverse (or direct). Conjunct SAP→3 and 3→SAP forms were not originally either direct or inverse, instead showing an agreement pattern that can be called NEUTRAL (Oxford 2023). Neutral forms lack the characteristic inverse theme sign **-ekw* and often have a portmanteau central suffix, as in the Moose Cree forms in (10).

(10) Moose Cree 1p↔3 conjunct (Ellis 1971): neutral agreement

a. *wa:pamakiht*			b. *wa:pamiyamiht*		
wa:pam	-Ø	-akiht	wa:pam	-i	-yamiht
see.TA	-3OBJ	-1p:3	see.TA	-1OBJ	-3:1p
'We see him/her.'			'S/he sees us.'		

The corresponding independent forms, however, have always been direct and inverse, and some languages have analogically rebuilt (some of) the conjunct forms on the direct/inverse pattern, as in the Plains Cree forms in (11) (see discussion in Dahlstrom 1989 and Collette 2019).

(11) Plains Cree 1p↔3 conjunct (Dahlstrom 1989): direct/inverse agreement

a. *wa:pama:ya:hk*			b. *wa:pamikoya:hk*		
wa:pam	-a:	-ya:hk	wa:pam	-iko	-ya:hk
see.TA	-3OBJ	-1p	see.TA	-INV	-1p
'We see him/her.' (direct)			'S/he sees us.' (inverse)		

In the direct/inverse pattern, the central suffix indexes the argument that ranks highest on the person hierarchy. Direct forms always have a simple central suffix indexing only the actor, as in (11a), and inverse forms always have a simple central suffix indexing only the primary object, as in (11b). The extension of direct/inverse agreement will thus sweep aside any preexisting portmanteau central suffixes in the affected forms.[5] In such cases, the loss of portmanteau agreement needs no special explanation: It is simply collateral damage from the extension of direct/inverse agreement.

3. Use a simple suffix in marked modes. A more interesting type of portmanteau loss occurs when a language fails to use a portmanteau suffix in a marked mode even though the portmanteau suffix exists in the indicative, as in the Northern Algonquin data in (2) above, repeated in (12). The language has a 1s→3 portmanteau *-ik*, as shown by the 1s→3 indicative form in (12b), but this portmanteau fails to appear in the 1s→3 dubitative form in (12c), which instead has the simple 1s suffix *-a:n*, the same as in the AI 1s form in (12a).

(12) Some Northern Algonquin conjunct forms

a. *takoššina:n*	b. *sa:ki:hik*	c. *sa:ki:ha:wa:ne:n*
takoššin -a:n	sa:ki:h -Ø -ik	sa:ki:h -a: -w -<u>a:n</u> -e:n
arrive.AI -1s	love.TA -3OBJ -1s:3	love.TA -3OBJ -W -<u>1s</u> -DUB
'I arrive.'	'I love him/her.'	'I might love him/her.'

We refer to the phenomenon exemplified in (12c) as PORTMANTEAU BLOCKING, defined as the replacement of a portmanteau central suffix by a simple central suffix in forms that include a negative/irrealis marker. Unlike the other two types of portmanteau loss, blocking does not have an independent explanation; it seems to reflect some property intrinsic to portmanteau agreement.

Survey of Portmanteau Robustness Patterns

We now survey the robustness of portmanteau agreement in w-mode and k-mode paradigms across the family. We distinguish three degrees of robustness: (i) FULL ROBUSTNESS, in which all portmanteaux are robust; (ii) PARTIAL ROBUSTNESS, in which 3→SAP portmanteaux and some SAP-actor portmanteaux are robust while other SAP-actor portmanteaux are blocked; and (iii) MINIMAL ROBUSTNESS, in which 3→SAP portmanteaux are robust but all SAP-actor portmanteaux are blocked.

The relevant w-mode and k-mode inflections from across the family are gathered in Tables 2 and 3, which employ the following conventions: Central suffixes are shown in boldface; "×" indicates that the form lacks a portmanteau because the relevant portmanteau has been eliminated from the language; "INV" indicates that the form lacks a portmanteau because the form has become inverse in the relevant mode (but not in the conjunct indicative); "?" indicates that the form is not given in our sources; "—" indicates that the argument combination is not possible in the relevant paradigm; and gray shading indicates the phenomenon of interest in this paper: The portmanteau is blocked.

Survey of w-Mode Patterns

The "w-modes" descend from PA paradigms in which **-w-* appeared in the negative/irrealis slot between the theme sign and the central suffix. Across the modern languages there are w-modes serving three different functions: (i) the CONJUNCT NEGATIVE (< PA **-w-* 'NEG' or PA **-hs(i)-w* 'DIM-NEG', Goddard 2006) in Ojibwe, Miami-Illinois, Eastern Algonquian, and Cheyenne; (ii) the CONJUNCT DUBITATIVE (< PA **-w-...-e:ni* 'NEG-...-DUB'), also known as the INTERROGATIVE ORDER (Bloomfield 1946:102–103), in Cree-Innu-Naskapi, Ojibwe, and Meskwaki-Kickapoo; and (iii) the PROHIBITIVE or negative imperative (< PA **-w-* 'NEG') in Munsee Delaware.

Table 2 presents the w-mode inflections in the daughter languages for argument combinations for which a portmanteau central suffix existed in PA.[6] Recall that shaded cells indicate forms in which portmanteaux are blocked. The overall tendency is for portmanteaux to be robust in the w-modes, with many languages showing full robustness, a few showing partial robustness, and only two—Munsee and Passamaquoddy—showing minimal robustness. We discuss each pattern in turn.

Full robustness in w-modes. Most of the languages surveyed show full robustness in the w-modes, with no portmanteau blocking whatsoever. This is the case in most varieties of Cree-Innu-Naskapi (Swampy/Moose Cree, Atikamekw, Southern East Cree, Mamit Innu), most varieties of Ojibwe (Southwest Ojibwe, Nishnaabemwin, Nipissing), Kickapoo, Old Illinois, Delaware, Massachusett, and Cheyenne. The fact

TABLE 2. Survey of potential portmanteau forms in w-modes

	1s:2p *-akokw	1s:3 *-ak	2s:3 *-at	1p:3 *-akent	X:3 *-ent	3:1p *-ament	3:2p *-a:kw
FULL ROBUSTNESS							
Sw./M. Cree (DUB)	-it-akok-wa:w-e:	-a:-w-ak-w-e:	-a:-w-at-e:	-a:-w-akiht-e:	-a:-w-iht-e:	-i-yamiht(-w)-e:	-it-a:kw-e:
Atikamekw (DUB)	-it-akok-wa:w-e:n	-a:-w-ak-w-e:n	-a:-w-at-e:n	-a:-w-akitt-e:n	?	-i-yamitt-e:n	-it-a:kw-e:n
S. East Cree (DUB)	-it-akuč-e:	-a:-w-č-e:	-a:-w-t-e:	-a:-w-čiht-e:	×	INV	-it-a:kw-e:
Mamit Innu (DUB)	-it-uw-a:wa:č-e:	-a:-w-ač-e:	-a:-w-ač-e:	-a:-w-ači:č-e:	×	-i-mi:k-w-e:	-it-a:kw-e:kw-e:
Shesh. Innu (DUB)	-it-u-kut-e:	-a:-w-č-e:	-a:-w-č-e:	-a:-w-(a:w)či:č-e:	×	INV	-it-a:ku-Ø
SW Ojibwe (DUB)	?	-a:-w-ak-e:n	-a:-w-at-e:n	-a:-w-ankit-e:n	-a:-w-int-e:n	-i-w-ankit-e:n	×
SW Ojibwe (NEG)	-issinow-akok	-a:-ssiw-ak	-a:-ssiw-at	-a:-ssiw-ankit	-a:-ssiw-int	-i-ssiw-ankit	×
Nishnaabemwin (DUB)	-inin-akokw-e:nh	-a:-w-ak-e:nh	-a:-w-at-e:nh	-a:-w-ankit-e:nh	-a:-w-int-e:nh	-i-w-ankit-e:nh	×
Nishnaabemwin (NEG)	-issino:n-akok	-a:-ssiw-ak	-a:-ssiw-at	-a:-ssiw-ankit	-a:-ssiw-int	-i-ssiw-ankit	×
Nipissing (DUB)	-in-Ø-okokw-e:n	-a:-w-ak-e:n	-a:-w-at-e:n	-a:-w-ankit-e:n	-a:-w-int-e:n	-i-w-amint-e:n	?
Kickapoo (INT)	-en-ako-Ø-e:ni	-á-Ø-ak-e:ni	-á-Ø-at-e:ni	-á-Ø-aket-e:ni	-a:-t-e:ni	-í-Ø-amek-w-e:ni	-en-o-a:kw-e:ni
Old Illinois (NEG)	-ehso:l-akok	-a:-hsi:w-ak	-a:-hsi:w-at	-a:-hsi:w-akint	×	-i-hsi:w-amint	-ehso:l-a:kw
Delaware (NEG)	×	-a:-w-ak	-a:-w-at	×	-a:-w-ənt	×	×
Massachusett (NEG)	×	-ã:-Ø-ak	-ã:-Ø-at	-ã:-Ø-akət	-ã:-Ø-ət	×	×
Cheyenne (NEG)	×	-ó-hev-o	-ó-hev-ose	×	×	×	×
PARTIAL ROBUSTNESS							
N. East Cree (DUB)	-iti-w-a:kw-a:	-a:-w-ič-a:	-a:-w-it-a:	-a:-w-ičihč-a:	×	-i-yimihč-a:	×
Pessamit Innu (DUB)	-ət-uw-a:wəč-e:	-a:-w-əč-e:	-a:-w-əč-e:	-a:-w-a:č-e:	×	-ə-mək-w-e:	-ət-a:ku-kw-e:
Golden Lk. Alg. (DUB)	-in-ik-w-e:n	-a:-w-akw-e:n	-a:-w-at-e:n	-Ø-ankit-e:n (1p) -a:-w-a:nkw-e:n (21)	-Ø-ik-w-e:n	INV	INV
Northern Alg. (DUB)	-in-Ø-okk-w-e:n	-a-w-a:n-e:n	-a-w-an-e:n	-Ø-ak-w-e:n	×	-ičih-emič	×
Meskwaki (INT)	-en-ow-e:kw-e:ni	-a:-w-ak-e:ni	-a:-w-at-e:ni	-a:-w-aket-e:ni	-a:-t-e:ni	-i-yamek-w-e:ni	-en-ow-a:kw-e:ni
later Miami-Ill. (NEG)	-ehso:l-akok	-a:-hsi:w-ak	-a:-hsi:w-an	-a:-hsi:w-akint	×	-i-hsi:w-amint	-ehso:l-a:kw
Penobscot (NEG)	×	-α-w-a(n)	-α-w-at	?	-α-mohk	?	×
Mi'kmaq (NEG)	×	-a-Ø-q	-a-w-t	-a-Ø-qat	-a-m-mək	-in-amewk	×
MINIMAL ROBUSTNESS							
Munsee Del. (PRH)	×	×	-a:-w-i:	×	×	×	×
Passamaquoddy (NEG)	×	-a-w-an	-a-w-ən	-a-w-ehk	-a-muhk	-in-əməhkw	-əlin-ahkw

that full robustness is the most prevalent pattern, attested in Plains, Central, and Eastern languages, may suggest that full robustness should be reconstructed for PA.

Partial robustness in w-modes. More interesting are the languages with partial robustness. In the languages surveyed, we see between one and three of the possible SAP-actor portmanteaux blocked in the w-modes, yet strikingly no 3→SAP portmanteaux are ever blocked. Within the partially robust languages, more robustness is more common than less robustness: There are more languages with only one portmanteau blocked than those with two or three. In particular, one portmanteau is blocked in Northern East Cree (1s:2p), Pessamit Innu (1p:3), Meskwaki (1s:2p), later Miami-Illinois (2s:3), and Mi'kmaq (X:3); two portmanteaux are blocked in Golden Lake Algonquin (1s:2p, 21:3) and perhaps Penobscot (1s:3, X:3)—though in Penobscot there are no attestations of the 1p:3 negative conjunct, so we do not know if that portmanteau would be blocked as well; and three portmanteaux are blocked in Northern Algonquin (1s:3, 2s:3, 1p:3). The distribution of blocked SAP-actor portmanteaux seems essentially random: We cannot identify any particular pattern, either synchronically or diachronically.

Minimal robustness in w-modes. Finally, there are only two languages with minimal robustness, in which all SAP-actor portmanteaux are blocked: Munsee Delaware in the prohibitive order (which is a w-mode in Munsee, an innovation compared to the k-mode prohibitives found elsewhere in the family) and Passamaquoddy. Again, 3→SAP portmanteaux are never blocked. Munsee is particularly interesting because it has two w-modes with different patterning: The prohibitive w-mode is minimally robust but the negative conjunct w-mode is fully robust. This difference indicates that portmanteau blocking cannot be triggered by the mode morpheme itself, since the prohibitive and the negative conjunct both have the same *-w-* and yet their blocking properties differ. Blocking must therefore be conditioned by some more abstract difference between modes.

Survey of k-Mode Patterns

The "k-modes" descend from PA paradigms in which *-(*h*)*k*- appeared in the negative/irrealis slot. The modern languages have k-modes serving various functions: (i) the PROHIBITIVE or negative imperative in Ojibwe, Meskwaki-Kickapoo, and Eastern Algonquian; (ii) the DELAYED/FUTURE IMPERATIVE in Cree-Innu-Naskapi, Ojibwe, Meskwaki, and Miami-Illinois; (iii) the POTENTIAL in Meskwaki-Kickapoo; and (iv) the CONDITIONAL in Mi'kmaq.

In the languages that retain k-modes only in imperative paradigms, the k-mode often only has forms for second-person actors. In such paradigms, the only relevant portmanteau is 2s→3 **at.* Only a few languages preserve k-modes with forms for non-second-person actors: Meskwaki-Kickapoo, Miami-Illinois, Unami Delaware, and Mi'kmaq. These languages are thus especially important for understanding portmanteau robustness in the k-modes.

Table 3 presents the k-mode inflections in the daughter languages for argument combinations for which a portmanteau central suffix existed in PA. In contrast to the w-modes, the vast majority of languages are minimally robust in the k-modes. We have found only one language with a fully robust k-mode (Unami Delaware) and only one language with partially robust k-modes (Meskwaki). We discuss each robustness pattern in turn.

Full robustness in k-modes. The only fully robust k-mode in our survey is the Unami prohibitive paradigm that uses a special prohibitive allomorph of the third person theme sign (from PA **-iye:*, also found in Nipissing, Meskwaki, and Kickapoo but regularized to **-a:* in the other languages). This paradigm has the 2s→3 form *-əye:-k-**ač*** '3OBJ-PRH-**2s:3**', with the portmanteau central suffix *-ač* '2s:3', a palatalized version of the portmanteau *-at* '2s:3' that appears elsewhere. Note that Unami also has an alternate prohibitive paradigm that is minimally robust: There the 2s→3 form is *-a:-h-**an*** '3OBJ-PRH-**2s**', with the simple central suffix *-an* '2s' rather than a portmanteau.

Partial robustness in k-modes. The only partially robust k-modes in our sample are the Meskwaki prohibitive and potential, where all the portmanteaux are blocked except for the 1s→2p suffix, which has a unique robust shape that is only found in the k-modes, *-a:wa:* (possibly composed from the prohibitive 1s suffix *-a:* plus the pluralizer *-wa:*).

Minimal robustness in k-modes. All the other k-mode paradigms in our survey are minimally robust. In the most common case, this just means that the 2s→3 portmanteau **-at* is blocked, as the majority of the k-modes are imperatives. Importantly, in Kickapoo, Miami-Illinois, and Mi'kmaq, which have a full(er) range of k-mode forms, all SAP-actor portmanteaux are blocked in the k-modes, yet, just as in the w-modes, the 3→SAP portmanteaux remain robust.

TABLE 3. Survey of potential portmanteau forms in k-modes

	1s:2p *-akokw	1s:3 *-ak	2s:3 *-at	1p:3 *-akent	X:3 *-ent	3:1p *-ament	3:2p *-a:kw
FULL ROBUSTNESS							
Unami Del. 1 (PRH)	—	—	-əye:-k-ač	—	—	—	—
PARTIAL ROBUSTNESS							
Meskwaki (PRH)	-en-ak-a(:wa)	-iye:-k-a	-iye:-k-an-i	-iye:-k-a:k-e	-iye:-k-i:k-e	-iy-amehkič-e	-en-ak-a:kw-e
Meskwaki (POT)	-en-ak-a:wa:-hi	-iye:-k-a:-ha	-iye:-k-ap-a	-iye:-k-a:k-ehe	-e-ne:-ha	-iy-ames-a	-en-wa:s-a
MINIMAL ROBUSTNESS							
Swampy/Moose Cree (DEL)	—	—	-a:-hk-an	—	—	—	—
Atikamekw (DEL)	—	—	-a:-kk-an	—	—	—	—
Northern East Cree (DEL)	—	—	-a:-hk-in	—	—	—	—
Southern East Cree (DEL)	—	—	-a:-hk-an	—	—	—	—
Pessamit Innu (DEL)	—	—	-a:-k-ən	—	—	—	—
SW Ojibwe (DEL)	—	—	-a:-kk-an	—	—	—	—
SW Ojibwe (PRH)	—	—	-a:-kk-e:n	—	—	—	—
Nishnaabemwin (DEL)	—	—	-a:-kk-an	—	—	—	—

Generalizations

Three interesting generalizations arise from our empirical survey of portmanteau robustness across Algonquian: (i) 3→SAP portmanteaux are always robust, even in the otherwise fragile k-modes; (ii) w-modes show much more robustness than k-modes; and (iii) the robustness of portmanteaux correlates with the distribution of the 3PL central suffix supplement (< PA *-*wa:w*).

3→SAP Portmanteaux Are Always Robust

A strikingly exceptionless generalization arises from our survey: 3→SAP portmanteaux are never blocked, even in the minimally robust languages, as first

	1s:2p *-akokw	1s:3 *-ak	2s:3 *-at	1p:3 *-akent	X:3 *-ent	3:1p *-ament	3:2p *-a:kw
MINIMAL ROBUSTNESS							
Nishnaabemwin (PRH)	—	—	-a:-kk-e:	—	—	—	—
Nipissing (DEL)	—	—	-a:-kk-an	—	—	—	—
Nipissing (PRH)	—	—	-iye:-kk-e:n	—	—	—	—
Northern Alg. (DEL)	—	—	-a-kk-an	—	—	—	—
Meskwaki (DEL)	—	—	-a:-hk-an-i	—	—	—	—
Kickapoo (PRH)	-en-ak-a	-ie:-k-a	-ie:-k-an-i	-ie:-k-a:k-e	-ie:k-i:k-i	-í-amehkič-i	-en-wa:hkič-i
Kickapoo (POT)	-en-ak-a:-ha	-ie:-k-a:-ha	-ie:-k-ap-a	-ie:-k-a:k-eha	-e-ne:-ha	-í-ameθ-a	-en-wa:θ-a
Miami-Illinois (DEL)	?	?	-a:-hk-an-i	?	?	-i-amihkič-e	-el-wa:hkič-e
Unami Del. 2 (PRH)	?	?	-a:-h-an	?	?	?	×
Massachusett (PRH)	—	—	-ã:-hk-an	—	—	—	—
Penobscot (PRH)	—	—	-ɑ-hk-ač	—	—	—	—
Passamaquoddy (PRH)	—	—	-a-hk-əč	—	—	—	—
Mi'kmaq (CND)	×	-ie-kk-Ø	-a-qq-Ø	-a-q-ekk	-a-ne-ss	-in-amət-s	×
Cheyenne (DEL)	—	—	-o-Ø-o'o	—	—	—	—

observed by Bondarenko (2020) for Passamaquoddy. Here we consider whether this generalization can be explained on functional grounds.

A possible functional reason why SAP→3 portmanteaux are more expendable than 3→SAP portmanteaux could involve the fact that SAP→3 portmanteaux are redundant with the theme sign while 3→SAP portmanteaux are not. In an SAP→3 form like (13a), for example, the portmanteau *-akint* '1p:3' indicates that the object is third-person, but this information is already conveyed by the theme sign (*-a:* '3OBJ'), so no information would be lost from the verb form as a whole if the portmanteau suffix *-akint* '1p:3' were replaced by the simple suffix *-a:nk* '1p'. In a 3→SAP form like (13b), in contrast, the portmanteau *-amint* '3:1p' conveys two pieces of information that are not expressed by the first-person object theme sign: (i) the first-person object is plural and (ii) the actor is third-person. Here the replacement of the portmanteau with a simple suffix would result in the loss of information: If *-amint* '3:1p' were replaced by the simple suffix *-k* '3' indexing only the actor, the inflection would no longer indicate that the first-person object is plural, and thus the form would be ambiguous between 3→1p and 3→1s; alternatively, if *-amint* '3:1p' were replaced by the simple suffix *-a:nk* '1p' indexing only the object, the inflection would no longer indicate that the actor is third person, and thus the form would be ambiguous between 3→1p and 2→1p.

(13) Miami-Illinois 1p↔3 conjunct negative (Costa 2003)

a. *wa:pama:hsi:wakinči*

wa:pam	-a:	-hsi:w	**-akint**	-i
see.TA	-3OBJ	-NEG	**-1p:3**	-IND

'We don't see him/her.'

b. *wa:pamihsi:waminči*

wa:pam	-i	-hsi:w	**-amint**	-i
see.TA	-1OBJ	-NEG	**-3:1p**	-IND

'S/he doesn't see us.'

Thus, blocking an SAP→3 portmanteau does not result in a loss of information, but blocking a 3→SAP portmanteau does. This difference might help to explain the fact that 3→SAP portmanteaux are never blocked: Languages might naturally tend to resist changes that create ambiguity, such as the loss of 3→SAP portmanteaux.

However, this cannot be the full explanation for 3→SAP robustness, as there is no inviolable diachronic constraint against changes that would create ambiguity. For instance, the Kickapoo 1s→2p portmanteau central suffix *-ako* is blocked in the k-modes, where the central suffix instead indexes the 1s actor (*-en-ak-**a**(:)* '-2OBJ-K-**1s**'), resulting in forms that are ambiguous between 2s and 2p objects. The fact that ambiguity is tolerated in this SAP→SAP form indicates that the systematic blocking of similar changes in 3→SAP forms must have an explanation that is specific to 3→SAP scenarios, rather than reflecting an overall ban on changes that create ambiguity.

Another illustrative case is found in Mi'kmaq, which totally lost both of the 2p-object portmanteaux (PA 3→2p *-*a:kw*, 1s→2p *-*akokw*). In both contexts, Mi'kmaq replaced the portmanteau with a simple central suffix indexing the 2p object, resulting in homophony of the 3→2p and 1s→2p forms:

(14) Mi'kmaq 2p object homophony (Francis and Hewson 2016)
nemu:loq
nem -u:l -oq
see.TA -2OBJ -2p
'S/he/they see(s) you.PL' or 'I see you.PL'

The Mi'kmaq change manifested in (14) affected 3→SAP forms but is not a case of 3→SAP portmanteau blocking under our definition, because in Mi'kmaq the 2p-object portmanteaux were completely lost from the language as a whole, whereas portmanteau blocking involves the loss of a portmanteau only in marked modes. The fact that 3→SAP portmanteaux can be lost globally, as in Mi'kmaq, but are nevertheless impervious to blocking in marked modes indicates that the explanation for their robustness must be tied closely to the blocking phenomenon.

While functional pressures relating to information loss and ambiguity creation must surely play a role in ensuring the rarity of such changes, the Kickapoo and Mi'kmaq examples demonstrate that these pressures cannot be the full story for 3→SAP robustness: There must be some particular property of 3→SAP portmanteaux and portmanteau blocking specifically that leads to 3→SAP robustness. A promising line of inquiry may lie in formal work on the distribution of SAP arguments, where it has been found that configurations involving a structurally low SAP argument are often subject to special grammatical restrictions, such as the Person-Case Constraint (PCC). It might be that the special treatment of 3→SAP portmanteaux is a product of the same mechanisms that have been proposed to give rise to PCC effects, such as person licensing (Bejar and Rezac 2003; Anagnostopoulou 2005) or feature gluttony (Bondarenko 2020; Coon and Keine 2021). We leave investigation of this intriguing parallel between two superficially quite different phenomena (portmanteau robustness and PCC effects) to future work.

w-Modes Are More Robust than k-Modes

Our survey reveals that w-modes are mostly fully or partially robust while k-modes are mostly minimally robust. The attested robustness patterns are summarized in Table 4. Looking across these patterns, we can draw the following implicational generalization: No language's k-modes are more robust than its w-modes. The one pattern predicted by the implicational robustness generalization but lacking from our survey is a language with fully robust w-modes but partially robust k-modes;

we assume this is lacking simply because of the rarity of partially robust k-modes in general.

We have no concrete explanation to offer for the asymmetry in robustness between w-modes and k-modes, but we note that the asymmetry could conceivably be explained on either diachronic or functional grounds. Diachronically, the fact that the vast majority of k-modes are minimally robust might suggest that the PA k-modes were minimally robust as well. The k-modes showing further robustness (Meskwaki, Unami) would then be innovations. In Unami, the one robust k-mode portmanteau, *-ač* '2s:3', could have been created by analogy with the portmanteau *-at* '2s:3' that appears in non-k-mode paradigms, and in Meskwaki, the one robust k-mode portmanteau, *-a:wa:* '1s:2p.PRH', could have been pieced together from the k-mode 1s suffix *-a:* plus the pluralizer *-wa:* that commonly appears in 3PL forms. The fact that the pluralizer is absent in the corresponding 1s:2p form in Kickapoo lends support to the idea that Meskwaki is innovative here. The proposal that the k-modes of PA were less robust than its w-modes could also be supported by the fact that in at least some cases, the loss of robustness seems to have spread from k-modes to w-modes: the loss of the 2s→3 portmanteau *-at* in the Miami-Illinois w-mode may reflect influence from the minimally robust k-modes, which already had the simple 2s suffix *-an* in the same cell.

Alternatively, from the perspective of markedness, we observe that portmanteau blocking makes TA forms more regular by replacing special portmanteaux with the same simple central suffixes that occur in AI and TI forms. The fact that such regularization is most advanced in the highly marked k-modes is consistent with the general tendency for more marked paradigms to be more regular (Tiersma 1982:833). This kind of explanation would be compatible with the k-modes being fully robust in PA; we could say that k-modes simply lost robustness more quickly

TABLE 4. Attested clines of robustness across modes

	W-MODE	K-MODE
Unami	fully robust	fully robust
Kickapoo	fully robust	**minimally robust**
Meskwaki	partially robust	partially robust
Mi'kmaq	partially robust	**minimally robust**
Passamaquoddy	**minimally robust**	**minimally robust**

over time than the w-modes due to their more marked status, resulting in the asymmetric situation reflected in Table 4.

Plural Supplements Correlate with Robustness

The final generalization involves an affix that we have not yet discussed. In conjunct forms, third-person plurality is often expressed by supplementing the central suffix **-t* '3' with a plural marker reflecting either PA **-wa:w* '3PL' (in Central) or PA **-h-etwi* 'CAUS-RECIP' (in Eastern) (Goddard 1980:154). This PLURAL SUPPLEMENT is found across the family in the AI conjunct forms:

(15) 3p in SW Ojibwe AI conjunct

a. *ma:ča:t*	b. *ma:ča:wa:t*
ma:ča: -t	ma:ča: -<u>**wa:**</u> -t
leave.AI -3	leave.AI -<u>**3PL**</u> -3
'She leaves.'	'They leave.'

(16) 3p in Passamaquoddy AI conjunct

a. *mačahat*	b. *mačahahtit*
mačaha -t	mačaha -<u>**hti**</u> -t
leave.AI -3	leave.AI -<u>**3PL**</u> -3
'She leaves.'	'They leave.'

In TA paradigms, some languages, such as Ojibwe (Nichols 1980:315–329) and Cree (in the subjunctive and iterative; Wolfart 1973:42), use the plural supplement in both 3→SAP and SAP→3 forms, as illustrated for Ojibwe in (17): *-wa:* '3PL' appears no matter whether the third person is the actor, as in the 3p→1s form in (17a), or the object, as in the 1s→3p form in (17b).

(17) Plural supplement in 1↔3p in SW Ojibwe

a. *wa:pamiwa:t*				b. *wa:pamakwa:*		
wa:pam	-i	-<u>**wa:**</u>	-t	wa:pam -Ø	-ak	-<u>**wa:**</u>
see.TA	-1OBJ	-<u>**3PL**</u>	-3	see.TA -3OBJ	-1s:3	-<u>**3PL**</u>
'They see me.'				'I see them.'		

In most languages, however, the supplement has a more restricted distribution, shown for Passamaquoddy in (18): *-hti* '3PL' appears in 3p→1s forms like (18a), where the third person is the actor, but never when the third person is the object, as in the 1s→3 form in (18b), which cannot take a plural supplement and thus does not indicate whether the object is singular or plural.

(18) Plural supplement only in 3p→1 in Passamaquoddy

a. *lapəmihtit*	b. *lapəmuk*
lapəm -i -<u>hti</u> -t	lapəm -Ø -uk
look.TA -1OBJ -<u>3PL</u> -3	look.TA -3OBJ -1s:3
'They look at me.'	'I look at her/them.'

When we consider the distribution of the plural supplement across languages, we can make a striking observation: portmanteaux that can co-occur with a 3p supplement, such as Ojibwe *-ak* '1s:3' in (17b), are always robust in the w-modes, while portmanteaux that cannot co-occur with a 3p supplement, such as Passamaquoddy *-uk* '1s:3' in (18b), may or may not be robust in the w-modes. We can thus formulate the generalization in (19).[7]

(19) *3p supplement generalization:* If a 3p central suffix supplement co-occurs with a portmanteau P in the conjunct indicative, then P is robust in the w-modes.

The generalization must be expressed in terms of particular portmanteau suffixes, not in terms of languages as a whole, because Northern East Cree and Pessamit Innu both have certain portmanteaux that are blocked in the w-mode (NEC *-ikut* '1s:2p', Innu *-əčət* '1p:3') while other portmanteaux remain robust—and, crucially, the portmanteaux that are blocked in these languages also do not co-occur with the 3p supplement **-wa:w*.[8] The correlation between the 3p supplement and robust portmanteau suffixes thus operates on a portmanteau-by-portmanteau basis, not a language-by-language basis. Informally, it seems that for any given SAP→3 argument combination for which a portmanteau suffix exists, if the verb's commitment to agreeing with the third-person object is strong enough to permit the use of a 3p supplement, then it is also strong enough to guarantee the robustness of the SAP→3 portmanteau in the w-mode. Refinement and interpretation of this observation must be left to future work.

TABLE 5. Portmanteau robustness in 3→SAP and SAP→3 forms

ROBUSTNESS PATTERN	3→SAP	SAP→3	
		W-MODE	K-MODE
Pattern I (Unami)	robust	robust	robust
Pattern II (Kickapoo)	robust	robust	**blocked**
Pattern III (Passamaquoddy)	robust	**blocked**	**blocked**

Conclusion

This paper has examined a previously underdescribed empirical phenomenon in Algonquian verb inflection: the blocking of portmanteau agreement suffixes in marked paradigms. Three important generalizations arise from our survey: (i) 3→SAP portmanteaux are always robust, as first observed for Passamaquoddy by Bondarenko (2020); (ii) a language's k-modes cannot be more robust than its w-modes (generalizations (i) and (ii) are synthesized in Table 5); and (iii) if a 3p central suffix supplement co-occurs with a portmanteau in the conjunct indicative, then that portmanteau is robust in the w-modes. Diachronic and functional factors are likely to play some role in accounting for the generalizations, but the intricacy and systematicity of the patterns seem to exceed what can be explained by these factors alone.

NOTES

1. We are grateful for helpful feedback from audiences at the 54th Algonquian Conference and WSCLA 26.
2. Abbreviations for features of verbal arguments: 1s = first-person singular, 2s = second-person singular, 1p = exclusive first-person plural, 21 = inclusive first-person plural, 2p = second-person plural, 3 = animate third person, 3p = animate third-person plural, 0 = inanimate third person, X = unspecified actor, SAP = speech-act participant (1st/2nd person). Abbreviations for argument combinations, exemplified for a TA verb whose arguments are 1p and 3: 1p→3 = 1p acts on 3, 1p↔3 = 1p and 3 interact (either 1p→3 or 3→1p), 1p:3 = agreement marker indexing 1p actor and 3 object, 1p,3 = agreement

marker indexing 1p and 3. Grammatical abbreviations: AI = animate intransitive, CND = conditional, DEL = delayed imperative, DUB = dubitative, IC = initial change, IND = indicative, INT = interrogative, INV = inverse, K = mode suffix reflecting PA *-(*h*)*k*-, * NEG = negative, OBJ = primary object, PL = plural, POT = potential, PRH = prohibitive, TA = transitive animate, TI = transitive inanimate, W = negative/irrealis suffix reflecting PA *-*w*- 'NEG'.

3. The X:3 portmanteau *-*ent* cannot be segmented as *-*en* 'X' plus *-*t* '3', despite the existence of both of these suffixes elsewhere in the system, because the sequence of *-*en* plus *-*t* would surface as **-*enk* rather than attested *-*ent* (cf. Goddard 1969:132; Costa 2003:386, note 68).
4. For simplicity, we consider only forms with ANIMATE third-person actors. The portmanteau *-*a:kw* '3:2p' in fact occurs with animate (3), inanimate (0), and unspecified (X) actors. The portmanteau *-*ament* '3:1p' has the variant *-*amenk* '0/X:1p' for inanimate and unspecified actors.
5. An exception to this statement in Parry Island Ojibwe is discussed in Oxford (2024: §2.2.2).
6. Our presentation of Sheshatshiu Innu 3→SAP forms in Table 2 differs from that in Clarke (1982). Clarke provides the following 3→SAP dubitative conjunct forms: -*ika:kwe:* '3:1p', -*ita:ku* '3:21', and -*ikwa:če:* '3:2p'. However, we wonder if these may be mislabeled—we suspect that -*ika:kwe:* is the 3→21 form with inverse theme sign -*ik* and simple 21 suffix *a:kw*; *ita:ku* is the 3→2p form with second person theme sign -*it* and 3:2p portmanteau *a:kw*; and -*ikwa:če:* is the 3→1p form with inverse theme sign -*ikw* and simple 1p suffix -*a:t*. Under this analysis, the 3→1p and 3→21 dubitative forms have become inverse (a change that also happened in Southern East Cree) and the 3→2p dubitative form contains a robust portmanteau.
7. We are aware of one exception to this generalization: Northern Algonquin uses the 3p supplement throughout much of the TA paradigm but is only partially robust in the w-modes.
8. The blockable Northern East Cree portmanteau -*ikut* '1s:2p' cannot co-occur with a 3p supplement because no third person is involved. The blockable Pessamit Innu portmanteau -*əčət* '1p:3' could conceivably co-occur with a 3p supplement, since the supplement does co-occur with some portmanteaux in the language, like robust -*ək* '1s:3' and -*a:t* '2s:3', but it is an arbitrary fact about the language that the 3p supplement does not appear in 1p→3p forms, not even in the conjunct indicative.

REFERENCES

Anagnostopoulou, Elena. 2005. Strong and Weak Person Restrictions: A Feature Checking Analysis. *Clitic and Affix Combinations: Theoretical Perspectives*, ed. by Lorie Heggie and Francisco Ordóñez, pp. 199–235. Amsterdam: Benjamins.

Aubin, George F. 1984. Some Verb Paradigms in Golden Lake Algonquin. *Papers of the 15th Algonquian Conference*, ed. by William Cowan, pp. 217–224. Ottawa: Carleton University.

Aubin, George F. 1989. Some Verb Paradigms in Golden Lake Algonquin: II. *Actes du vingtième congrès des algonquinistes*, ed. by William Cowan, pp. 1–16. Ottawa: Carleton University.

Baraby, Anne-Marie, and Marie-Odile Junker. 2011–2020. Innu Verb Conjugations, 4th ed. http://verb.innu-aimun.ca.

Bejar, Susana, and Milan Rezac. 2003. Person Licensing and the Derivation of PCC Effects. *Romance Linguistics: Theory and Acquisition*, ed. by Ana Teresa Pérez-Leroux and Yves Roberge, pp. 49–62. Amsterdam: Benjamins.

Béland, Jean-Pierre. 1978. Atikamekw Morphology and Lexicon. PhD thesis, University of California, Berkeley.

Bloomfield, Leonard. 1946. Algonquian. *Linguistic Structures of Native America*, ed. by Harry Hoijer, pp. 85–129. New York: Viking Fund Publications in Anthropology.

Bondarenko, Tanya. 2020. Feature Gluttony for Algonquian: Agreement in Passamaquoddy. PhD generals paper, Massachusetts Institute of Technology.

Brouillard, Edmond, and Marie Dumont-Anichinapeo. 1987. *Grammaire algonquine respectant les règles langagières et coutumières propres aux communautés du Lac Simon ainsi que du Grand Lac Victoria*. Lac Simon, QC: Centre culturel Amikwan.

Clarke, Sandra. 1982. *North-West River (Sheshātshīt) Montagnais: A Grammatical Sketch*. Canadian Ethnology Service Paper no. 80. Ottawa: National Museums of Canada.

Collette, Vincent. 2019. Paradigm Leveling in South East Cree Verbal Inflections. *Papers of the 48th Algonquian Conference*, ed. by Monica Macaulay and Margaret Noodin, pp. 33–52. East Lansing: Michigan State University Press.

Coon, Jessica, and Stefan Keine. 2021. Feature Gluttony. *Linguistic Inquiry* 42:655–710.

Costa, David J. 2003. *The Miami-Illinois Language*. Lincoln: University of Nebraska Press.

Dahlstrom, Amy. 1989. Morphological Change in Plains Cree Verb Inflection. *Folia Linguistica Historica* 9:59–71.

Ellis, C. Douglas. 1971. Cree Verb Paradigms. *International Journal of American Linguistics* 37:76–95.

Francis, Bernie, and John Hewson. 2016. *The Mi'kmaq Grammar of Father Pacifique*. Sydney, NS: Cape Breton University Press.

Francis, David A., and Robert M. Leavitt. 2008. *Peskotomuhkati wolastoqewi latuwewakon: A*

Passamaquoddy-Maliseet Dictionary. Orono: University of Maine Press. http://pmportal.org.

Goddard, Ives. 1969. Delaware Verbal Morphology: A Descriptive and Comparative Study. PhD thesis, Harvard University.

Goddard, Ives. 1980. Eastern Algonquian as a Genetic Subgroup. *Papers of the 11th Algonquian Conference*, ed. by William Cowan, 143–158. Ottawa: Carleton University.

Goddard, Ives. 1994. *Leonard Bloomfield's Fox Lexicon: Critical Edition*. Winnipeg: Algonquian and Iroquoian Linguistics.

Goddard, Ives. 1995. Notes on Fox (Mesquakie) Inflection: Minor Modes and Incompletely Described Morphemes. *Papers of the 26th Algonquian Conference*, ed. by David H. Pentland, pp. 124–150. Winnipeg: University of Manitoba.

Goddard, Ives. 2000. The Historical Origins of Cheyenne Inflections. *Papers of the 31st Algonquian Conference*, ed. by John D. Nichols, pp. 77–129. Winnipeg: University of Manitoba.

Goddard, Ives. 2004. Meskwaki Verbal Affixes. *Papers of the 35th Algonquian Conference*, ed. by H. C. Wolfart, pp. 97–123. Winnipeg: University of Manitoba.

Goddard, Ives. 2006. The Proto-Algonquian Negative and its Descendants. *Actes du 37e Congrès des Algonquinistes*, ed. by H. C. Wolfart, pp. 161–208. Winnipeg: University of Manitoba.

Goddard, Ives. 2021. *A Grammar of Southern Unami Delaware (Lenape)*. Petoskey, MI: Mundart Press.

Goddard, Ives, and Kathleen J. Bragdon. 1988. *Native Writings in Massachusett*. Philadelphia: American Philosophical Society.

Jones, David. 1977. *A Basic Algonquin Grammar: For Teachers of the Language at Maniwaki, Quebec*. Maniwaki, QC: River Desert Band Council.

Junker, Marie-Odile, and Marguerite MacKenzie. 2010–2014. East Cree (Northern Dialect) Verb Conjugation, 3rd edn. http://verbn.eastcree.org.

Junker, Marie-Odile, and Marguerite MacKenzie. 2011–2014. East Cree (Southern Dialect) Verb Conjugation, 3rd edn. http://verbs.eastcree.org.

Leman, Wayne. 2011. *A Reference Grammar of the Cheyenne Language*. Lulu Press.

Nichols, John D. 1980. Ojibwe Morphology. PhD thesis, Harvard University.

Oxford, Will. 2023. Direct, Inverse, and Neutral: Refining the Description of Algonquian Transitive Verb Forms. *Papers of the 52nd Algonquian Conference*, ed. by Monica Macaulay and Margaret Noodin, pp. 223–244. East Lansing: Michigan State University Press.

Oxford, Will. 2024. *The Algonquian Inverse*. Oxford: Oxford University Press.

Quinn, Conor. 2015. Recovering the Penobscot TA Conjunct: Documentary, Analytical, and Revitalization Considerations. Paper read at the 47th Algonquian Conference, Winnipeg, October 24.

Tiersma, Peter Meijes. 1982. Local and General Markedness. *Language* 58:832–849.

Valentine, J. Randolph. 2001. *Nishnaabemwin Reference Grammar*. Toronto: University of Toronto Press.

Voorhis, Paul H. 1974. *Introduction to the Kickapoo Language*. Bloomington: Indiana University.

Voorhis, Paul H. 1979. *Grammatical Notes on the Penobscot Language from Frank Speck's Penobscot Transformer Tales*. University of Manitoba Anthropology Papers 24. Winnipeg: Department of Anthropology, University of Manitoba.

Wolfart, H. C. 1973. *Plains Cree: A Grammatical Study*. Transactions of the American Philosophical Society, n.s., vol. 63, part 5. Philadelphia.

Menominee Preverb Ordering Revisited

Andrew Kline, Monica Macaulay, and Jennifer Stoughton

This paper presents results of an examination of a large body of data involving co-occurrence and relative ordering of preverbs in Menominee.[1] Preverbs are bound prosodic words that precede a verb stem, and have a range of semantics including aspect, mood, and various adverbial meanings. Our results are contrasted with previous claims about Menominee preverb ordering: specifically, those found in Bloomfield (1962), a grammar that was edited posthumously by Charles Hockett, and those in Cook (2003). Bloomfield's grammar contains an unfinished section on the relative ordering of one set of preverbs, but leaves another set unordered. Cook reexamines the ordered set and proposes that the ordering is based on semantic factors.

Here, we provide an updated picture based on a database of 1,731 examples of multiple preverb usage drawn from a variety of sources. We find that Cook's ordering does not hold up, but that Bloomfield's partial ordering does, to a large degree. The preverbs that he left unordered appear very rarely in our database (and even more rarely co-occur), which may explain why he left them aside. We are also able to resolve a number of other questions that are left unanswered in Bloomfield's description.

The paper proceeds as follows: First, we provide background on Menominee preverbs, and walk through the somewhat confusing presentation of preverbs in Bloomfield's grammar. We then describe our methodology and findings. We conclude with directions for future research and a summary of what our data has shown.

Background

This section provides background first on Menominee preverbs in general, and second, on Bloomfield's (1962) treatment of the preverbs.

The Verbal Template and the "Preverb Space"

The verbal template for Menominee is schematized in Figure 1, where the asterisk in the second cell means (theoretically) any number, including zero. As Figure 1 shows, the verb stem and any preverbs that are present may be preceded by an optional prefix. The prefixes are part of the inflectional morphology of the Menominee verb, and mark person. Examples (1) and (2) have preverbs bolded.[2]

(1) Ne-**kēs-awēh**-esīqtawāw.
1-CMPL-go.to.do-I.visit.her
'I went to visit her.' (LT 8/26/08)

(2) **Cew-kēs-pemīm**-esiatuaq.
EPIS-CMPL-go.by-they.go.CONJ
'They must have been going by here.' (LB 1928:324)

Example (1) shows a verb with a person prefix, *ne-* 'first person', and two preverbs, *kēs-* 'completive' and *awēh-* 'go to do'. Example (2) is in a paradigm that does

(prefix-)	preverb-*	V stem	-suffix(es)

FIGURE 1. Menominee verbal template

not take a person prefix, and has three preverbs, *cew-* 'epistemic', *kēs-* 'completive', and *pemīm-* 'go by'.

We call the second cell in Figure 1 (the one that says "preverb-*") the PREVERB SPACE (following Shields 2005, and bolded in (1) and (2)). Occasionally the preverb space contains other material following one or more preverbs, for example, a demonstrative or particle, but we set that aside for a later section.

Preverbs in Bloomfield (1962)

Charles Hockett compiled Bloomfield's extensive notes and drafts into *The Menomini Language* (1962) after Bloomfield's death in 1949. The section on preverbs (1962:214–222; subsections 13.65–13.123) is one of the parts that Bloomfield had not finished, and Hockett includes a few editorial comments on what he found and what he surmised. In what follows we walk through the presentation of the preverbs fairly carefully because—presumably due to the state of the materials that Hockett was working with—it is internally inconsistent and contradicts itself in places.

After a few introductory remarks, in §13.67, Bloomfield says that there are two classes of preverbs. The ones in the first class, he says, "are limited in number; some of them have static vowel quantities; some combine in irregular ways with the personal prefixes and behave irregularly under initial change; and most of them occur only as preverbs" (1962:214–215).[3] The second class is open; any particle with a zero final (i.e., without any overt derivational suffixation) can be used in this way. Bloomfield isn't explicit that the preverbs of Class 1 precede those of Class 2 in linear order, should they co-occur, but that is implicit in the rest of the sections.

Section 13.68 provides Bloomfield's general introduction to the Class 1 preverbs. He says they're "extremely frequent," and that "the order is for the most part fixed" when there are more than one (1962:215).

Sections 13.69–13.73 cover the first five Class 1 preverbs, which according to a note from Hockett (described immediately below) is as far as Bloomfield got with the explicit ordering. The five preverbs and their relative order are shown in (3)[4]:

(3)	cew-	>	aw-	>	kew-	>	kēs-	>	katāēw-
	EPISTEMIC	>	IRREALIS	>	HABITUAL	>	COMPLETIVE	>	VOLUNTATIVE FUTURE

Between §13.73 and §13.74 (1962:217), Hockett inserts his editorial voice. He says that his summary of the 22 additional preverbs of Class 1 is just taken from

TABLE 1. Bloomfield's ordering of Class 1 preverbs

PREVERB	DEFINITION	PREVERB	DEFINITION
cew-	epistemic	*awēh-*	go to do
aw-	irrealis	*naehēh-*	skillfully, well able, given to
kew-	habitual	*ap-*	go off to do (and return)
kēs-	completive	*papām-*	going about
katāew-	voluntative future	*yōh-*	from there, for that reason
enem-	in the process, on the way, during the time	*wāep-*	begin (to)
pes-	coming (space, time)	*yāh-*	again; back
macēq-	bad, badly	*kāeqc-*	greatly, much, intensely
ahpēc-	so far, so long, to such a degree	*pāeqc-*	accidentally
nawāc-	before other action, first	*nōc-*	easily
es-, eses-	towards there, in that manner	*puaq-*	fail (to)
āec-	so far, so long a time	*yāhpec-*	completely, beyond repair
pemīm-	set about an act, go ahead and do; go by, past	*tasēh-*	there, then, through that length of time; without effect
māek-	ongoing action or state		

notes, but that he is confident that Bloomfield had intended them to be presented in the order given. The 27 total Class 1 preverbs are shown in Table 1.[5] Bloomfield's ordering is seen in the table by reading down the first two columns, then continuing at the top of the second two columns to the bottom of the table.

Hockett presents the rest of these preverbs in sections 13.74–13.96, and then includes another editorial note, in which he explains that the rest of the preverbs to be presented were not categorized by Bloomfield; that is, that there was no indication which were Class 1 and which were Class 2, if Bloomfield had even come to a conclusion. He says, "There is no way of determining Bloomfield's intention, though it is likely that a number of the following preverbs do belong to the first class" (1962:220). Sections 13.97–13.123 then provide what Hockett calls the "additional preverbs." He presents them alphabetically, to emphasize that this set is not ordered or classified.

Although this part of the grammar contains 27 preverbs, in fact there are 42 unclassified preverbs if we count the ones in Bloomfield's *Lexicon* (1975) in addition to the ones in the grammar. We begin our analysis, then, from the point provided in (4):

(4) Bloomfield (1962, 1975)
  a. 27 Class 1 preverbs, ordered
  b. 42 unclassified preverbs, not ordered ("other")

Methodology

We assembled all of the Menominee sources that were readily available to us and (relatively) easily searchable, and then identified all cases of verbal forms containing more than one preverb. Our sources appear in Table 2, which shows that the data span 100 years, from 1920 until 2020.

Altogether we collected 1,731 examples containing multiple preverbs. We placed them by type in an array to get a graphic view of the different orderings. Figure 2

TABLE 2. Sources of data

AUTHOR	PUBLICATION DATE	SOURCE AND DATE OF DATA
Bloomfield, Leonard	1928, 1962, 1975	fieldwork 1920–1921, supplemented by interactions with speakers until 1949
WNALP texts	1973–1976	stories collected from five speakers in Milwaukee, WI
Misc. community materials	n/a	precise source unknown; probably 1970s or 1980s
Guile	2001	data collected in the 1980s
Macaulay database	n/a	fieldwork 1997–2020

cew-	aw-	kew-	kēs-	kata͞ew-	enem-	pes-	macēq-	ahpēc-	nawāc-	es-	a͞ec-	pemīm-	ma͞ek-	awēh-	naehēh-	ap-	papām-	yōh-	wa͞ep-	yāh-	ka͞eqc-	pa͞eqc-	nōc-	puaq-	yāhpec-	tasēh-
X1	X2																									
X2	X1																									
X1		X2																								
X1			X2																							
X2			X1																							
X1				X2																						
X1					X2																					
X1						X2																				
X1								X2																		
X1									X2																	
X1										X2																
X2											X1															
X1												X2														
X1													X2													
X1														X2												
X1																	X2									
X1																		X2								
X2																		X1								
X1																			X2							

FIGURE 2. Partial data array

provides a screenshot of part of the array, showing some of the Class 1 preverbs. Cells marked X1 indicate that the preverb is found as the first in a pair, while cells marked X2 are cases where the preverb occurs second. Shaded cells indicate cases that violate the predicted ordering. We discuss these further below.

Findings

This section describes our findings in the context of Cook (2003) and Bloomfield (1962). We present counterexamples to their proposed orderings and discuss our findings regarding the ordering of the "other" category of preverbs.

Cook (2003)

Cook (2003) provides a semantic classification of Menominee preverbs.[6] She looks at Bloomfield's Class 1 preverbs and four preverbs of the "other" class, using a relatively small data set.[7] She organizes them into four main semantic categories,

TABLE 3. Cook's (2003) semantic categories and classification of preverbs

MODAL	ASPECTUAL	SPATIAL	ADVERBIAL
Pure modal *cew-* 'EPIS' *aw-* 'IRR'	Endpoints *kēs-* 'CMPL' *wāep-* 'begin'	Directed motion *enem-* 'during' *pes-* 'coming' *pemīm-* 'go by' *awēh-* 'go to do' *ap-* 'go and return' *papām-* 'going around' *yōh-* 'source, reason'	Manner *macēq-* 'badly' *es-* 'manner' nōc- 'easily' *pāec-* 'properly'
Control *katāew-* 'VOL' *naehēh-* 'well able' *puaq-* 'fail' *natāw-* 'try'	Internal structure *kew-* 'HAB' *māek-* 'ongoing' *yāh-* 'again' *yāpec-* 'repeatedly'	Spatial orientation *āec-* 'so far' *wāeh-* 'source, reason' *pemīm-* 'go by' *tasēh-* 'there'	Degree *ahpēc-* 'to that degree' *kāeqc-* 'much' *yāhpec-* 'completely'
	Temporal ordering *nawāc-* 'before' *anīh-* 'finished'		

shown in Table 3 (where we have abbreviated the preverb glosses): Modal, Aspectual, Spatial, and Adverbial. She then divides Modal into pure modal (such as epistemic and irrealis) and control (where the translations are control verbs in English); Aspectual into endpoints and internal structure; Spatial into directed motion (e.g., 'coming') and spatial orientation (e.g., 'go by'); and Adverbial into manner and degree.

Cook claims that when preverbs co-occur, they are ordered as in the headers in Table 3: Modal > Aspectual > Spatial > Adverbial. She is not claiming that Bloomfield's ordering of the entire set of Class 1 preverbs (as illustrated in Table 1) occurs in this order, but just that when preverbs co-occur they follow the ordering she suggests. She further claims that members of these main categories can co-occur, but that the members of the subcategories cannot, except for the adverbials.

Our data shows counterexamples to both claims. First, (5) provides examples which violate the proposed ordering of the main categories:

(5) *Attested violations of* MODAL > ASPECTUAL > SPATIAL > ADVERBIAL

a. SPATIAL > ASPECTUAL: *pes-mǣk-* 'coming-on.going'

b. SPATIAL > MODAL: *ap-aw-* 'go.and.return-IRR'

c. ADVERBIAL > MODAL: *kǣqc-katǣw-* 'much-VOL'

d. ADVERBIAL > SPATIAL: *es-pes-* 'manner-coming'

e. ASPECTUAL > MODAL: *kew-naehēh-* 'HAB-well.able'

Cook's second claim, that members of the subcategories (aside from adverbial preverbs) cannot co-occur, was also counterexemplified in our larger corpus of examples. Consider (6):

(6) *Co-occurrence of Members of Subcategories: Examples*

a. Tāq taeh yōm **cew-aw-esēqtayan?**
what and this EPIS-IRR-I.do.CONJ
'How shall I deal with this?' (HV 118:35)

b. 's **kew-mǣk-pahpēseyan**
AOR HAB-on.going-you.hunt.CONJ
'while you are on a hunt' (TG 0079-0080)

c. **Enem-yōh-espīpesit.**
during-source-he.speeds.upwards.CONJ
'(He) leaped up aloft.' (WAW 472:20)

TABLE 4. Co-occurrence of members of Cook's (2003) subcategories

MODAL		ASPECTUAL		SPATIAL		ADVERBIAL	
Pure modal	✓	Endpoints	✓	Directed motion	✓	Manner	✓
Control	✓	Internal structure	✓	Spatial orientation	×	Degree	×
		Temporal ordering	×				

In (6a), two members of Cook's "pure modal" subcategory co-occur, in (6b) two members of "internal structure" co-occur, and in (6c) two members of "directed motion" co-occur.

Table 4 shows our overall results with respect to the subcategories. In the table, a check means that we found members of a subcategory co-occurring, while an 'X' means that we did not. The table shows that members of six of the subcategories do display internal co-occurrence, and that only three do not, invalidating Cook's second claim.[8]

Cook's work served as a useful first discussion and classification of the semantics of Menominee preverbs, but her two claims about their ordering and constraints on that ordering do not hold up against a larger corpus.

Bloomfield (1962)

In his introduction to the discussion of preverbs, Bloomfield says, "There is no restriction on the number of preverbs which may be compounded with a single verb stem" (1962:214). However, even with the large corpus that we assembled, the maximum number of preverbs we found co-occurring was four.[9] Examples (7) and (8) demonstrate:

(7) **aw-kew-yōh-māēhnow-ītuaq**
IRR-HAB-source-well-they.stay.CONJ
'(so that) they would get well from (them)' (MH 006)

(8) **Cew-kēs-pes-eses-nānōhtawatuaq.**
EPIS-CMPL-coming-manner-RED.they.hear.it.CONJ
'They must have always heard it.' (CAN 002)

As laid out above, Bloomfield's (1962) section on Menominee preverbs was brief and not completed. He did, however, provide the ordering of the Class 1 preverbs that we showed in Table 1. Our data largely confirm Bloomfield's ordering of these Class 1 preverbs, although there are some exceptions. In total, we found 34 counterexample tokens and 24 counterexample types. Of these, the majority were single occurrences (Table 5); however, there were a number with multiple

TABLE 5. Counterexamples with one occurrence

aw-cew 'IRR-EPIS'	*kēs-cew* 'CMPL-EPIS'	*āēc-cew-* 'so.far-EPIS'	*yōh-cew-* 'source-EPIS'
kew-aw- 'HAB-IRR'	*kēs-aw-* 'CMPL-IRR'	*pes-aw-* 'coming-IRR'	*awēh-aw-* 'go.to.do-IRR'
kēs-kew- 'CMPL-HAB'	*katāēw-kēs* 'VOL-CMPL'	*macēq-kēs-* 'badly-CMPL'	*māēk-enem* 'on.going-during'
es-pes- 'manner-coming'	*es-macēq* 'manner-badly'	*kāēqc-naehēh* 'much-well.able'	*es-kew-* 'manner-HAB'

TABLE 6. Counterexamples with multiple occurrences

ap-aw- 'go.and. return-IRR'	*āēc-aw-* 'so.far-IRR'	*katāēw-kew* 'VOL-HAB'	*kāēqc-katāēw* 'much-VOL'
māēk-katāēw 'on. going-VOL'	*māēk-pemīm-* 'on. going-go.by'	*yōh-pes-* 'source-coming'	

occurrences as well (Table 6). With the exception of *ap-aw* (discussed immediately below), the number of tokens in Table 6 was two for each combination.

The combination *ap-aw-*, shown in Table 6, occurred five times in one story with the same verb. One of these instances is shown in (9):

(9) **Ap-aw-cēqnapamācen.**
go.and.return-IRR-he.looks.at.it.CONJ
'[He will be the first] to go look at it.' (RS 211)

While we are unsure of the exact reason for this ordering, the repetition may just be a rhetorical device, as the sentences come at significant points in the development of the plot of the story they are contained in.

In his discussion of the ordering of the first five preverbs of Class 1, Bloomfield did note one case of variable ordering, involving *katāēw-* 'voluntative future'. He says it normally comes in the position we have shown it in (in Table 1), as the last of the first set of five, and means that "the actor . . . has an inner tendency to the action which he will presumably carry out" (1962:216). However, he says that it can also follow all other preverbs in Class 1, in which case it means "a strong tendency of the actor . . . without regard to its fulfillment in action" (1962:217)—presumably intended as a distinction of telicity or completion. However, when we searched our corpus, we only found three such examples in the data from Bloomfield: two from the grammar where he brings this up, and one in a text. These are shown in (10) and (11):

(10) Bloomfield (1962:217)

a. **Ne-kāēqc-katāēw-mīcehsim.**
1-much-VOL-I.eat
'I very much want to eat.'

b. **Ne-kēs-kāēqc-katāēw-nepām.**
1-CMPL-much-VOL-I.sleep
'I very much wanted to sleep.'

(11) **Enecewak kāēh pes-katāēw-naeqnat mamāceqtaw!**
it.must.be.that of.course coming-VOL-you.kill.him.CONJ human
'It would really seem that you have come here to kill men!' (LB 1928:568)

We do not see in these examples any real evidence (at least, as given in the translations) that would support Bloomfield's claim that this order of preverbs is distinct in meaning from the much more common order where *katāēw-* 'voluntative future' precedes the other preverbs.[10]

One example of *katāēw-* following another Class 1 preverb is found in a story from the 1970s, shown in (12):[11]

(12) **Kenīs taeh āwew new 's aw-māēk-katāēw-enes-akēmāēw**
a.long.time and it.is EMPH AOR IRR-on.going-VOL-there-he.counts
ēh-akom maskūcīhsak.
here-these beans
'It must have been a long time they were there counting those beans.' (ONE 018)

Katāēw- 'voluntative future' is predicted to follow irrealis *aw-* (as it does here), but it is predicted to precede *māēk-* 'on-going' (which it does not do here). This, then, should be an example of Bloomfield's second definition ("a strong tendency of the actor . . . without regard to its fulfillment in action," 1962:217). In this example, though, the semantic contribution of *katāēw-* is obscure, and it is impossible to assign either definition to it with certainty.

Finally, the second author did do some elicitation with speakers in 2004 about the relative ordering of *katāēw-* and other preverbs. The results were inconclusive: the speakers said *katāēw-māēk-* 'voluntative-on.going' and *māēk-katāēw-* 'on.going-voluntative' were both acceptable, but that there was no meaning difference. They also accepted both *katāēw-yāh-* 'voluntative-again' and *yāh-katāēw-* 'again-voluntative' without any meaning difference, although in this case they said the first was preferable.

We conclude, then, that the semantic distinctions involving *katāēw-* that Bloomfield claimed to correlate with a distinction in relative ordering are not supported by our data.

Another unexpected finding concerns four examples of doubled preverbs, cases where a given preverb occurs twice in the preverb space. See (13) and (14) show the first two examples:

(13) Aw-pes-yōm-aw-naeqnīhtwatowak.
IRR-coming-this.INAN-IRR-they.share
'They can come (tomorrow) and share (this meat).' (LB 1928:492)

(14) kew-yōs-kew-piat
HAB-here-HAB-he.comes.CONJ
'whenever anyone comes here' (LB 1928:460)

In example (13), we see two occurrences of *aw-* 'irrealis', and in (14), two occurrences of *kew-* 'habitual'. Recall that we said above that occasionally other elements are included in the preverb space. Both (13) and (14) are examples of this; each one also has an included demonstrative (*yōm* 'this inanimate' and *yōs* 'here'). Example (13) additionally includes the preverb *pes-* 'coming', which is predicted to follow *aw-*. It is not clear whether the speaker in each case intended to repeat the preverb, or whether these were just false starts that Bloomfield did not note as such.

Example (15) shows another, slightly different kind of repetition:

(15) a. Yōh-waēh-pīmakah.
reason-reason-it.comes.CONJ
'This is the reason why this came.' (FND)

b. **wāēh-yōh-āwek**
reason-reason-it.is.CONJ
'why it is' (LRB 002)

Wāēh- is the changed conjunct form of *yōh-* 'reason' (that is, it has initial change, discussed in note 4), so they do in fact represent the same lexeme, and are further examples of doubling. But both *wāēh* and *yōh* also occur as independent particles, so it is possible that the second occurrence in each example is just a particle in the preverb space. This still does not explain why the repetition occurs, however.

Ordering of the "Other" Category of Preverbs

Recall that Hockett's presentation of Bloomfield's classification leaves the 43 preverbs of the "other" class unordered. We found that these occur infrequently and follow those of Class 1 in almost all instances.

Bloomfield points out a difficulty in the analysis of forms containing these preverbs. Because they all also function as independent particles, and particles can be included in the preverb space, there is no way to distinguish an "other" preverb from the homophonous particle when the form follows a Class 1 preverb. Example (16) illustrates this potential ambiguity with Class 1 *aw-* 'irrealis' and the form *osām* 'too much':

(16) Kat 's **aw-osām-**pāqtek.
NEG AOR **IRR-too.much-**it.is.dry.CONJ
'It would not be too dry.' (PF 067)

There is simply no way to know, in an example like (16), whether *osām-* is functioning as a preverb (it is one that appears in the "other" class) or a particle. In fact, the only way to be sure an element from this class is a preverb is when it occurs first in the preverb space and is immediately preceded by a person-marking prefix, or bears initial change, because only a preverb could appear in these contexts.

This can be seen by Bloomfield's one example of an "other" class preverb showing true preverb behavior. Consider (17):

(17) *Sekāc- as a Preverb* (*Bloomfield 1962:215*)

a. Ne-**sāēkāc**-pīhāw.
   1-impatiently-I.wait.for.him
   'I impatiently await him.'

b. (aneh) **sāēkāc**-pīhācen
   that.AN impatiently.IC-he.waits.for.him.CONJ
   '(that one) whom he impatiently awaits'

In (17a), *sekāc-* 'impatiently' is the only preverb, and is preceded by the first person prefix, showing that it is truly a preverb.[12] In (17b), it is again the only preverb, and initial change has applied (accounting for the change in the first vowel), which likewise means that it has to be functioning as a preverb. Neither of these would be possible if it was an independent particle that just happened to precede the verb.

But aside from this example, we have no parallel evidence for any of the "other" preverbs: We did not find a single example with a prefix or initial change as in (17). This leaves us with an unanswerable question: Did Bloomfield actually have positive evidence that everything in his "other" class was a preverb, or was that part of what never got checked for this set? In the absence of any evidence either way, for the purposes of this project, we have assumed that they are all actually preverbs.

Setting this aside, we found only five examples (four types) out of the 1,731 tokens in our corpus where preverbs of the "other" class co-occurred. The first three are shown in (18)–(20):

(18) Eneq taeh 's **ām-pāēc**-kaehkēnaman.
   that's.it and AOR almost-properly-I.know.CONJ
   'And that's almost all I know well.' (PE 018)

(19) awāēhsaeh, **oskēh-tepēh**-apēw āwewen,
   bear first-alone-he.sits it.is.said.to.be
   'a young bear—one that had made its first den' (SM 504:34)

(20) **Anīh-tāēp**-āwew.
   finished-enough-he.is
   'He's beyond the age.' (MF, SS 2/26/04)

The first example is from a story written in a letter to Bloomfield by a fluent speaker named Amos Striker, and the second is from one of Bloomfield's published (1928) texts.[13] The third is from elicitation in 2004, and unfortunately has no further context.

The other two examples of co-occurring preverbs of the "other" class both contain *anīh-āpaehtaw-* 'finished-half':

(21) eneh-peh taeh **kayēs-anīh-āpaehtaw-nēpeh**
that-time and IC.CMPL-finished-half-it.is.summer.CONJ
'and at the time after the fourth of July' (TG 2001:241)

(22) **Anīh-āpaehtaw-tepāēhkah** cew-āwew.
finished-half-it.is.night.CONJ EPIS-it.is
'It was after midnight.' (ONE 16)

In both cases, however, *āpaehtaw-* 'half' forms a constituent with the verb that follows it: *āpaehtaw-nēpeh* is literally 'half-it is summer', or 'July', and *āpaehtaw-tepāēhkah* is literally 'half-it is night' or 'midnight'. Thus, the sequence *anīh-āpaehtaw-* 'finished-half' is not a legitimate case of co-occurrence, and this reduces our set to only three.

Given this lack of data, drawing any conclusions about the relative ordering of the "other" preverbs is simply not possible.

Examples where "other" preverbs follow Class 1 preverbs are more common—we found 68 different combinations and 222 examples. Examples (23)–(26) illustrate the most frequent of the combinations we found:

(23) Eneq 's **kēs-anīh-māwan.**
it's.then AOR CMPL-finished-I.cry.CONJ
'Then I stopped crying.' (HRN 021)

(24) 's **aw-māēhnow-wītūhkatit**
AOR IRR-well-they.work.together.CONJ
'so that they can treat each other well' (ODD 051)

(25) **Kēs-pāēc-esēkemakat.**
CMPL-properly-it.works
'It worked well.' (MH 017)

(26) **kēs-tāēp-nāēwakuaq**
CMPL-enough-I.see.them.CONJ
'(until) I've seen them enough' (CTM 007)

These four combinations represent 124 of the 222 examples, or almost 56%. Specifically, 55 are instances of *kēs-anīh-* 'completive-finished' (23), 42 are of *aw-māēhnow-* 'irrealis-well' (24), 16 are of *kēs-pāēc-* 'completive-properly' (25), and 11 are of *kēs-tāēp-* 'completive-enough' (26).

At this point, we can ask whether, based on our data, any "other" class preverbs could be shifted to Class 1. Examples where a preverb of the "other" class precedes a Class 1 preverb might provide evidence, but there are very few such examples. Examples (27) and (28) are two of the few that we have found:

(27) **Kēs-osām-katāēw-āwaek.**
CMPL-too.much-VOL-they.use.it
'They would use too much of it.' (LKL 008)

(28) **Anīh-māēk-anāmehawak.**
finished-on.going-they.pray
'(They) just finished (praying).' (MF, SS 2/26/04)

In (27), *osām-*, from the "other" class, is sandwiched between two preverbs of Class 1. This could easily be explained as a particle in the preverb space, however. In (28), "other" class *anīh-* 'finished' precedes Class 1 *māēk-* 'on-going'. However, this comes from a 2004 elicitation session in which the opposite order (*māēk-anīh-* 'on.going-finished') was also judged acceptable.

With such sparse evidence, no case can be made for moving any "other" class preverbs into Class 1.

Future Research

We turn now to topics for future research. First, while it would be interesting to look at preverb ordering across the family, we have found that relative order of preverbs is not often discussed in the literature. Furthermore, Pentland (2005:329) points out that there are few preverb cognates across the family, which would preclude comparison.

A second area of interest is the semantics of combinations of preverbs. Other works (Cook 2003; Shields 2005, 2008) have focused on the semantics of individual preverbs in Menominee, but the variable ordering we found with some of the preverbs leads to questions of scope and other semantic topics.

Finally, two aspects of our data set raise questions that are worth further examination. One is whether there are additional sources that could be added to the data. There are archival documents going back to the early 1800s that have not yet been examined on this topic. It would also be worth investigating Bloomfield's original notebooks to see whether he has additional relevant data. The fact that the lexicon contains many more preverbs than Bloomfield lists in his grammar indicates that there might be. A second avenue of approach is diachronic: Because our corpus combines data from various sources spanning almost a century, it would be worth investigating whether there are differences in preverb use and combination over time.

Conclusion

This paper has examined previous claims about preverb ordering in Menominee against a corpus of 1,731 examples containing more than one preverb per verb. We considered Cook's (2003) semantics-based ordering hypothesis and found numerous counterexamples.

However, Bloomfield's (1962) ordering of Class 1 preverbs did, for the most part, hold up, and we were able to resolve a number of questions raised by the grammar's section on preverbs, as follows:

- Although Bloomfield talks in an early section about dividing the preverbs into Class 1 and Class 2, what Hockett presents is Class 1 and an unordered "other" set. As mentioned above, Hockett speculates that "it is likely that a number of the ["other"] preverbs do belong to the first class" (1962:220). We have shown that this does not appear to be the case, and in fact Bloomfield may have stopped where he did with Class 1 because he saw the patterns that we have found in this study.

- Relatedly, we found no strong evidence for any relative ordering among the "other" preverbs, primarily due to a lack of instances of co-occurrence.
- While the ordering of the Class 1 preverbs was largely supported, we did find a modest number of counterexamples, which may point to greater flexibility in the ordering of preverbs in Menominee than Bloomfield's grammar indicates.
- Bloomfield does discuss variable ordering in the case of *katǣw-* 'voluntative future', claiming that there is a subtle difference in meaning between the two possible placements of this preverb. However, we found only three examples of *katǣw-* appearing in a different order than the predicted one, and the translations of the examples did not reveal any difference in meaning. Thus, this claim of Bloomfield's is not supported.
- Bloomfield (1962:214) also says that there is "no restriction on the number of preverbs" that can occur with a given verb, but in practice four is the maximum found.
- There are quite a few more of the uncategorized preverbs than are given in the grammar; these can be found in the *Lexicon* (1975).

Overall, our examination of a large corpus of verbs bearing multiple preverbs resulted in numerous new generalizations about their relative ordering. It also allowed us to verify most of Bloomfield's claims about preverb ordering, and to resolve numerous questions that the grammar leaves open.

NOTES

1. Menominee is presently spoken by only one or two first-language speakers, but many new speakers are being created through the tribe's vibrant language-teaching programs. We thank the fluent first-language speakers with whom the second author worked, Marie Floring, Sarah Skubitz†, and Larry Tomow†, whose knowledge of the language contributed to this paper, and the Menominee Language and Culture Commission for its guidance. We are also grateful to the audience at our UW-Madison dry run, the audience at the 54th Algonquian Conference, Joe Salmons, and two anonymous reviewers for their

comments and suggestions. The authors' names appear in alphabetical order.

2. Abbreviations used in glosses are: AN = animate, AOR = aorist, CMPL = completive, CONJ = conjunct, EMPH = emphatic, EPIS = epistemic, HAB = habitual, IC = initial change, INAN = inanimate, IRR = irrealis, NEG = negative, RED = reduplication, VOL = voluntative future. The symbol '>' is used to mean 'precedes' in linear ordering. Our source abbreviations include "LB" for Leonard Bloomfield's works, and codes for specific stories from Bloomfield (1928) that have been glossed and analyzed: CTM = Conversation of Two Men, HRN = How Red Cloud Woman Got Her Name, HV = A Husband's Vengeance, MH = Medicinal Herbs, ODD = Origin of the Dream Dance, PF = Puberty Fast, RS = Red Swan, SM = The Snake-Man, and WAW = Wäwapikuahsemit. Two stories are from Bloomfield's notebooks, CAN = Cannibalism and PE = Personal Experiences, and three are from the WNALP (1973–1976) texts, FND = Forty-Nine Dance, LKL = Legend of Keshena Lake, and ONE = Here's One for You, Here's One for Me. Abbreviations also include "TG" for Guile (2001), and LRB = Legend of the Rainbow, a story from the collection of tapes from the 1970s or 1980s. Examples also come from the second author's fieldwork with speakers Marie Floring (MF), Sarah Skubitz (SS), and Larry Tomow (LT).
3. Initial change refers to a set of morphophonological processes that apply to the first syllable of the verbal complex (the verb stem, if there is no preverb, or the first preverb if any are present). The details will not concern us here; see Bloomfield (1962:98).
4. According to Bloomfield (1962:216–217), *katāēw-* has variable ordering. We address this below.
5. The definitions given are combinations of those given in Bloomfield (1962, 1975), in some cases slightly altered by the second author.
6. Shields (2005, 2008) followed up on Cook's discussion of the semantics of preverbs in Menominee, but since Shields was not concerned with relative order, we set her work aside for present purposes.
7. The four from the "other" category are *natāw-* 'try', *yāpec-* 'repeatedly', *anīh-* 'finished', and *pāēc-* 'properly'.
8. Recall that these results are based on textual examples. If fieldwork were still possible, we could explicitly test the members of the three categories where we did not find co-occurrence, and our results might be different.
9. Cook (2003:49) also found a maximum of four in the data she examined.
10. Differences due to relative scope may account for the differences in readings; we leave this for future research.
11. There's an inconsistency in this example, in that the verb is preceded by the aorist *'s*, which requires a following conjunct order verb, yet the verb is in independent order. This

could be a performance error, or possibly just a transcription error.

12. The vowel quality and quantity change that the first syllable of the preverb undergoes is a regular effect of the metrical rules in (17a).
13. There is a footnote on the English translation of (19) that says, "Literally, 'fresh-den-sitter'; a year-old bear" (1928:505).

REFERENCES

Bloomfield, Leonard. 1928. *Menomini Texts.* Publications of the American Ethnological Society 12. New York: G.E. Stechert.

Bloomfield, Leonard. 1962. *The Menomini Language*, ed. by Charles F. Hockett. New Haven, CT: Yale University Press.

Bloomfield, Leonard. 1975. *Menominee Lexicon*, ed. by Charles F. Hockett. Milwaukee Public Museum Publications in Anthropology and History 3. Milwaukee, WI: Milwaukee Public Museum Publications.

Cook, Clare. 2003. A Semantic Classification of Menominee Preverbs. *Papers of the 34th Algonquian Conference*, ed. by H.C. Wolfart, pp. 35–56. Winnipeg: University of Manitoba.

Guile, Timothy. 2001. *An Anthology of Menominee Sayings*. Munich: Lincom Europa.

Pentland, David H. 2005. Preverbs and Particles in Algonquian. *Papers of the 36th Algonquian Conference*, ed. by H.C. Wolfart, pp. 323–338. Winnipeg: University of Manitoba.

Shields, Rebecca. 2005. Menominee Preverbs as Functional Categories. *Papers of the 36th Algonquian Conference*, ed. by H.C. Wolfart, pp. 383–406. Winnipeg: University of Manitoba.

Shields, Rebecca. 2008. The Functional Hierarchy in Menominee: Preverbs and Adverbs. *CLS 41: The Main Session*, ed. by Rodney L. Edwards, Patrick J. Midtlyng, Colin L. Sprague, and Kjersti G. Stensrud, pp. 431–444. Chicago: The Chicago Linguistic Society.

Wisconsin Native American Languages Project (WNALP). 1973–1976. University of Wisconsin–Milwaukee Archives Department. http://digital.library.wisc.edu/1711.dl/wiarchives.uw-mil-uwmmss0020.

Temperature Expressions in the Miami-Illinois Corpus

Hunter Thompson Lockwood

Miami-Illinois is an academic cover term for a tightly related group of varieties attested from the late 17th to the mid 20th century in documentation that now serves as the foundation for a vibrant and growing base of language speakers (Costa 2003, 2021).[1] This paper presents the results of an investigation into the linguistics of temperature in Miami-Illinois, as part of a broader investigation into measurement and scalar terms in Miami-Illinois requested by language teachers and learners of the Myaamia Center. The findings support prior theories of temperature typology: A full suite of basic temperature components denoting 'hot', 'warm', and 'cold' can be found for ambient, tactile, and personal-feeling temperature categories (cf. Lockwood and Vejdemo 2015 for Ojibwe).

Positionality Note

I begin by briefly describing my relationship to the question at hand (which, as Rice 2022 notes, is offered even by Bishop Baraga's grammar of Ojibwe). I am a settler, a non-Native linguist who grew up on land ceded by Ottawa and Ojibwe people in the 1836 Treaty of Washington. I have worked with Ojibwe speakers since 2007 and Potawatomi speakers since 2010, and since 2015 have been involved with various Miami-Illinois language projects. Today, I work for the Miami Tribe of Oklahoma, as a research linguist under David Costa in the Language Research Office of the Myaamia Center at Miami University in Oxford, Ohio.

The Miami-Illinois Language

As the name may imply, the corpus of Miami-Illinois can be divided into a Miami half, gathered in the 1800s and 1900s by mostly nonlinguists working among Miami, Peoria, and Wea people in what is now Oklahoma and Indiana, and an older Illinois half, gathered by French missionaries in the late 1600s and early 1700s working among Peoria, Kaskaskia, and Tamaroa people (Costa 2003:2–7). The oldest sources form the majority of the documentation.

Citation Practices

Examples cited in this paper follow a four-line glossing standard illustrated below:

(1) a. Example in community orthography
b. 'gloss or translation in single quotes'
c. Document (Page#-Line#-Phrase#)
d. <original script> 'original gloss' (retranslation)

Lines one (1a) and two (1b) provide my analysis of the form and meaning, following the standards used by the speech community today. Everything below that line is bibliographic, marked by line three (1c), which is the source of the form. Line four (1d) contains a transcription of the form as it was written in that source, and, when the occasion demands it, a retranslation of the French into English.

An actually attested example, given in this format, is as follows:

(2) lipansiinwi
'It is not cold.'
Largillier (511-20-2)
<ripansin8i> 'Il ne fait pas froid.'

In this straightforward case, we can see both the phonemicized forms in the modern community orthography (line 1) and the original transcription from the primary source (line 4, in angle brackets). In other cases, for a variety of historical and linguistic reasons, either the form or the gloss in line 4 (or both) may not match what we give in lines 1 and 2. Presenting examples in this manner and giving the name of the document and page, line, and phrase numbers (on line 3) enable readers to navigate directly to the example under discussion as it was originally written, hosted on the Indigenous Language Digital Archive (ILDA) interface (discussed below), with the caveat that occasionally page, line, and phrase numbers fluctuate as analysis continues.[2]

Structure of the Miami-Illinois Verb

Because there is no lexical class of adjectives, all expressions of temperature use verbs in the language, so a brief overview of Algonquian verbal morphology is crucial to understanding the expression of temperature in Miami-Illinois.

In Algonquian languages, a verb stem is typically understood to be composed of at most three pieces conventionally called components. The three components are INITIALS, MEDIALS, and FINALS, and they are named for their position.

An example with all three is given next; the initial and final are bolded.

(3) **kiišoo**kam**iteewi**
'It is warm liquid.'
LeBoullenger (130-21-3)
<kich8gamite8i> (unglossed in original)

Initials typically have the broadest swath of meanings and are sometimes considered an open lexical class. In the example above, the initial appears as *kiišoo-* and means 'warm'. Medials are typically the most restricted, usually just to verbal classifiers or nominal meanings like body parts. In the example above, the medial appears as *-kam-* and means that the verb is describing a liquid, like water or coffee. Finals often carry lexical meanings but also encode grammatical category. For verbs, the finals establish four verb categories based on animacy and transitivity: inanimate intransitive (inanimate subject, intransitive verb); animate intransitive (animate subject, intransitive verb); transitive inanimate (inanimate object, transitive verb); and transitive animate (animate object, transitive verb). In the example above, the final appears as *-itee*, and it is an inanimate intransitive verb final that means something like 'it is hot or warm'. I revisit this initial and final in the discussion below.

The basic temperature components of Miami-Illinois are all either initials or finals. This is the expected situation, following the summary just given, and it matches precisely the grammatical situation for temperature-denoting expressions in Ojibwe-Potawatomi (Lockwood and Vejdemo 2015).

In more traditional linguistic terms, these components are the surface constituents in primary derivation, and roughly map to morphemes. However, as we will see below, the components themselves can sometimes appear to consist of multiple morphemes, which I take here as evidence of historical change rather than of internal complexity (for extended discussion and a proposal, see Macaulay and Salmons 2017).

Methodology and the ILDA Corpus

As mentioned above, the Miami-Illinois corpus spans several centuries and multiple language varieties. In order to organize these thousands of manuscript pages and create language resources for community members, the Myaamia Center created and hosts the Indigenous Languages Digital Archive, or ILDA (Miami Tribe of Oklahoma 2023). As of the time of this writing, there are over 90,000 entries, each one a token of language as recorded from a speaker who unfortunately is not known in most instances. The text in these documents has been made freely available to the public through a searchable Web interface, connecting the research output of the Myaamia Center with community members in a direct and visible way. Note, however, that data entry and analysis on ILDA are ongoing, so not all sources have been entered at equal paces. As such, I will avoid giving quantitative analyses, which quickly change as more data continues to come online, and encourage interested readers to visit the ILDA web interface (Miami Tribe of Oklahoma 2023) to explore the language for themselves.

On the Study Itself

Data for this study come from several primary and secondary sources. First and foremost, I used the ILDA platform to search for English and French temperature terms which are in common use (hot, cold, warm, etc.). After establishing a list of potential temperature-denoting components, the ILDA platform was then used to search for these specific parts of words. I then examined Costa's published and unpublished documentary material on Miami-Illinois, especially the grammar (Costa 2003) and his manuscript etymological dictionary (cited as Costa 2022), with discussions with community language educators (e.g., at a brownbag lunch on the topic), and by reviewing various tribally developed educational materials like the dictionary (Miami Tribe of Oklahoma 2023).

Some Limitations of the Method

While typological studies of temperature expressions in Indigenous languages usually involve fieldwork and direct elicitation from native speakers (Bowern and Kling 2015; Lockwood and Vejdemo 2015), this is not possible in Miami-Illinois. As such, we are instead forced to glean the semantics of temperature expressions from translations into 19th century English or Early Modern French. The latter situation is far more common; not only is most of the Miami-Illinois corpus from the Illinois period, as mentioned above, but while the bulk of the work for this paper was being done (2021–2022), the ILDA corpus had a more complete collection of the old Illinois material than the modern Miami material. As such, the current analysis focuses heavily on the oldest sources from the first quarter of the 18th century: Largillier (n d.; ca. 1700), LeBoullenger (n.d.; ca. 1725), and Pinet (n.d.; ca. 1702).

Typologizing Temperature

In this section, I define and contextualize the core concepts that guided my analysis.

Basic Temperature Terms

For practical purposes, temperature typology begins with Estonian linguist Urmas Sutrop's paper (1998:60) exploring the extent to which the notion of basic color terms (after Berlin and Kay 1969) might have an equivalent across another sense (see also Koptjevskaja-Tamm and Rakhilina 2006 for a contemporary acknowledgment of Sutrop's influence). The concept of a basic temperature term is mapped to the domain of temperature directly from Berlin and Kay's notion of a basic color term. Thus, following the famous color studies, Sutrop (1998:61) postulated that a basic temperature term has three basic properties. First, it should be "psychologically salient." Despite this notion being a central part of his model, he does not define or illustrate what that might mean. Second, a basic temperature term should be "in most cases morphologically simple." This criterion would come under fire from later scholars including Koptjevskaja-Tamm and Rakhilina (2006), who note the need to distinguish diachronic from synchronic complexity, and Lockwood and Vejdemo (2015), whose study of Ojibwe argues against the complexity criterion entirely. The least controversial criteria are that the basic temperature terms should be "[in most cases] native," as opposed to borrowed, and that a basic temperature term "generally denotes the quality of temperature," applicable equally to all domains, from weather to animate or inanimate objects.

Basic Temperature Categories: Types of Temperatures

Perhaps the most significant update to Sutrop's initial exploration of basic temperature terms comes from Koptjevskaja-Tamm and Rakhilina (2006), who compare temperature terms in Swedish and Russian. They found that languages may distinguish TACTILE from non-tactile temperature expressions, either across the entire temperature spectrum or only for a subset of the broader scale. For instance, they argued, in Russian, the 'hot' domain distinguishes tactile from non-tactile temperature in a way that the 'cold' domain does not, unlike Swedish. Later work brings in other languages (see Koptjevskaja-Tamm 2015 for a more thorough exposition) and goes on to further subdivide the non-tactile category into AMBIENT and PERSONAL-FEELING temperature expressions.

That is the approach taken in this paper, as summarized in (4) here:

(4) a. AMBIENT temperature expressions are non-referential descriptions (e.g., cold weather, cold temperature in a room)

b. PERSONAL-FEELING temperature expressions involve sentient experiencers (e.g., feeling cold)

c. TACTILE temperature expressions describe thermal properties of an entity (e.g., cold cup of coffee, cold ice cream)

These "basic temperature frames" (Koptejvskaja-Tamm 2022) are widely shared cross-linguistically, and in Algonquian have been documented at least for the Ojibwe-Potawatomi subgroup (Lockwood and Vejdemo 2015) and, as I will show in the following, for Miami-Illinois.

Previous Studies of Temperature in Algonquian Languages

Few studies of Algonquian temperature terms exist. Pentland's work on "verbs of precipitation" (Pentland 1996) is a near exception. However, Pentland's goal there was to examine a particular set of verbs having to do with natural processes like rain and snow. To be sure, there are overlaps between precipitation and temperature expressions; however, the lexical-semantic typology approach to temperature outlined above forces us to ignore words that denote weather. A more holistic investigation of Miami-Illinois temperature would have to take verbs of precipitation into account.[3]

General reference sources on particular Algonquian languages sometimes do not discuss temperature or weather expressions in depth or at all; Lockwood and Vejdemo (2015) relied heavily on a few pages of temperature expressions collected by Valentine (2001) to form the basis for their investigation of temperature terms in a variety of Ojibwe spoken by a fluent speaker from Manitoulin Island, Ontario. Using acceptability judgments, they constructed temperature scales in the three basic temperature frames and found they were clearly differentiated in the grammar; for instance, classifiers were practically required in the expression of tactile temperature but had limited acceptability with personal feeling temperature expressions.

Most centrally, Lockwood and Vejdemo (2015) found that the basic temperature-denoting unit in Ojibwe was the component rather than the word or stem; there were clear instances of temperature-denoting components in use across ambient, tactile, and personal-feeling temperature expressions but few whole words. These basic temperature components, rather than basic temperature words, are initials and finals that otherwise meet all of Sutrop's criteria for basicness. This turns out to be a useful frame with which to approach the Miami-Illinois material; most of the basic temperature components discussed by Lockwood and Vejdemo (2015) in their study of Ojibwe are shared widely across the family and have clear cognates in the Miami-Illinois forms given below, like Ojibwe *giizhoo-* 'hot' and Miami-Illinois *kiišaw-* 'warm'. I return to the question of a comparison of the two systems in the conclusion, but a full reconstruction of Algonquian temperature morphology is beyond the scope of this paper.

Summary of Findings: Inventory by Domain

A full suite of temperature-denoting components can be found in the archival material, across all the basic temperature frames. The rest of this section walks through the most likely candidates for basic temperature components in Miami-Illinois, beginning first with the 'hot' domain and finishing with the 'cold' domain.

Expressions of Heat

In the 'hot' domain, there are commonly used initials and finals that are basic temperature components. The three basic temperature initials are given here:

(5) *kišaapihk-* 'hot'

(6) *ap-* 'warm'

(7) *kiišaw-* 'warm'

I discuss each in turn.

The initial *kišaapihk-* 'hot' must be historically derived from the collocation of initial *kiš-* 'hot' plus the classifier medial *-aapihk-* 'metal, inorganic solid'. But even going back to the earliest records of the language, temperature expressions with *kišaapihk-* 'hot' are used in the absence of any nouns to classify.

Frustratingly, the nature of the data—mostly dictionaries and wordlists—is such that there are many ambiguous examples.

(8) **kiišaapihkiteeki**
'It (inan.) is hot.'
Trowbridge (192-5-1)
<Kishōpekitaak> 'hot (applied to tangible substances)'

In this word, *-aapihk-* could be functioning as a medial, but without context it is impossible to know. However, in the example below it is used for an expression of personal feeling temperature (see Costa 2003 for discussion of the changes in dependent verbs).

(9) **kiišaapihkisita**
'S/he has a fever.'
Largillier (188-31-1)
<Kichabikisita> 'qui rostit, malade qui est en feu en sa fievre' (who roasts, a sick person on fire because of their fever)

There is no possible interpretation of this word where *-aapihk-* can function as a medial. In the example below, *kiišaapihk-* 'hot' appears in an expression of ambient temperature.

(10) **kiišaapihk**kaahkoteeki kaahkiihkwe
'It is a hot day.'
Gatschet (1895:712-4-1)
<kishapkaxkutätí káxkikwe> 'heat of the day. Said also of the heated area around a big fire, house burning, etc.'

Again, there is no possible interpretation of this sentence where *-aapihk-* is a medial. The older form *kiš-* 'hot' also appears in the record, as below, but does not recur across every basic temperature frame the way the basic temperature components do.

(11) nin**kiš**ahaan
I heat it up.'
LeBoullenger (356-37-2)
<nikichahan> 'Je fais rechaufer cela.' (I reheat this.)

In the example above the initial *kiš-* 'hot' appears without initial change, in one of the few instances where it is attested.

There are two forms that are glossed as 'warm': *ap-* 'warm' and *kiišaw-* 'warm'. The differences between them are not entirely clear. Beginning with *ap-*, the Early Modern French gloss on the temperature expression below, which strikes me as ambiguous between tactile and ambient temperature, may indicate that *ap-* is hotter than *kiišaw-*.

(12) **apeteewi**
'It is warm, hot.'
Largillier (46-7-1)
<Apete8i> 'chaud, rechauffé' (hot, reheated)

These effects are not consistent and may just be an artifact of translation; the personal feeling temperature expression below does not necessarily hint at being particularly warm.

(13) **nintapinehkiisi**
'I warm my hands.'
Largillier (48-36-1)
<nitapinekisi> '[Je presente] les mains [au feu].' (I warm my hands by the fire.)

Further research may shed light on this.

The second 'warm' component, *kiišaw-*, appears below in an expression of personal feeling temperature.

(14) **ninkiišawapi**
'I sit warmly.'
Largillier (189-13-1)
<Nikicha8api> 'Je suis chaudement.' (Lit. 'I am warmly')

Because the phonetic content of the original Old Illinois word has been so clearly recorded, the derivational structure ('warm' plus 'sit') can be easily reconstructed, with a meaning composed straightforwardly (cf. Ojibwe *giizhoobi* 's/he sits in a warm place, live in a warm house'). But the original French gloss deserves a remark; "I am warmly" is marginally grammatical in both the English and French forms presented above. Despite lacking a full philological exploration of the French in these manuscripts, we can confidently describe at least two potential explanations for this mismatch. First, because these dictionaries are handwritten, the scribes frequently employ shorthand (including a dizzying array of Latin abbreviations). The original writer may have simply omitted a word that was obvious in his original context.

Second is the simple issue of grammatical variation in Early Modern French, some combination of syntactic and regional; similar alternations of adjective and adverb persist in both English and French.

Kiišaw- 'warm' also appears in expressions of tactile temperature, as below where it appears alongside a classifier medial, realized here as *-kam-*, which restricts the reference of the verb to liquids (cf. Lockwood and Vejdemo 2015 for discussion of Ojibwe classifier medials in temperature expressions).

(15) **kiišoo**kamiteewi
'It is warm liquid.'
LeBoullenger (130-21-3)
<kich8gamite8i> (unglossed in orig.)

Further research may be able to establish a distinction between these two 'warm' components.

The 'by heat' finals are very common and cognates are shared across the family.

(16) the 'by heat' final
a. inanimate intransitive *-etee*
b. animate intransitive *-esi*
c. transitive inanimate *-esam*
d. transitive animate *-esw*

We have seen several examples of this already; two are repeated below. In the first, an inanimate intransitive verb attested from the modern Miami materials is explicitly glossed as a tactile temperature expression.

(17) kiišaapihk**iteeki**
'It (inan.) is hot.'
Trowbridge (192-5-1)
<Kishōpekitaak> 'hot (applied to tangible substances)'

Since inanimate intransitive verbs can also be used without referencing a subject, they can be ambiguously tactile or ambient; clarifying glosses and appropriate context are not always provided. In the next example, the animate intransitive verb 'have a fever' uses this same component.

(18) kiišaapihkisita
'S/he has a fever.'
Largillier (188-31-1)
<Kichabikisita> 'qui rostit, malade qui est en feu en sa fievre'

Expressions of Cold

There are two 'cold' initials, listed below.

(19) lip- 'cold'

(20) tahk- 'cold'

At present, I am not confident in a distinction between these, and it does not appear to be the case that one is especially colder than the other. In the first example below, *lip-* 'cold' appears with initial change in a personal feeling temperature expression.[4]

(21) leepacita
'S/he is cold.'
Largillier (505-15-1)
<Ripatchi8a> 'frilleux a Nirepatchi' (sensitive to cold, from "Nirepatchi")

The original French gloss is peculiar here in two ways. First, the scribe's choice to spell *frileux* with <ll> would have been an archaic practice even at the time of writing; second, our choice was to translate *frileux* 'susceptible to cold' as the relatively neutral 'cold', which is closer to the etymological sense of its Latin source. Archaisms like this are fairly common; the authors of these manuscripts knew and frequently used Latin.[5]

In the next example, *lip-* appears in an expression that in English and Miami-Illinois is ambiguous between ambient and tactile temperature; in French, it is unambiguously ambient.

(22) lipansiinwi
'It is not cold.'
Largillier (511-20-2)
<ripansin8i> 'Il ne fait pas froid.'

The example of *tahk-* 'cold' below is a tactile temperature expression:

(23) teehkaahkwahki
'It is frozen wood.'
Largillier (534-7-1)
<tacacat8i> 'bois froid, gelé, ou autre chose froide couverte par desus de frimas' (cold wood, frozen, or some other cold thing covered in hoarfrost)

Currently, the clearest examples of *tahk-* I have are tactile; further research will have to confirm whether that is (or is part of) the distinction between the two 'cold' forms.

There is also a full set of finals, which I conventionally gloss as 'by cold'. The gloss is, admittedly, awkward, which reflects a somewhat awkward status.

(24) the 'by cold' final
a. inanimate intransitive *-aten*
b. animate intransitive *-aci*
c. transitive inanimate *-acitoo*
d. transitive animate *-acim* or *-atem*

In the example below, the transitive animate 'cold' final is used in a personal feeling temperature expression.

(25) nintayiilatemikwa
'He makes me cold.'
Largillier (23-27-2)
<Nitaïratemig8a> 'Il me fait avoir froid.'

In the next example, it is used in what is likely a tactile temperature expression.

(26) ciilatenwi
'It is extremely cold.'
Largillier (561-25-1)
<Tchiraten8i> 'bien gelé'

Although this form could be ambiguously ambient in English, the gloss strongly hints that this form is referential.

Conclusion

This paper presents an investigation of the linguistics of temperature in Miami-Illinois, as part of a broader investigation into measurement and scalar expressions, one of many such requested by members of the community. I round out the discussion with a brief comparison of the Miami-Illinois temperature term system with Ojibwe, one of the few Algonquian languages where temperature terms have been studied in detail.

As noted, Lockwood and Vejdemo argue that there are only basic temperature components rather than words in Ojibwe, and that they are all either initials or finals. Miami-Illinois certainly fits into that mold; it makes more sense to talk about basic temperature initials and basic temperature finals than basic temperature words or stems. With that adjustment to the concept of basic temperature terms, we have seen that the finals attest a two-term system, a simple hot–cold binary with one component for each, conventionally referred to here as the 'by hot' and 'by cold' finals. The initials attest five terms, one in the 'hot' category and two each in the 'warm' and 'cold' categories, although currently I am unable to differentiate these terms. This is basically the same as Lockwood and Vejdemo's analysis of Ojibwe, although they did not at that time find sufficient examples of the 'cold' final to analyze it in detail and entirely missed the presence of the Ojibwe cognate for Miami-Illinois *ap-* 'warm'. And of course, unlike Ojibwe, Miami-Illinois has *kišaapihk-* 'hot' as basic, replacing *kiš-* (cognate of Ojibwe *gizh-* 'hot'), which still appears in a limited number of forms.

Like Ojibwe, the corpus attests the use of the final meaning 'lay, lie, fall' to denote falling or fallen temperatures, as in the example here:

(27) Sakaanki teehkihsenki.
'Eventually, it cooled off.'
Gatschet (1895:363-11-1)
<sakángi teksengi> 'quite a while | cooled off'

Like Ojibwe, basic, generic temperature words tend to be initial–final structure where both pieces denote temperature, but unlike Ojibwe, classifier medials do not seem to be as strongly required, although the evidence is still limited here. Finally, Ojibwe has a system of describing neutral temperatures by using the preverb *mino-* 'good'; no similar system appears to exist in the Miami-Illinois documentation.

NOTES

1. I am grateful to everyone at the Myaamia Center for their comments and questions along the way as this paper developed, to two anonymous reviewers for their helpful and formative feedback, and to the editors of this volume.
2. An additional discovery aid comes in the form of ILDA's tag system; a search of "temperature" in the Semantic field will reveal hundreds of examples of temperature expressions that have been appropriately tagged.
3. In this paper, I do not address the extent to which cultural, ideological, spiritual, and/or discursive factors in the co-construction of language documentation play a role in temperature expressions, although I wonder whether Pentland was potentially correct in noting that "the English preoccupation with the weather appears to be unique" (Pentland 1996:339).
4. The scribe added *a Nirepatchi* to provide a comparison to <Ripatchi8a>; we did not include that in the retranslation.
5. I would probably translate "sensitive to cold" with the secondary final *-ihki* 'habitually' (the so-called "verb of addiction").

REFERENCES

Berlin, Brent, and Paul Kay. 1969. *Basic Color Terms*. Berkeley: University of California Press.

Bowern, Claire, and Laura Kling. 2015. Bardi Temperature Terms. *The Linguistics of Temperature*, ed. by Maria Koptjevskaja-Tamm, pp. 815–831. Amsterdam: John Benjamins Publishing.

Costa, David. 2003. *The Miami-Illinois Language*. Lincoln: University of Nebraska Press.

Costa, David. 2021 sk and sp in Illinois. 53rd Algonquian Conference, Ottawa, Canada, October 14.

Costa, David. 2022. Miami-Illinois Etymological Dictionary. Unpublished manuscript, Myaamia Center at Miami University, Oxford, OH.

Gatschet, Albert. 1895. Notes on Peoria. Manuscript 236, National Anthropological Archives, Smithsonian Institution.

Koptjevskaja-Tamm, Maria (ed.). 2015. *The Linguistics of Temperature*. Amsterdam: John Benjamins Publishing Company.

Koptjevskaja-Tamm, Maria. 2022. Semantic Maps and Temperature: Capturing the Lexicon-Grammar Interface across Languages. *Zeitschrift für Sprachwissenschaft* 41(1):125–177.

Koptjevskaja-Tamm, Maria, and Ekaterina V. Rakhilina. 2006. "Some Like it Hot": On the Semantics of Temperature Adjectives in Russian and Swedish. *Language Typology and*

Universals 59(3):253–269.

Largillier, Jacques S. J. [n.d., ca. 1700] Illinois–French Dictionary. Manuscript, Watkinson Library, Trinity College, Hartford, CT.

LeBoullenger, Antoine-Robert, S. J. [n.d, ca. 1725] French and Miami-Illinois Dictionary. Manuscript at the John Carter Brown Library, Brown University, Providence, RI.

Lockwood, Hunter, and Susanne Vejdemo. 2015. "There Is No Thermostat in the Forest"—The Ojibwe Temperature Term System. *The Linguistics of Temperature*, ed. by Maria Koptjevskaja-Tamm, pp. 721–741. Amsterdam: John Benjamins Publishing.

Macaulay, Monica, and Joseph Salmons. 2017. Synchrony and Diachrony in Menominee Derivational Morphology. *Morphology* 27:179–215.

Miami Tribe of Oklahoma. 2023. *The Indigenous Languages Digital Archive*. ilaatawaakani.org.

Pentland, David H. 1996. Verbs of Precipitation in Algonquian. *Nikotwâsik Iskwâhtêm, Pâskihtêpayih! Studies in Honour of H. C. Wolfart*, ed. by John D. Nichols and Arden C. Ogg, 337–354. Winnipeg: Manitoba.

Pinet, Pierre-François. [n.d., ca. 1702] French–Miami-Illinois dictionary. Manuscript, Archives des jésuites au Canada, Montréal, Québec.

Rice, Mskwaankwad. 2022. Power and Positionality: A Case Study of Linguistics' Relationship to Indigenous Peoples. *Proceedings of the Linguistic Society of America* 7(1):5295.

Sutrop, Urmas. 1998. Basic Temperature Terms and Subjective Temperature Scale. *Lexicology* 4:60–104.

Trowbridge, Charles. [n.d.] Notes on the Kickapoo. Manuscript at the Bentley Historical Library, University of Michigan, Ann Arbor.

Valentine, J. Randolph. 2001. *Nishnaabemwin Reference Grammar*. Toronto: University of Toronto Press.

Relational Meanings in Ojibwe

Richard A. Rhodes

When I first started at the University of California, Berkeley, Len Talmy was building a theory about how language structures space and how motion is lexicalized across languages (Talmy 1983, 1985).[1] In the hope of incorporating Ojibwe in his theory, he asked me to translate one of his standard sentences into Ojibwe. The sentence was: *The bottle floated into the cave*. He wanted to know how the spatial relationship between the bottle and the cave is expressed and how aspects of the bottle's motion are coded in the Ojibwe verb. I immediately recognized that any straightforward translation would be awkward Ojibwe, so I declined to give one. At the time I couldn't put my finger on what the problem was, but now, 30-plus years later, I finally understand enough Ojibwe structure to give a coherent account of the problem. How are spatial relations expressed in Ojibwe? And how are the various aspects of motion coded? This paper will focus on the former question.

In most languages, the kinds of spatial relationships Talmy was interested in are primarily expressed with adpositional constructions. In Talmy's sentence the relationship between the bottle and the cave is expressed in the prepositional phrase *into the cave*. Of course, most languages have a range of constructions for expressing spatial relations. Many elaborate simple adpositional phrases. In English, for example, we see several such constructions in (1). All crucially involve prepositions or adverbial particles morphologically related to prepositions.

(1) English constructions expressing containment
  a. The ball is **in** the box.
  b. The ball is **inside** (**of**) the box.
  c. Put the ball **in**(**to**) the box.
  d. Put the ball **in**.

Even though the basic syntax of adpositional phrases is alike, it is important to recognize that the syntax of adpositional morphemes is not a direct reflection of the spatial configuration. Even in the case where adpositions refer to closely related spatial configurations, their syntax may differ. Take, for example, English *in* and *out*, which are both relations with respect to containment but *out* is only a particle while *in* is either a particle or a preposition.

(2) Differences between *in* (particle/preposition) and *out* (particle)
  a. Particle syntax

He walked **in**.	He walked **out**.
He walked **into** the room.	He walked **out of** the room.

  b. Prepositional syntax

He walked **in** the room.	*He walked **out** the room.

The crucial takeaway is that even for prepositions for which the syntax is not particularly complex, the morphosyntax is not just a simple reflection of the semantics. This is important for understanding the morphosyntax of Ojibwe spatial relations, which employs a range of constructions with radically different syntax than adpositional phrases. There is almost no literature directly on this topic. What there is appears incidentally in work on a different research point. See, for example, Kilroe (1991).

Most languages use adpositional constructions as the primary means of specifying spatial relations. But Ojibwe and Algonquian in general make almost no use of adpositions (Rhodes 2010a). The Ojibwe morphology expressing spatial relationships shows up most often as the root or initial in the verb, or as a complex adverbial, or both. A typical example of this can be seen in a sentence from a story by Anna Gibbs (2010), where the pieces of morphology that correspond are highlighted in parallel, either underlined or in bold.[2]

(3) Examples of Ojibwe spatial relations in text

Agongos giiwed waabamaad abinid mitgoon **imaa mitakamig**,

agongos	giiwe-d	waabam-aa-d	abi-ni-d	mitgw-an	**imaa mita-kamig**
chipmunk	return-3	see.AN-3.OBJ-3	be.there-OBV-3	tree-OBV	there bare-ground

zhaaboba'iwed bagonezinind **mitigoon**

zhaabw-iba'iwe-d	bagonezinind	**mitigoon**
through-run.from-3	have.hole-OBV-3	tree-OBV

'While escaping the chipmunk saw a log there on **the bare ground**, and ran away through **the log** but it had a hole.'[3] (Gibbs 2010:78[4])

The constructions of interest in (3) abstracted from their respective clauses are given in (4) with their word class and morphosyntactic roles indicated.

(4) Ojibwe spatial relation constructions

a. tree in relation to the ground

...	abi[nid]	mitigoon	imaa mitakamig
gloss:	be.there	tree	there on.bare.ground
word class:	verb	noun	adverbial
morphosyntax:	relative root	subject	relative root complement

b. chipmunk in relation to the tree

...	zhaabo-ba'iwe[d]	Ø	mitigoon
gloss:	through-run.from	(chipmunk)	tree
word class:	verb	Ø	noun
morphosyntax:	initial	subject	secondary object

The fact that these Algonquian constructions are typologically rare (Rhodes 2006, 2010b) can make the data seem more complex than they are. All that is important to understand at this point in the discussion is that verbs and adverbials rather than adpositions are central to the Ojibwe expression of spatial relations. To understand how these constructions work we need to understand how the spatial relations are structured cognitively, so we turn to Talmy's work on that subject.

One of the most important results from Talmy's work on spatial relations is the recognition that such relations are perceptually asymmetric. In his groundbreaking study "How Language Structures Space" (Talmy 1983:230–231), Talmy shows that the effect of this asymmetry is to impose an interpretation on spatial and geometrical relationships between objects not present in the physical world. We think we are speaking objectively if we say The glass is on the table. But, as Talmy points out, there is a significant conceptual asymmetry between the glass and the table (1983:232–233). Based on what we know about glasses and tables, we automatically foreground the glass and background the table, and we express that asymmetry in language. We locate the glass with respect to the table and not vice versa. It is truly odd to say The table is under the glass.

There is a widely accepted terminology for the conceptual roles in spatial expressions. It is due to Langacker (1987:217ff). The foregrounded role is called the TRAJECTOR and the backgrounded role the LANDMARK. Talmy and Langacker both focused on English, where spatial relationships are expressed primarily as prepositions, but the Ojibwe constructions require a way to talk about the conceptual role specifying the relationship, that is, the role prepositions play in languages that work the way English does. We use the term RELATOR to label that role. In Ojibwe there are various ways relators are realized.

One important consequence of the fact that landmarks are backgrounded is that they tend to occur in limited morphosyntactic configurations. Trajectors on the other hand appear in a wide variety of morphosyntactic configurations with respect to the relator–landmark complex. In the example sentences in (5) we see that the morphosyntactic treatment of the landmark underlined is the object of a preposition, but the morphosyntactic relation between the preposition phrase and the trajector (in boldface) is different in each sentence. Note that in all the sentences in (5) the conceptualization of the spatial relation between the glass and the table is the same.

(5) Different syntactic configurations for trajectors (in bold) and landmarks (underlined)
The glass is on the table.
There is **a glass** on the table.
Bring me **the glass** that is on the table.
The glass on the table is dirty.

In English there are a few morphologically bound relator–landmark pairs. Some examples are given in (6).

(6) Fused landmarks and relators

home (= at home)

ashore (= on the shore)

asea (= at sea) (mostly metaphorical now)

abed (= in bed) (archaic)

In Ojibwe such one-word locative expressions are a regular way of jointly realizing relators and landmarks. They occur in two variants: initial–final constructions, as in (7), and prenoun–noun constructions, as in (8).

(7) Examples of relator and landmark in initial+final construction

aajisag	'in the next room'	(aaj-isag	partition-wood)
agaamajiw	'across on the other hill'	(agaam-ajiw	other.side-hill)
anaamaabik	'under a/the rock'	(anaam-aabik	under-rock)
biindoonag	'in a/the boat'	(biind-oonag	in-boat)
ishkwekana	'at the end of the road/trail'	(ishkwe-kana	at.the.end-path)
jiigaakwaa(ng)	'near the woods'	(jiig-aakwaa	near-woods)
mishawikwam	'out on the ice'	(mishaw-ikwam	in.open.area-ice)
naawagaam	'in the middle of the lake'	(naaw-agaam	in.middle.of-water)
ogidaagonag	'on top of the snow'	(ogid-aagonag	on.top.of-snow)
zaagidaw	'at the mouth of a/the river'	(zaag-idaw	out-??)

(8) Examples of relator and landmark in prenoun+noun construction

agaami-oodena	'across town'	(agaami=oodena	across=town)
anaami-nibaagan	'under the bed'	(anaami=nibaagan	under=bed)
biinji-waazh	'in a/the den/cave'	(biinji=waazh	in=cave)
ishkwe-minis	'at the end of the island'	(ishkwe=minis	at.the.end=island)
jiigi-baawitig	'by the rapids'	(jiigi=baawitig	near=rapids)
naawi-ziibi	'in the middle of the river'	(naawi=ziibi	in.middle.of=river)
ogiji-odoopowin	'on the table'	(ogiji=odoopowin	on.top.of=table)

Coming from English there is a temptation to look at the forms in (7) and (8) and think that the Ojibwe construction is just a kind of funny prepositional phrase. But it should be noted that Algonquian initial–final and prenoun–noun constructions are normally used for encoding modifier–modificand, as exemplified in (9).

The expression of the relator–landmark complex simply piggybacks on general morphosyntactic constructions.

(9) a. Modifier as initial in initial+final noun construction

ozaawakik	'brass kettle'	(ozaaw-akik	yellow-kettle)
amikwayaan	'beaver pelt'	(amikw-ayaan	beaver-hide)
niswaabik	'three dollars'	(nishw-aabik	three-metal)

b. Modifier as noun in prenoun+noun construction

misko-waagosh	'red fox (Vulpes vulpes)'	(misko=waagosh	red=fox)
wiigwaasi-jiimaan	'birchbark canoe'	(wiigwaasi=jiimaan	birchbark=boat)
niizho-biboon	'two years'	(niizho=biboon	two=winter)

Because landmarks are backgrounded, they are often underspecified and the exact reference needs to be calculated pragmatically. When a landmark is fully backgrounded an initial–final construction is used, with the whatchamacallit root *ay-* as the final. *Ay-* otherwise only appears as a nominal root in the forms given in (10).

(10) Whatchamacallit pronominals

aya'aa	NA	'whatsisname, whatsername'
aya'ii	NI	'whatchamacallit'
(in)daya'iim	NID	'(my) stuff' (stem -aya'iim)
odaya'iimi	VAI	'he has property' (verb of possession)
odaya'aami	VAI	'he has dependents' (verb of possession)

Examples of the implicit landmark construction are given in (11).

(11) Implicit landmark construction

naawaya'ii	'in the middle (of it)'	(naaw-aya'ii	in.middle.of-thing)
zhaabwaya'ii	'through (it)'	(zhaabw-aya'ii	through=thing)
ishkwe-aya'ii	'at the end (of it)'	(ishkwe-aya'ii	at.the.end=thing)
ogij-aya'ii	'on top (of it)'	(ogij-aya'ii	on top=thing)

Here's an example of the use of an implicit landmark in a sentence.

(12) Textual example of an implicit landmark construction
Ogii-kikenimaa' anaamaya'ii danwewidaminid.
o-gii=gikenim-aa-a' **anaam-aya'ii** dan-wewidam-ini-d.
3.PST=know-3.AN-OBV.PL under-thing there-speak.noisily-OBV-3.CONJ
'She knew by the sound of their voices that they were down inside.' (Jones 1917:4)

Sometimes the spatial relation can be calculated from the nature of the landmark and/or the frame referenced by the verb and no relator is used. Ojibwe commonly uses simple nouns inflected as locatives in this way, leaving the spatial relation between the landmark and its trajector unspecified. Such locatives function syntactically as adverbials and semantically as landmarks, as in (13). Nothing in the morphology in (13) specifies the spatial relation between the trajector, *awiya* 'someone', and the landmark, *obikwan* '(Nenabozh's) back'.

(13) Textual example of an unspecified relator
Baanimaa go miinawaa obikwanaang owiya nwaandawaad.
baanimaa go miinawaa **o-bikwan-aang** owiya cc.noondaw-aa-d.
later emph again 3.POSS-back-LOC someone cc-hear-3.AN-3.CONJ
'Again, a bit later, right behind him he heard some creature.' (Jones 1917:114)

When we translate such locatives, English demands the specification of an explicit locative relationship, but it is only pragmatically calculated in Ojibwe.

Before turning from adverbials to verb constructions, we need to note that a common syntactic construction for locative adverbials is to stack them as appositives, as in (14) and (15). The use of *imaa* in such construction has a force similar to that of definiteness. Limitations of space preclude a fuller discussion.

(14) Appositive locative adverbial with *imaa*
Gaawiin wiikaa ningoji izhaasii, mii go apane imaa biindig ayaad.
gaawiin wiikaa ningoji izhaa-sii-w
not never somewhere go.there-NEG-3

mii go apane **imaa biindig** ayaa-d.
EMPH EMPH always there inside be.there-3.CONJ
'He never goes anywhere, he just remains indoors.' (Jones 1917:2)

(15) Stacked appositive locative adverbials

Miish ayaayaan gaa-izhi-gimoodiyaan bezhig a'aw gichi-zaasakokwaan ji-asag imaa anaamayi'ii imaa ingodaashenzhishing.

miish ayaa-yaan cc.gii=izhi=gimoodiyaan
EMPH be.there-1.SG.CONJ CC.PST=EMPH=steal-1.SG.CONJ

bezhig a'aw gichi=zaasakokwaan
one that.AN big=fry.bread

ji=as-ag **imaa anaamayi'ii imaa in-godaash-enzh-ish-ing**
FUT=put.there-1>3.AN.CONJ there under-thing there 1.POSS-skirt-DIM-PEJOR-LOC

'While I was there, I stole a big piece of frybread to stick under my little old skirt.' (Kegg 1978:58)

Now let us turn our attention to spatial relations expressed in verb morphology. Morphemes expressing spatial relations occur either as the root of a simplex stem, as in (16), or as the initial in a bipartite stem, as in (17).

(16) Roots expressing spatial relations

boozi 's/he gets in [a vehicle]'
agoozi 's/he is perched [there]
ayaa 's/he is [there]'
daa 's/he lives [there]'

(17) Initials expressing spatial relations

a. biindigebatoo
biindige-batoo-w
go.in-run-3
's/he runs in'

b. zaagaagone
zaag-aagon-e-w
out-snow-VBLZR-3
'it is sticking out of the snow'

c. zhaabonang
zhaabw-in-am-g
through-use.hand-INAN-3.CONJ
'to put it **through**'

d. onjigaa
ond-igaa-w
from-drip-3
'it drips/leaks **from** [there]'

A subclass of the relators that appear in verb stems are relative roots. As a quick reminder, a relative root is a morpheme that adds a syntactic slot to the verb case frame, as can be seen by comparing the sentences in (18), which have the same root verb with and without an added relative root.

(18) a. Simple transitive
Ngii-waabmaa waawaashkeshi.
n-gii=waabam-aa waawaashkeshi
1-PST= see-3.AN deer
SBJ OBJ.AGR PRIMARY OBJ
'I saw a deer.' (Bloomfield 1958:155, sentence 256)

b. Transitive with relative root
Niniing-sh go naa wgii-naabmaan niwi mnidoon.
[aniniw-ing]=sh go naa o- gii= in- aabam- aa-an niwi manidooj-an.
man-LOC=EMPH 3- PST= like- see- 3.AN-OBV this spirit-OBV
[REL ROOT COMP] SBJ REL.ROOT OBJ.AGR PRIMARY OBJ
'He saw the spirit in the form of a man.' (Piggott and Kaye 1973, Text 3, sentence 20)

It should be noted that there is ample evidence that relative roots are *not* applicatives. A full argument can be found in Rhodes (2010b).

The relator–landmark construction with the spatial relation realized by a relative root and one realized by a nonrelative root are superficially identical, as shown in (19) and (20). The difference is in the syntactic structure.

(19) Relative root relator–landmark construction
Imaa odinimaanganaang ningii-asig.
[imaa o-dinimaangan-aang] nin-gii=as-ig
there 3.POSS-shoulder-LOC 1-PST=**put.there**-INV
[rel root comp] rel.root
landmark relator
'He put me on his shoulders.' (Kegg and Nichols 1983:11)

(20) Adverbial adjunct relator–landmark construction
Waasa zhigwa ani-dagwishinoon biindigese endaanid;
waasa zhigwa ani-dagwishinoon **biindige**-se-w CC-daa-ni-d
far already away-arrive-3-obv go.in-fly-3 [where-live-OBV-3.CONJ]
relator adverbial adjunct
'(Seeing) from afar that the other had arrived, he flew into his house.' (Jones 1917:338, 12)

However, for the initials that are not relative roots there is another possible morphosyntactic configuration for the landmark. It can be realized as a medial, as in the examples in (21).

(21) Medials as landmarks
a. with *biind-* 'in'
i. biindige
biind-ig-e
in-house-VBLZR-3
'S/he goes **into** [an enclosed space].'
ii. biindaabikinang
biind-aabik-in-am-g
in-metal-use.hand-INAN-3.CONJ
'to put it **in** the oven'
b. with *zaag-* 'out'
i. zaagaagone
zaag-aagon-e-w
out-snow-VBLZR-3
'It is sticking **out of** the snow.'

ii. zaagibii

zaag-ibii-w

out-water-3

'It is sticking **out of** the water.'

c. with *zhaab-* 'through'

zhaabwaanakwad

zhaabw-aanakwad-w

through-cloud-3

'The clouds can be seen **through.**'

d. with *zhiibaa-* 'under'

zhiibaazigwa'asabii

zhiibaa-zigw-a'-asaby-e-w

under-ice-use.instr-net-VBLZR-3

'S/he sets a net **under** the ice.'

It should be noted that this is not the most common semantic configuration for medials. Medials mostly realize absolutives or more rarely instrumentals, as exemplified in (22).

(22) Morphosyntactic functions of medials

a. Absolutives

(i) Subjects of transitives

wiin**iingwe**

wiin-**iingwe** -w

dirty-**face**-3

'His/her **face** is dirty.'

(ii) Objects of transitives

wiikw**aanikwe**binaad

wiikw-**aanikwe**-bin-aa-d

pull-**hair**-pull-3.AN.OBJ-3.CONJ

'to pull his/her hair'

b. Instrumentals

ikw**aabiig**inang

ikw-**aabiig**-in-am-g

move.upwards-**string**-use.hand-INAN-3.CONJ

'to pull it up with a rope'

There are a few frequent forms with medials realizing landmarks that have specialized relators. The two most common are given in (23).

(23) Specialized relators

a. madaabii
madaa-bii-w
to.open.area-water-3
'S/he goes (down) **to** the water.'
madaako
madaa-ko-w
to.open.area-ice-3
'S/he goes (out) **on** the ice.'

b. bakobii
bakw-ibii-w
in-water-3
'S/he goes **into** the water.'

The initials *madaa-* and *bakw-* only occur in these forms. *Madaa-* is unique, but *bakw-* has a homonym meaning 'to peel or skin', exemplified in (24).

(24) Homonymous *bakw-* meaning 'peel'

a. bakonang
bakw-in-am-g
peel-use.hand-IN.OBJ-3
'to peel it'

b. bakonaad
bakw-in-aa-d
peel-use.hand-AN.OBJ-3
'to skin him/her'

Water in the landscape has long been an important feature of Ojibwe life, being located historically and, for most varieties, contemporarily in the lake country surrounding the Great Lakes. So it only makes sense that the initial referring to water as a landmark, *bakobii* and *madaabii*, are recycled as initials for a large number of verbs of motion or implied motion with respect to water. A small sample of each is given in (25) and (26).

(25) *bakobii* as initial (sample)

bakobiibatoo	'S/he runs into the water.'	(-batoo	'run')
bakobiise	'It falls in the water.'	(-se	'move quickly')
bakobiimo	'The road leads into the water.'	(-amo-	'be a road')
bakobiidaabaanaad	'to drag him/her into the water'	(-daabaaN-	'drag him/her')
bakobiiwebinang	'to throw it into the water'	(-weebin-	'throw him/her')

(26) *madaabii* as initial (sample)

madaabiibizo	'S/he drives to the shore.'	(-bizo	'drive')
madaabiigozi	'She moves to the shore.'	(-gozi	'move residence')
madaabiimo	'The road leads down to the shore.'	(-amo-	'be a road')
madaabiiyaanimad	'There is an offshore breeze.'	(-aanimad	'the wind blows')
madaabiiwidood	'To carry it down to the shore.'	(-wid(oo)-	'carry it')

It's worth noting that there is an interesting extension of *madaabii* as an initial in Southwest Ojibwe where no water is involved. Instead, the initial+medial combination reflects the original meaning of the initial *madaa*(*w*)- as 'clearing; open space'. This meaning is still attested in Plains Cree.

(27) Remnant of original meaning of *madaa-*
madaabiishkosiwe 'S/he goes out into a meadow.' (mashkosi 'meadow')
cf. Plains Cree: matâwisiw 'S/he comes (out) into an open area.'

Returning to the importance of water in the landscape and therefore its use as a landmark, just as there are words that treat water as a goal, *bakobii* 'into the water' and *madaabii* 'down to the water', there are forms that treat the water as a source. In other words, they express 'out of the water' and 'away from the water'. A few examples of water as a landmark with relators in opposite meanings are given in Tables 1 and 2.

There are two morphemes that treat water as a landmark but have lexicalized the relator and landmark as a single morpheme, *agwaa-* and *gop-*. Since there is no explicit morphology to fix the landmark, in some contexts they are ambiguous

TABLE 1. *bakobii-* 'into the water' versus *agwaa-* 'out of the water; on to shore'

FULL VERB	GLOSS	FULL VERB	GLOSS
bakobii	'S/he goes into the water.'	*agwaazii*	'S/he comes out of the water.'
bakobiiyaasin	'It is blown into the water.'	*agwaayaasin*	'It is blown ashore.'
bakobiidaabaanaad	'to drag him/her into the water'	*agwaadaabaanaad*	'to drag him/her ashore'
bakobiiwebinang	'to throw it into the water'	*agwaawebinang*	'to throw it ashore'

TABLE 2. *madaabii-* 'to the water' versus *gop-* 'away from the water; (moving) inland'

FULL VERB	GLOSS	FULL VERB	GLOSS
madaabii	'S/he runs to the shore.'	*gopii*	'S/he goes up from the water.'
madaabiibizo	'S/he drives to the shore.'	*gopibizo*	'S/he drives inland.'
madaabiikawe	'S/he leaves tracks down to the shore.'	*gopikawe*	'S/he leaves tracks heading inland.'
madaabiiwidood	'to carry it down to the shore'	*gopiwidood*	'to carry it inland'

between source and goal interpretations. To come out of landscape water is normally to come onto the shore. To move away from the landscape water is to go inland, often to go into the woods.

(28) Source-oriented interpretation

a. agwaa- 'out of water'

b. gop- 'away from the water'

(29) Goal-oriented interpretation

a. agwaa- '(on)to shore'

b. gop- 'inland, into the bush'

Certain forms containing these morphemes have semantic extensions clearly based on goal reading.

(30) Goal-oriented semantic extensions

a. agwaa'oodood 'to unload a boat or vehicle'

b. i. gopa'o 'S/he paddles upstream.'

ii. gopinizhikawaad 'to chase him/her into the woods'

The morpheme *agwaa-* is not limited to referring to water on the landscape. It equally well means out of water in a container.

(31) agwaa'ang
agwaa-a'-am-g
out.of.water-use.INSTR-INAN-3.CONJ
'to dip him/her out of the water'

However, the lexeme in (31) has further metonymical extensions arising out of the prototypical scene in which one would take something out of water with an instrument, namely, when something is cooking in water/liquid. To take something out of water is to take it out of the kettle. To take something out of a kettle, is to take it off of/out of the fire. *Agwaa'ang* can be used to mean any of those specific meanings.

(32) Metonymic extensions of *agwaa'ang*

1) take it off the water or fire (using something)
2) take it out of the pot (using something)
3) dip it out

The extension of water as a landmark to fire is found across the family in languages that have exact cognates of the lexeme *agwaa'waad/agwaa'ang*, as the examples in (33) show.

(33) Cognates of *agwaa'ang*

a. Menominee
akwuahɛɛw/akuaham
'He takes him/it out of a vessel or medium [water or fire][4] by tool.'

b. Meskwaki
akwâhwêw/akwâham
'fishes him/it out of water, fire (as, with a stick)'

c. Plains Cree
akwāhwāw/akwāham
'S/he takes him/it from water or fire by tool.'

d. Cheyenne
é-onóhnóho /é-onóha
'knock him/it out by tool [of the water or fire]'[5]

The initial *agwaa-* also appears in a few stems with the water medial. They are listed in (34) with the medial in bold for clarity. Note that even with the water medial, some of these can also mean 'off the fire'.

(34) *agwaa-* with medial
agwaa**bii**daabaanaad 'to drag him/her out of the water'
~ agwaadaabaanaad
agwaa**biiga**'ang 'to take it off/out of the water using something'
~ agwaa**bii**'ang ~ agwaa'ang
agwaa**biig**inang 'to take it off the fire; take it off the water'

The bleaching of medial meaning in relator–landmark construction also happens with *biindige* 'enter [a structure or enclosed space]', for which the structure is shown in (35).

(35) *biindige*
biind-ig-e-w
in-house-VBLZR-3
's/he enters'

This has been grammaticalized in Ojibwe as an initial meaning simply 'into'. Here's a list of some representative verb stems with *biindige* as the initial. The forms in (36a) have motion finals, but those in (36b) are built on non-motion finals.

(36) *biindige* as a productive initial

a. With finals indicating motion

biindigebatoo 'run in'

biindigejiwan 'flow in'

biindigejiishkiwagishkige 'track mud in'

b. With finals not otherwise implying motion

biindigedemo 'come/go in crying'

biindigedebii 'come/go in drunk'

biindigeyaanimizi 'come/go in in fear'

For those forms in (36b), it is the presence of *biidige* as an initial that imparts a motion reading, like the caused motion construction in English, where the presence of an appropriate prepositional phrase turns a verb that does not express motion into the understood cause of motion, either literal or figurative.

(37)

Non-motion	Caused motion
She sneezed.	She sneezed the napkin off the table.
He hit the book.	He hit the book off the shelf.
She squeezed the orange.	She squeezed the juice out of the orange.
They laughed.	They laughed him off the stage.

And that brings us back to Len Talmy's original question: How would you say *The bottle floated into the cave* in Ojibwe? The complication is that in English one can either use float as a verb of motion or not.

(38)

Non-motion	Motion
The ball floats.	The ball floats away.

There's much more to this than we can discuss here. Usually, English non-motion intransitives require a special construction to get the implied motion.

(39)

Non-motion	Motion
He sang.	He sang his way down the street.

However, in Ojibwe *agonde* 'it floats' cannot have a motion reading. In Ojibwe how the inanimate thing comes to be moving must be specified. The closest rendering of Talmy's sentence is that given in (40), which came out of a discussion with a group of Anishinaabe language teachers.[6]

(40) Waanzhing biindigeyaaboode wi mooday.

waanzh-ing	biindige-yaaboode-w	wi	mooday
cave-LOC	in-carry.on.current-3	that	bottle

'The bottle was carried into the cave on the current.'

In conclusion, there remains one important point regarding the syntax of landmarks. Landmarks sometimes show up as secondary objects, especially if the initial is the relator but not a relative root, for example, (4b), repeated here as (41), with relator and landmark explicitly indicated.

(41) Chipmunk (trajectory) located in relation to the tree (landmark)

	... zhaabo-ba'iwe[d]	Ø	mitigoon
Gloss:	through-run.from	(chipmunk)	tree
Morphosyntax:	initial	subject	secondary object
Semantic function:	relator		landmark

Several AI+O verbs with landmark objects are given in (42) from Southwest Ojibwe. Noting dialect for this construction is important because this morphosyntactic strategy varies significantly among varieties of Ojibwe.

(42) Landmarks realized as objects of AI+O verbs

a. odapabin

od-ap-abi-n

3.ERG-on-sit.[there]-OBJ

'S/he sits **on** it.'

b. omadaakon

o-madaa-ko-n

3.ERG-**to.open.area**-ice-OBJ

'S/he goes **to** it out on the ice.'

c. odizhaanan

od-iN-yaa-nan

3.ERG-to-go-AN.OBJ

'S/he goes **to** him.'

There is much more to say about this topic, but there is also a practical application. When I was learning Ojibwe, elders repeatedly said that when they speak Ojibwe, they see pictures. The analysis presented here, based in cognitive linguistics, depends on seeing whole scenes, putting academic flesh on the elders' wisdom. The kind of analysis in this paper requires a holistic view of the world. Language teaching often breaks it down into its smallest parts. Thereby we miss that words reference gestalts—what the elders call pictures. We would do well to consider that in future curriculum planning.

NOTES

1. The ideas in this paper are deeply influenced by my discussions with Len Talmy and Eve Sweetser over the course of decades, but also more recently by my participation in the Tyndale House Workshop in Greek Prepositions in Cambridge, England, in the summer of 2017, and discussions with Steve Runge, Michael Aubrey, and Rachel Aubrey. All mistakes, misinterpretations, and lapses of memory are mine alone.

   The data for this paper are primarily from Southwest Ojibwe sources, Kegg (1978), Kegg and Nichols (1983), Gibbs (2010), and the Ojibwe People's Dictionary (n.d.). Data from Odawa comes from Bloomfield (1958) and Piggott and Kaye (1973). Data from northern Ontario varieties are from Jones (1917). Data from other languages are drawn from Bloomfield (1975) for Menominee, Fisher et al. (2017) for Cheyenne, Goddard and Thomason (2014) for Meskwaki, and Wolvengrey (2001) for Plains Cree. Unless otherwise noted, all single word citations are Southwest Ojibwe drawn from the Ojibwe People's Dictionary (n.d.).
2. Glossing follows Leipzig rules (Bickel et al. 2015), with the added abbreviations: AN = animate, INAN = inanimate, and OBV = obviative.
3. The translation provided is unclear. The whole paragraph is:

   > Agongos giiwed waabamaad abinid mitgoon imaa mitakamig, zhaaboba'iwed bagonezinind mitigoon. Mii igo ani-maajiiba'iwed agongos. Mii igo gookooko'oon gii-ani-gaashkibinigod obikwaanaang.

   A translation that makes clear what is being expressed in Ojibwe reads like this: 'Chipmunk started running toward home and safety and saw a fallen tree out on the open ground, not noticing that there was a hole in it. So, he ran off into the log. Owl reached in through the hole, trying to grab Chipmunk as he ran through, but only managed to rake his back.' (And that's why chipmunks have stripes on their back today.)

4. Bloomfield uses the term "medium" as a cover term for any of water/liquid, air, or fire. It is clear, in this case, that air is not intended. If only water or liquid were meant, then he would have translated 'liquid' or 'water', as in his gloss for *akuapiihεεw/akuapiiham* 'he takes him, it out of a liquid by tool' and *akuaqtaw* 'he moves out, gets out of the water'. Note that his gloss of an Odawa word with a cognate initial is explicit, *ekwa·pwe·peʔank* 'he throws it out of a medium (water, fire) by tool' (Bloomfield 1958:236).
5. The entry in Fisher et al. (2017) reads: "**onóh(n)** *vta.* remove; knock out s.o. by tool. **tséstaéšema'ėho'hetsėse é'-onóhnósesto** After (the rock; obv.) got red hot he knocked it out (of the fire) (with a stick)."
6. This sentence was elicited by asking for a translation, as Talmy had. The ensuing discussion opened mirroring my initial reaction—that such wording is not how Ojibwes talk about such situations. At first, the younger speakers had trouble with the final and produced some novel solutions for the final. But the discussion ended when the older speakers honed in on the version given here. The speakers in question are Odawa speakers from Wikwemikong, Ontario.

REFERENCES

Bickel, Balthasar, Bernard Comrie, and Martin Haspelmath. 2015. The Leipzig Glossing Rules: Conventions for Interlinear Morpheme-by-Morpheme Glosses. https://www.eva.mpg.de/lingua/pdf/Glossing-Rules.pdf.

Bloomfield, Leonard. 1958. *Eastern Ojibwa: Grammar, Texts, and Word List*, ed. by Charles Hockett. Ann Arbor: University of Michigan Press.

Bloomfield, Leonard. 1975. *Menomini Lexicon*, ed. by Charles Hockett. Milwaukee, WI: Milwaukee Public Museum Press.

Fisher, Louise, Wayne Leman, Leroy Pine, Sr., and Marie Sanchez. 2017. *Cheyenne Dictionary*. Lame Deer, MT: Chief Dull Knife College.

Gibbs, Anna C. 2010. How the Chipmunk Got Its Stripes. *Oshkaabewis Native Journal* 7(2):78–81.

Goddard, Ives, and Lucy Thomason. 2014. *A Meskwaki-English and English-Meskwaki Dictionary*. Petosky, MI: Mundart Press.

Jones, William. 1917. *Ojibwe Texts, Part 1*, ed. by Truman Michelson, *Publications of the American Ethnological Society Volume VII*. Leyden: E.J. Brill.

Kegg, Maude. 1978. *Gabekanaansing: At the End of the Trail*, ed. by J. Nichols. *Occasional Publications in Anthropology: Linguistics series no. 4*, University of Northern Colorado

Museum of Anthropology, Greeley, CO.

Kegg, Maude, and John D. Nichols. 1983. *Nookomis gaa-inaajimotawid.* Occasional Publications no. 11, Minnesota Archaeological Society, St. Paul, MN.

Kilroe, Patricia. 1991. Spatial-Marking Affixes and the Expression of Time in Ojibwa. *Papers of the 22nd Algonquian Conference*, ed. by William Cowan, pp. 193–202. Ottawa: Carleton University.

Langacker, Ronald. 1987. *Foundations of Cognitive Grammar*, vol. I. Stanford, CA: Stanford University Press.

Ojibwe People's Dictionary [n.d.] https://ojibwe.lib.umn.edu.

Piggott, Glynne L., and Jonathan D. Kaye. 1973. *Odawa Language Project: Second Report.* Linguistic Series 1, Toronto: Centre for Linguistic Studies, University of Toronto.

Rhodes, Richard A. 2006. *Clause Structure, Core Arguments, and the Algonquian Relative Root Construction*, pp. 1–29. The 1998 Belcourt Lecture, University of Manitoba.

Rhodes, Richard A. 2010a. Missing Obliques: Some Anomalies in Ojibwe Syntax. *Hypothesis A/Hypothesis B: Linguistic Explorations in Honor of David M. Perlmutter*, ed. by Donna B. Gerdts, John C. Moore, and Maria Polinsky, pp. 427–455. Current Studies in Linguistics 49. Cambridge, MA: MIT Press.

Rhodes, Richard A. 2010b. Relative Root Complement: a Unique Grammatical Relation in Algonquian Syntax. *Rara & Rarissima: Documenting the Fringes of Linguistic Diversity* (Empirical Approaches to Language Typology), ed. by Michael Cysouw, Orin Gensler, and Jan Wohlgemuth, pp. 305–324. Berlin: de Gruyter.

Talmy, Leonard. 1983. How Language Structures Space. *Spatial Orientation: Theory, Research, and Application*, ed. by Herbert Pick and Linda P. Acredolo, pp. 225–282. New York: Plenum Press.

Talmy, Leonard. 1985. Lexicalization Patterns: Semantic Structure in Lexical Forms. *Language Typology and Syntactic Description* 3(99):36–149.

Wolvengrey, Arok. 2001. *Nêhiyawêwin: Itwêwina, Cree: Words* (Volumes 1 and 2). Regina: University of Saskatchewan Press.

Incorporation and Classification in Ojibwe

Some Key Distinctions and Potential Explanations from Formal Syntax

Anna Whitney

Ojibwe exhibits a robust capacity for verbal classifiers and noun incorporation, as well as medials that cannot be clearly categorized as either.[1] Where these processes have been covered in the generative syntax (Principles and Parameters) literature, noun incorporation dominates the discussion—Ojibwe has been used as an example in theoretical debates on noun head/phrase movement in incorporation (see, e.g., Barrie and Mathieu 2016, following Baker 2009).[2] Verbal classifiers and medials that appear to undergo noun incorporation despite being bare roots offer further insight into the Ojibwe verbal complex and could supplement this debate. This analysis suggests that some bare root medials originate within the vP layer while incorporated nouns originate lower, within the VP, and undergo raising, but both phenomena are methods of fulfilling the Extended Projection Principle (EPP). This theory could also provide syntactic evidence for a diachronic transition from incorporation to classification (Mithun 1986). Some medials that otherwise seem to be in the middle of the cline from incorporation to classification (Biedny et al. 2021; O'Meara 1990), such as environmental and body part medials, also resist clear syntactic explanation and offer room for further research.

Background

Ojibwe is known to make use of both verbal classifiers and noun incorporation. In both the Algonquianist and formal syntax traditions, these processes have often been considered separately. In the most typical characterization, noun incorporation involves making an otherwise independent noun (such as *zhooniyaa* 'money' in (2)) into a part of the verb (as in (3)):[3]

(1) asigin[4]
asig-in
collect-act.on.him/her.by.hand.VTA
'collect him/her'

(2) zhooniyaa
money.AN
'money'

(3) asigizhooniyaawe
asig-i-zhooniyaa-e
collect-EPEN-money-INCORPORATING.VAI
'S/he collects money as a donation.'

Verbal classifiers, on the other hand, are morphemes that modify the verb or a noun with which they occur. In (4), *aniibish* 'tea' falls within the class of liquids, and the verbal classifier *-aagam-* 'liquid' makes the verb specific to that class:

(4) Jiikaagamin iwe aniibiish.
jiik-aagam-i iwe aniibish
pleasant-liquid.CL-VII DEM tea.IN
'The tea was real good.'

This paper aims to posit a unified formal syntactic explanation of some instances of both phenomena. While the literature in formal syntax has extensively investigated noun incorporation (as discussed in the following section of this paper), there is still much to know about the syntax of verbal classifiers and other medials.[5] To further complicate this picture, some research has found that the distinction between incorporation and classification is murky at best. Historically speaking, there is strong evidence that classification arose from robust use of noun incorporation (Mithun 1986). Even synchronically, there is a cline between incorporation and classification (Biedny et al. 2021; O'Meara 1990), such that medials may exhibit traits that seem at once indicative of incorporation and classification. There exist bare root medials that could never occur as standalone nouns outside of the verb, which might indicate that they are classifiers—except for the fact that some of those very same medials cannot co-occur with overt nouns, which would typically suggest that the medial is the product of incorporation. In the cline between prototypical examples of noun incorporation and prototypical examples of classification, such bare root medials are thought to be somewhere in the middle.

This presents a puzzle for syntactic analysis. Generative syntax has been explored extensively to analyze gradual clines and historical processes, and that analysis can be extended to those processes related to incorporated nouns and verbal classifiers. To do this, a formal account would need to describe several syntactic structures that appear similar in surface form but are in fact underlyingly different and could thus explain movement along the cline over time. This paper will integrate some existing syntactic analyses with other descriptions of noun incorporation and verbal classification to posit such a formal syntactic analysis. The present work will begin with a review of some prior work on the topic, then offer an explanation of incorporated bare roots before turning to other medials, including verbal classifiers. We will conclude with cases that require further analysis.

Previous Formal Analysis

Much of the canon on noun incorporation in generative syntax (within Principles and Parameters) was pioneered by Mark Baker (see especially Baker 1985, but also Baker 1996 and 2003). In his early analyses, noun incorporation was limited to the movement of a phrase head—whole phrases were strictly excluded from this process. This permits the incorporation of bare nouns or even bare stems, but nothing else. Baker has since come to argue that noun incorporation is not a unified phenomenon cross-linguistically, but head movement is still necessary for a generative explanation (Baker 2009).

In contrast, Barrie and Mathieu (2016) suggest that noun incorporation targets whole phrases. Their analysis is also distinct in that Ojibwe, and Algonquian languages generally, form part of their foundational evidence and examples. They propose that many verbs incorporate whole nominal phrases (nPs, dPs, DPs, KPs, and CPs) that perhaps only appear to be heads because they are usually packaged in a single word. Examples of this occur with nominalizers, such as the nominalizer *-an* in (5), as well as with adjectives, such as *gichi-* 'big', which operates as an adjectival prefix in (6).

(5) bkwezhganke
bakwezhig-an-ke-w
bread-NOM-make.VAI-3
'He/she makes bread.' (Barrie and Mathieu 2016:16)[6]

(6) ngii-gchi-gwiiwzensiw
n-gii-gichi-gwiiwzens-wi
1-PST-big-boy-be.VAI
'I was a big boy.' (Barrie and Mathieu 2016:18)

However, Barrie and Mathieu suggest their analysis does not extend to what would otherwise appear to be the incorporation of bare roots. Body part medials would be one example of this, as in (7); *-jaan* 'nose' would require possessor marking to stand as an independent noun. There are some classifier-like medials that also appear to be incorporated bare roots, as in (8); *-is-* 'wood' also cannot function as an independent noun outside of the verb. Barrie and Mathieu consider this to be a separate phenomenon, which they term root–root merger.

(7) bookjaane
booko-jaan-e
break-nose-INCORPORATING.VAI
'S/he has a broken nose.' (Pedchenko et al. 2003, cited in Barrie and Mathieu 2016:23)

(8) mnise
man-is-e
chop-wood-INCORPORATING.VAI
'chop firewood' (Valentine 2001, cited in Barrie and Mathieu 2016:23)

A Theory of Incorporated Bare Roots

This account will now turn toward these "bare roots" that otherwise appear to be incorporated and investigate potential formal explanations. If a verb appears to show incorporation, if it ends in incorporating *-e* and it follows Baker's rules of noun incorporation, how can we explain it using a Barrie and Mathieu view on noun incorporation? How might it be different from the phrases that Barrie and Mathieu find typical to noun incorporation?

The answer lies in the mechanics and motivation of noun incorporation. Although they mention it only in passing, Barrie and Mathieu follow prior research suggesting that noun incorporation is motivated by the Extended Projection Principle, or EPP (Massam 2001). Under this logic, a *v* head can require a nominal element—not necessarily an NP, a DP, or even a noun that can stand on its own, but something with a nominal referent. In Ojibwe, the verb final acts as the *v* head and the nominal element must merge into the specifier of the *v* head. Incorporation in Ojibwe is closely associated with the *v* head/verb final known as INCORPORATING *-E*, which forms verbs that can be animate intransitive and/or inanimate intransitive, depending on context. Therefore, we can posit a structure like in Figure 1.

Barrie and Mathieu's work focuses on examples where the nominal element is taken from the existing body of the tree and moved into this specifier position. However, this need not be the case. If we took incorporating *-e* and other incorporating verb finals to be syntactic probes, that would indeed be a requirement, but that is not the argument made in Barrie and Mathieu (2016) and Massam (2001). In some

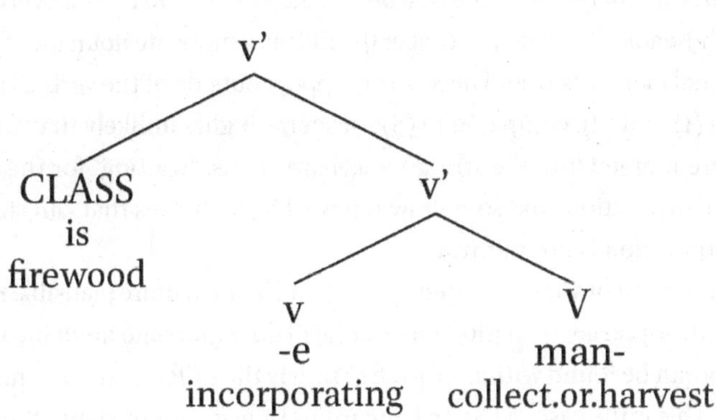

FIGURE 1. Tree diagram for *manise* 'S/he harvests, cuts firewood.'

ways, their arguments' use of the EPP anticipates the existence of incorporation-like medials. The EPP does not require movement from the c-commanded domain into the specifier position, but allows the lexical insertion (without movement) of new nominal elements to fill the necessary slot in the syntax. (This is, for example, how the EPP is fulfilled by *it* in the English sentence *It is raining*.) The existence of medials that behave in this way—much like the pronominal "dummy subjects" common to the EPP—validates the conceptual arguments made in Barrie and Mathieu (2016) and Massam (2001), even if they do not necessarily extend their analyses to these kinds of medials.

Expanding Barrie and Mathieu's logic to these new examples shown in (8) and Figure 1, the bare noun stem may enter the syntactic tree as a medial, fulfilling the EPP without already being present in the *v* head's domain. In fact, this distinction is what allows bare stems, as opposed to noun or determiner phrases, to act as medials. Because medials of this type emerge in the specifier of a bare verb final that also cannot stand alone, the medial is never at risk of standing alone itself, and thus the bareness of the stem is no issue. Compare this to the targets of traditional noun incorporation as described by Barrie and Mathieu. In traditional noun incorporation in Ojibwe, the nominal element begins life as a potential subject or object, and it enters the syntactic tree "prepared" to stand alone (without incorporation). The bare stem is not suitable for this kind of true incorporation, but not because of the EPP or the *v* head. Bare stems are not suitable for the noun incorporation described in Barrie and Mathieu because their analysis focuses on nominal elements that are already present in the syntactic tree at the time the *v* head is introduced. These nominal elements must be phrases, but only because of their position in the tree; these phrases are merged into the tree before the *v* head, and for the overwhelming majority of *v* heads (which do not trigger the EPP and motivate noun incorporation), these nominal elements would necessarily appear outside of the verb, as a separate word (as in (1) and (2), compared to (3)). It seems highly unlikely that all nominal elements are merged into the structure as bare stems, "waiting" for the *v* head to motivate incorporation, and somehow repaired into phrases that can stand alone when incorporation is not motivated.

From this point of view, bare stem medials are a much more plausible reparative strategy for the opposite scenario: When a *v* head does motivate noun incorporation but nothing can be found within the tree to satisfy the EPP, a bare stem medial may fill the slot. This is the case in Figure 1; incorporating *-e* is merged into the structure before any nominal elements, and without any nominal to move into the specifier position, *-is-* 'wood' is inserted into the structure, satisfying the EPP as a bare root. As long as the grammar assumes noun incorporation to be the exception, rather than the rule, this reparative strategy is sufficient.

Implications for Other Medials

So far, this analysis has focused on medials (like the aforementioned *-is-* 'wood') that are incorporation-like, meaning they occur with a very small set of *v* heads known to trigger incorporation and they do not classify or modify other nouns with which they co-occur. This still leaves many other medials, which pair with different *v* heads and may or may not be acting as classifiers, unexplained. The present paper cannot offer explanations for every medial but will offer some potential routes for future syntactic investigation.

One possibility is that classificatory medials are inhabiting the same slot that would otherwise be occupied by an incorporated nominal, even if the *v* head does not require or motivate anything of the sort. In other words, the EPP does not need to be triggered for this position to be available for a medial. This theory is corroborated by work in semantics, such as Riccomini (2019), which elaborates a template for Ojibwe verbs, featuring "slots" for multiple argument roles. Riccomini does not focus on medials in her work but instead focuses on how person, number, and animacy marking fills these slots. Although it differs in some key ways from previous trees included in this paper, Riccomini's original diagram is reproduced here as Figure 2 for ease of reference. Additionally, Riccomini offers examples of Ojibwe sentences according to this structure. One is reproduced in (9), with the matching tree diagram in Figure 3.

(9) ndazhtamaag
ni-azhi-it-amaw-igw
1-make-**cause**.VTI-APPL.VTA-3>1
'She is making it for me.' (Valentine 2001:700, cited in Riccomini 2019:61)

We can imagine a classificatory medial serving a role much like that of the person, number, and animacy marking in these verbs. Much like person/number/animacy marking, a classifier can be a bound morpheme and be coreferential with a stand-alone noun outside the verb. This would also provide order to the coreferentiality

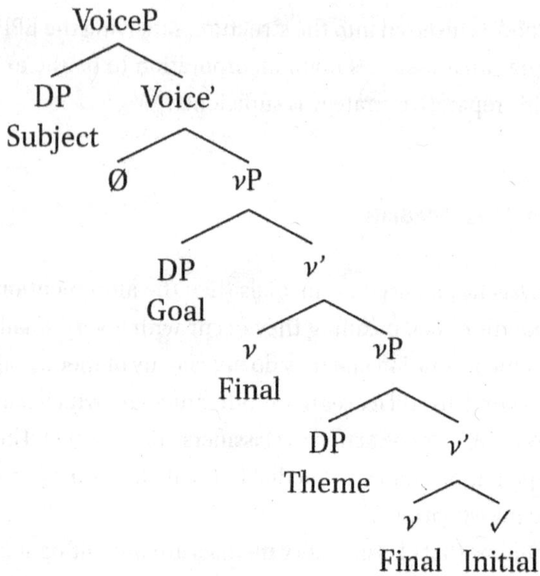

FIGURE 2. Riccomini's template for Ojibwe verbs (Riccomini 2019:103)

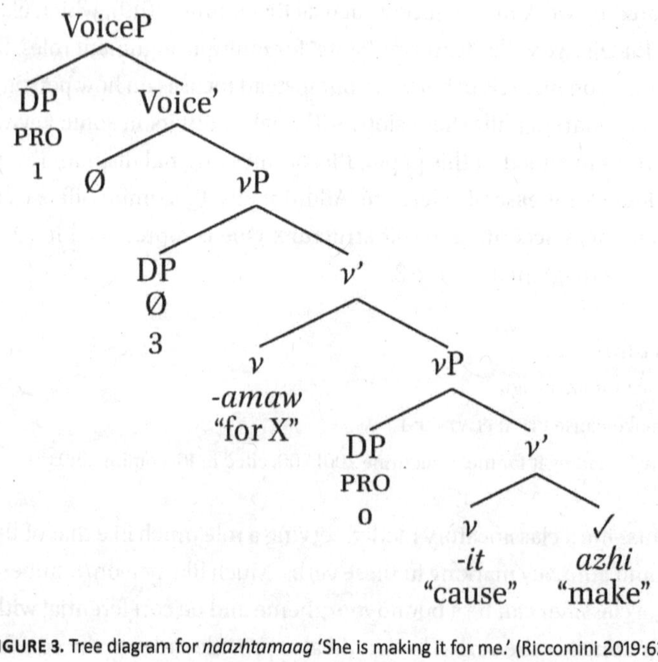

FIGURE 3. Tree diagram for *ndazhtamaag* 'She is making it for me.' (Riccomini 2019:62)

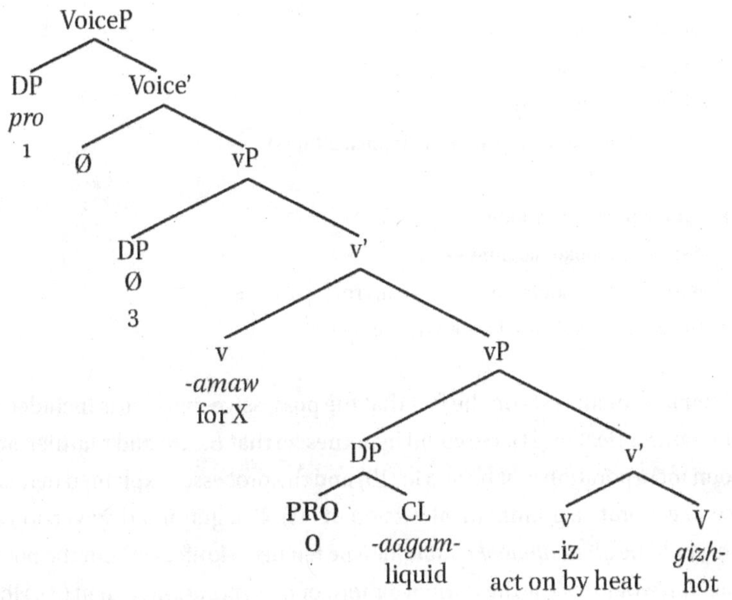

FIGURE 4. Tree diagram for *gizhaagamizamaw* 'Heat (it) (a liquid) for h/.' in the style of Riccomini (2019)

found between medials and overt nouns—they both correspond to the same argument role. In Figure 4, the classifier *-aagam-* 'liquid, body of water' is imagined sharing the theme spot with the same unpronounced pronominal seen in Figure 3. Admittedly, more theoretical and cross-linguistic work is needed to understand any potential mechanics of classifiers within verb-internal DPs, but the tree in Figure 4 at least demonstrates one potential point of origin for verbal classifiers.

Somewhat different from classificatory medials, body part medials also warrant further examination. Body part medials, although likely adherent to one of the structures described in this paper, suffer from a confusion of origin. That is, it is unclear whether they are merged into the syntax early on as phrases, or whether they are merged later as bare stem medials. If they enter the syntax early, they are necessarily phrases, as body parts are inalienably possessed in Ojibwe and must carry possessor marking to be words that stand alone. Barrie and Mathieu successfully apply their theory of noun incorporation to other possessed nouns in Ojibwe, but only in cases of light verb incorporation, or verbs without verb initials. Their examples are included here:

(10) mookmaanimi
o-mookomaan-im-i-w
3-knife-POSS-have.VAI-3
'He/she has a knife.' (Barrie and Mathieu 2016:18)

(11) *gii-naajimookmaanime
gii-naad-i-mookomaan-im-e-w
PST-fetch-EPEN-knife-POSS-INCORPORATING.VAI/VII-3S
'He fetched his knife.' (Barrie and Mathieu 2016:19)

Their argument rests on the fact that the possessive marking is included in (10) but ungrammatical in (11). We could hypothesize that Barrie and Mathieu account for noun incorporation as it occurs in (10) and the processes explained in this paper suffice to generate a grammatical version of (11). The grammatical version of (11), which would be *gii-naajimookmaane* 'he/she fetched a knife', without the possessive marker *-im*, would follow the normal pattern of incorporation seen in (3). However, with body parts and some other inalienably possessed nouns, explanation becomes more difficult. Many body parts do not showcase an overt possessive marker like *-im* in (10) and (11), despite being inalienably possessed, as in (12):

(12) ojaan
o-jaan
3-nose.IN
'his/her nose'

Therefore, it is hypothetically possible that the whole DP 'his/her nose' is incorporated into a phrase like 's/he has a broken nose', and that the person marking features on the noun are repurposed for the person, number, and animacy marking on the verb. In (13), the unpronounced third person marking at the beginning of the verb is analogous to the third person possessor marking *o-* that we might otherwise expect to see on the body part, as in (12):

(13) bookojaane
ø-bookw-jaan-e
3-broken-nose-INCORPORATING.VAI/VII
'S/he has a broken nose.'

This explanation is especially tempting given the co-referential nature of the subject and the incorporated body part. Even when incorporating *-e* works as a postmedial and a transitive verb is formed (as in (14)), body part medials are always possessed by the theme of the verb. Notice that in (14), it is the recipient of the massage, rather than the agent, that possesses the foot. Even if the possessor is not marked directly on the medial, body part medials are still body parts and are still inalienably possessed by an argument of the verb.

(14) zinigozidebizh
zinigw-zid-e-biN
rub-foot-INCORPORATING-use.the.hands.on.him/her.VTA
'massage his/her foot'

However, these facts are not true for all medials that would otherwise be inalienably possessed nouns. Consider the following trio of examples. The light verb incorporation in (16) does not include the full DP shown in (15).[7] The medial is still translated as possessed in (17) but is not possessed by any person that would otherwise be marked on the verb.

(15) onaabeman
o-naabem-an
3-husband.AN-3'
'her husband'

(16) onaabemi
o-naabem-i
3-husband-have.VAI
'S/he has or gets a husband.'

(17) gimoojinaabeme
gimood-naabem-e
steal-husband-INCORPORATING.VAI/VII
'S/he steals somebody's husband.'

All of this is to suggest that some medials consistently resist neat categorization and still require further study.

Luckily, syntactic analysis clears a path for future research. Syntactic and semantic fieldwork could help categorize otherwise difficult examples like (13), (16), and (17). As Bliss (2018) demonstrates, constituency tests can uncover the relationship between nominals and verbs in cases of noun incorporation or pseudo-incorporation, especially when accompanied by research on the scope, definiteness, and specificity of those nominals. Hard-to-categorize medials in Ojibwe are ripe for similar investigation to determine the constituency of medials, and to better understand the semantic properties of medials on a more individualized, case-by-case basis to potentially uncover more qualities that are more concretely associated with incorporation versus classification and movement between those two poles on the cline.

Conclusion

Certain verb finals, or *v* heads, trigger incorporation via the Extended Projection Principle, or EPP. However, medials can also fulfill the EPP, even as bare stems that are merged into the syntax after the *v* head. There is still more work to be done explaining classifiers and other medials that are difficult to categorize purely in terms of incorporation and classification, in particular, body part medials and incorporated kinship terms. The generative syntax account outlined here does not perfectly divide the cline between noun incorporation and classification, but it does provide more tools for describing variation within that space. Syntactic description can hypothesize about the origins of medials within the syntactic structure and the effect of those origins on the qualities of medials. A syntactic explanation is not always readily available for every instance of every medial, but the hypotheses presented here lay the groundwork for constituency tests and semantic fieldwork. Such future work could more quantitatively describe the placement of medials along the cline between classification and incorporation. If research only seeks examples with known signs of classification, such as co-occurrence with overt nouns, this does not preclude the medial from being incorporated in other examples. Many signs of incorporation, such as the existence of a corresponding standalone noun and the absence of a co-occurring overt noun, do not prove that the medial never serves a classificatory role. This is especially important to keep in mind when we consider medials undergoing diachronic change, which may result in usage that more closely resembles classification or incorporation. A syntactic view allows us to examine examples individually, creating space for variation across speakers and examples.

NOTES

1. Many thanks to those whose comments and guidance aided in the refining of this paper, including Dr. Patrice Beddor, Dr. Acrisio Pires, and the staff at the Sweetland Writing Center. I am especially grateful to the two anonymous reviewers and the editors of this volume for their patient and resourceful advice. All remaining errors are my own.
2. "Ojibwe" is used throughout this paper as the label for several closely related language varieties. Much diversity exists within this broad characterization, including language varieties and communities that gravitate toward other, more specific labels, such as Anishinaabe, Chippewa, and Nishnaabemwin. The intention is to draw together theoretical arguments that have been made across communities to explain a potential shared underlying mechanism—but the phenomena discussed here likely vary greatly between groups of speakers. The author does not claim to represent any or all such communities. The author had the immense privilege of studying Ojibwe as a teenager over three years at Bemidji State University's Ojibwemowin Niibinishi Gabeshi and has been involved in collaborative research on Ojibwe at the University of Chicago and the University of Michigan since 2019.
3. Abbreviations used: 0 = inanimate, 1 = first person, 2 = second person, 3 = third person, 3' = third person obviate, APPL = applicative, AN = animate noun, CL = classifier, DEM = demonstrative, EPEN = epenthesis, IN = inanimate noun, NOM = nominalizer, POSS = possessive, PST = past, VAI = animate intransitive verb, VII = inanimate intransitive verb, VTA = transitive animate verb, VTI = transitive inanimate verb.
4. Unless otherwise noted, all examples come from the Ojibwe People's Dictionary and are accurate to that website as of August 25, 2023. This analysis comes out of an ongoing collaborative Ojibwe Classifiers Project (Whitney et al. 2023; Meyer and Whitney 2022), which has involved the systematic collection of all verbs in the Ojibwe People's Dictionary (n.d.) that contain a medial listed in their word parts. In addition to the present work, which offers a theoretical account of different medial qualities, work is ongoing to understand the individual qualities of each medial according to its semantics and its ability to combine with different verb finals and coreferential nouns. Some types of medials, in particular those with corresponding numeral classifiers, have admittedly received more attention compared to, for example, medials that pertain to environmental phenomena or body parts. Example sentences from the Ojibwe People's

Dictionary are given special consideration alongside dictionary entries.

5. For the purposes of this analysis, anything that systematically occurs between a verb initial (or V head) and a verb final (or *v* head) is considered a medial. This is a very broad characterization, intended to capture many different phenomena. As research in this area progresses, it may become more accurate to describe such "medials" with different terms (e.g., "pre-finals"). However, that delineation is outside the scope of the present paper.
6. Note that examples from Barrie and Mathieu (2016) and Riccomini (2019) may feature alternate forms or different spellings of verbs and morphemes when compared against examples from the Ojibwe People's Dictionary. The argument of this paper abstracts beyond these differences, which largely reflect phonological variation across dialect areas.
7. Barrie and Mathieu do note that noun incorporation may target nPs (categorized/nominalized stems) or dPs (modified N-stems), but it is still unclear how or why a portion of a targeted nominal phrase would be "lost," as appears to happen between (15) and (16).

REFERENCES

Baker, Mark C. 1985. Incorporation: A Theory of Grammatical Function Changing. PhD thesis, Massachusetts Institute of Technology.

Baker, Mark C. 1996. *The Polysynthesis Parameter.* Oxford: Oxford University Press.

Baker, Mark C. 2003. *Lexical Categories.* Cambridge: Cambridge University Press.

Baker, Mark C. 2009. Is Head Movement Still Needed for Noun Incorporation? *Lingua* 119(2):148–165.

Barrie, Michael, and Eric Mathieu. 2016. Noun Incorporation and Phrasal Movement. *Natural Language & Linguistic Theory* 34(1):1–51.

Biedny, Jerome, Matthew Burner, Andrea Cudworth, and Monica Macaulay. 2021. Classifier Medials across Algonquian: A First Look. *International Journal of American Linguistics* 87(1):1–47.

Bliss, Heather. 2018. Pseudo-Incorporation in Blackfoot. *International Journal of American Linguistics* 84(4):441–470.

Massam, Diane. 2001. Pseudo Noun Incorporation in Niuean. *Natural Language & Linguistic Theory* 19(1):153–197.

Meyer, Cherry, and Anna Whitney. 2022. Semantic Effects of VII Finals /-aa/ and /-ad/ on Medials. Paper read at the 54th Algonquian Conference, University of Colorado Boulder.

Mithun, Marianne. 1986. The Convergence of Noun Classification Systems. *Noun Classes and Categorization: Proceedings of a Symposium on Categorization and Noun Classification, Eugene, Oregon, 1983*, ed. by Colette G. Craig, pp. 379–397. Amsterdam: Benjamins.

Ojibwe People's Dictionary. [n.d.] Department of American Indian Studies. University of Minnesota. http://ojibwe.lib.umn.edu

O'Meara, John D. W. 1990. Delaware Stem Morphology. PhD dissertation, McGill University.

Pedchenko, Svetlana "Weshki-ayaad," Charlie J. Lippert, and Guy T. Gambill. 2003. *Freelang Dictionary—Ojibwe Language Module.* https://www.freelang.net/dictionary/ojibwe.php

Riccomini, Kate. 2019. The Syntax and Semantics of the Ojibwe Verbal Domain. PhD dissertation, University of Ottawa.

Valentine, Randolph J. 2001. *Nishnaabemwin reference grammar.* Toronto: University of Toronto Press.

Whitney, Anna, Garrett Johnson, and Cherry Meyer. 2023. A Survey of "Classificatory Medials" in Ojibwe: Classifiers versus Incorporation. *Papers of the Fifty-Second Algonquian Conference,* ed. by Monica Macaulay and Margaret Noodin, pp. 361–377. East Lansing: Michigan State University Press.

Contributors

Irene Appelbaum received a PhD in philosophy and an MA in linguistics from the University of Chicago. She is a professor of linguistics at the University of Montana in Missoula. Her research focuses on Ktunaxa language documentation and linguistics.

Antti Arppe is an associate professor of quantitative linguistics at the University of Alberta, as well as the founder of the Alberta Language Technology Lab and the Partnership Director of the SSHRC-funded partnership "21st Century Tools for Indigenous Languages."

John-Paul Chalykoff is an assistant professor in Anishinaabe Studies and chair of the Department of Modern Languages at Algoma University/Shingwauk Kinoomaage Gamig. He is a member of Michipicoten First Nation (Ojibwe).

David J. Costa is the program director for the Language Research Office at the Myaamia Center at Miami University of Ohio. He grew up in the San Francisco Bay Area and completed his PhD in linguistics at the University of California, Berkeley, in 1994. He has been studying the Miami-Illinois language since 1988.

Daniel Dacanay is a graduate student in the Department of Linguistics at the University of Alberta, whose research primarily focuses on the use of computational methods in the documentation of Canadian Indigenous languages.

Amy Dahlstrom is an associate professor of linguistics at the University of Chicago. Her research deals with issues of morphology, syntax, and information structure in Meskwaki and Plains Cree.

Ying Gong is currently a PhD candidate in linguistics at Boston University. Her study centers on morphosyntax, semantics, and language documentation.

Peter Grishin is a postdoctoral associate in linguistics at the Massachusetts Institute of Technology. His primary research interests lie in syntax and morphology, with a secondary interest in semantics. Since 2020, much of his work seeks to understand various morphosyntactic and semantic topics in Passamaquoddy on both a descriptive and a theoretical level.

Andrew Kline graduated with a BA in linguistics from the University of Wisconsin–Madison. His interests lie in Arabic, sociolinguistics, and Algonquian languages. He is currently a Peace Corps volunteer in Timor Leste.

Hunter Thompson Lockwood is a linguist in the Language Research Office in the Myaamia Center at Miami University in Oxford, Ohio. He has worked on Algonquian language documentation projects since 2007.

Monica Macaulay received her PhD in linguistics from the University of California, Berkeley. She is the Ada Deer Professor of Language Sciences at the University of Wisconsin–Madison and on the board of the Endangered Language Fund. She also works closely with the Menominee Indian Tribe of Wisconsin on language reclamation and revitalization.

Will Oxford is an associate professor of linguistics at the University of Manitoba. His research focuses on the morphosyntax of the Algonquian languages from comparative and theoretical perspectives.

Richard A. Rhodes has studied Ojibwe, especially the Ottawa dialect, intensively throughout his career. He has also contributed significantly to the documentation of other endangered languages: Métchif, and the Mexican language Sayula Popoluca. The focus of his work has ranged from morphology and descriptive syntax to lexical semantics and lexicography. Currently he is working on historical linguistic questions in Algonquian, particularly in Cheyenne.

Jennifer Stoughton graduated from the University of Wisconsin–Madison in 2023. Her interests include morphosyntax and the Algonquian languages.

Anna Whitney is a PhD student in the Department of Linguistics at the University of Michigan. Her research focuses on language variation and change, contact, and sociolinguistics.

